FROM ENDOGENOUS CONSTRAINTS TO ECONOMIC RESULTS: THE PASSAGE THROUGH MORALITY, UNCERTAINTY AND STRATEGIES

Mariateresa Fiocca has done research at the LUISS University, Rome. She has a Master degree in Economics from the University of York (UK). At present, she is lecturer in economics at the LUISS. She has published various works on the economics of uncertainty, on public sector economics and on the economics of altruism.

FROM ENDOGENOUS CONSTRAINTS TO ECONOMIC RESULTS: THE PASSAGE THROUGH MORALITY, UNCERTAINTY AND STRATEGIES

MARIATERESA FIOCCA
LUISS University, Rome

Dartmouth
Aldershot . Brookfield USA . Hong Kong . Singapore . Sydney

Published by
Dartmouth Publishing Company Limited
Gower House
Croft Road
Aldershot
Hants GU11 3HR
England

Dartmouth Publishing Company
Old Post Road
Brookfield
Vermont 05036
USA

British Library Cataloguing in Publication Data
Fiocca, Mariateresa
From Endogenous Constraints to Economic
Results: Passage Through Morality,
Uncertainty and Strategies
I. Title
170

Library of Congress Cataloging-in-Publication Data
Fiocca, Mariateresa, 1957-
From endogenous constraints to economic results : the passage through morality, uncertainty and strategies / Mariateresa Fiocca.
p. cm.
Includes bibliographical references and indexes.
ISBN 1-85521-190-4 : $57.95
1. Economics--Moral and ethical aspects. I. Title.
HB72.F45 1994
174—dc20 93-5190
CIP

ISBN 1 85521 190 4

Printed and Bound in Great Britain by
Athenaeum Press Ltd, Newcastle upon Tyne.

Contents

List of tables and figures

Introduction

This work is positive in that it tries to explain how morality and/or some other individual behavioural 'dispositions' operate as internal or subjective constraints on economic agents, binding their decision-making and hence their patterns of behaviour. Throughout the book, a 'cross sectional' analysis of these internal constraints is thus proposed – also by providing two case studies (see Parts II and III). Their role will be investigated in three different (but non-mutually exclusive) frames of the individual's decision-making: under uncertainty conditions, in the marketplace, and within a strategic framework with interdependent decision-making either among people or among 'selves'.

From this perspective, the decision-making process appears as the relevant outcome of complex interactions within which – together with the external environment, rationality, and preferences – internal constraints, which will be labelled '*endogenous*' hereafter, play an important role (though it will be argued throughout this work that, to some extent, *preferences and even rationality may be interpreted as particular kinds of endogenous constraints*).

Such an interpretation of preferences as internal constraints largely conflicts with the orthodox economic theory of preferences. As far as morality is concerned, in his paper '*Morality: Preference or Constraint?*', Vanberg (1988) summarises the economists' traditional position:

> 'Attempts to account for a dispositional variable like morality in economic explanations seem to be at odds with the standard economic classification of explanatory variables into either *preferences* or *constraints*. As normally understood, this classification corresponds to the 'subjective vs. objective' distinction: preferences are the subjective, intrapersonal determinants of choice, and constraints are the objective, external determinants. Given this system of reference, introducing morality into economic explanations as a variable would seem to require us either to classify morality as a subjective, intrapersonal preference-variable or as an objective, external constraint-variable' (p. 7).

However, the *preferences versus constraints* approach seems quite misleading: there is no dichotomy or dilemma of this type, no need to conceptualise morality as belonging to one of the two categories. There is not necessarily a conceptual tension between preferences and constraints in so far as sometimes they are just the same. The reason is two-fold: in the above orthodox approach, economic agents are regarded as dealing exclusively with *exogenous* constraints, namely with the objective dimension of their decision-making process. Generally, no room has been left in the theory for the other category of constraints, that is the internal ones; yet they exist and affect the behaviour of the economic agents.

Once allowing for endogenous constraints, the *preferences versus constraints* dichotomy seems even less fruitful. Actually, *to some extent*, preferences can be regarded or identified as constraints of an individual's behaviour: as long as actions are 'preference-oriented', preferences turn out to be (more or less strictly) binding constraints for the individual's behaviour.

In 1783, David Bernoulli introduced the notion of risk aversion, that in the modern psychological theory of preferences can be regarded as *one* of the types of preferences the individual is likely to display under uncertainty conditions. It is a 'standard' preference in all choice settings involving risk – the one typically assumed by the theory of uncertainty – but not the only possible one – as the current contributions in experimental economics highlight. There is no doubt that risk aversion, as a typical preference towards risk, constrains the individual behaviour, preventing some courses of action and inducing him/her to undertake some other behaviour patterns. Analogously, moral preferences constrain the individual not to lie, not to cheat, to keep a promise, etc.

Hence, we can argue that: (i) together with external constraints, there exists the equally important category of endogenous constraints; (ii) there is no necessary dilemma between preferences and constraints: for example, given some environmental conditions like uncertainty, or some personal disposition like one to act according to moral principles, preferences (towards risky prospects and a moral code) *are* constraints of the individual's decision-making and hence of his/her behavioural pattern. In this respect, then, preferences are translated into (internal) constraints. Obviously, also the other direction of causality may be true in that some (internal) constraints are translated into preferences: for instance some physical handicap may model the individual's preferences; bounded rationality shapes the individuals' preferences towards a satisfying rather than an optimal goal, and the like. This view seems consistent with the theory of cognitive dissonance: 'In general terms men tend to match their desires and beliefs to their means so as to avoid the intolerable situation of wanting what they cannot have or finding inescapable circumstances undesirable.' (Elster 1993, p. 55).

Within the 'typical' economic environment – namely the marketplace – transaction-cost economics, the economics of information, the principal-agent approach, the economics of uncertainty, and game theory have all focussed on the frictions hampering or precluding fruitful market exchanges: their most dangerous enemies are, as is well-known, absence of legally enforceable property rights, imperfect information about what is being traded and about agents' actions, and the like. In the face of these environmental frictions, the economic agent becomes a '*new*' and somehow more '*sophisticated*' economic agent. Following the lines suggested by Bowles and Gintis (1993), the new homo economicus is now less benign than his ancestor: 'Not satisfied with calculating marginal rates of substitution while shopping for groceries, he now optimizes while deciding how hard to work for his employer, how truthfully to transmit information to his exchange partners, and whether the benefits exceed the costs of defaulting on a loan' (p. 84). Such more demanding activities produce a double impact on the economic agent: on the one side his/her action is conditioned by his/her limited, bounded capacities; on the other side he/she needs a more sophisticated endowment to cope with economic transactions. From this perspective, thus even some deliberate restraints, that is some subjective self-imposed constraints, can be regarded as relevant tools belonging to this more complex individual endowment.

More generally, then, if we ask why endogenous constraints matter, our tentative answer is because the environment envisaged by economic agents is complex, uncertain and evolving; moreover, most of the times individuals experience social interactions that take the form of a PD. It is the environment, then, that is the first source of constraint-governed behaviour; it is the attempt of individuals to cope with it and to increase their adaption to it:[1] moral rules, rules of thumb, self-control rules, procedures, commitments, and routines are all the adaptive response to environmental complexities, uncertainty, evolution, and to the strategic interactions in recurrent social dilemma situations. In many circumstances then, the complexity of the world – that is, its evolution, the potentially innumerable relevant variables, the 'shadow' of the future – as well as the agent's limited resources – both economic and cognitive ones – favour the technology of rules over situational case-by-case decisions. To the extent that such a technology prevents a waste of resources, it turns out to be the most efficient: a routine pattern of behaviour avoids the information-gathering costs the individual would bear in a case-by-case strategy and prevents confusion and mistakes when uncertainty is pervasive; it avoids a bias in favour of short-run interests versus long-run ones; moreover, routine creates reputation, thereby rendering easier strategic control over opponent(s).[2]

The routine strategy applies even to morality for somewhat similar reasons. Allowing for some 'return' from a moral behaviour – such as others' fruitful reciprocal responses – a *moral routine* may be more efficient than a cost-benefit analysis in each situational choice:

'...the more reason a person has to care about his

> reputation, the more rational it may be for him to adopt the rule always to act morally, because it may simply be too costly to try to identify those situations in which rule violation would not be detrimental and/or because the risk of misidentifying such a situation may appear to be too high' (Vanberg 1988, p. 23-24).

The difficulty of representing the economic agent is that there does not exist a representative agent, and this, of course, makes any prediction less straightforward. From this viewpoint, the individual can be thought of as a 'de-centred' subject without an essential core defining him/her (Hargreaves Heap 1993). Edgeworth (1881) was already aware of such a conceptual difficulty: '...between the frozen pole of egoism and the tropical expanse of utilitarianism, there has been granted to imperfectly-evolved mortals an intermediate temperate region; the position of one for whom in a calm moment his neighbour's happiness as compared with his own neither counts for nothing, nor yet 'counts for one', but counts for a fraction... agreeing with the view suggested that the concrete nineteenth century man is for the most part an impure egoist, a mixed utilitarian' (p. 102-4). Likewise, we cannot predict economic agents following either of the two polar patterns of behaviour, pure routine versus situational case-by-case choice; rather they range among these two courses of action.

To justify a 'mixed' behaviour on the part of economic agents, we can use a public choice perspective as well as the rationality perspective. From the first perspective, the economic agent's situational and constitutional choices (both at the personal level and at the social level) are likely to diverge (Vanberg 1988, Vanberg and Buchanan 1990). At the social level the individual's constitutional choice reflects his/her preferences among alternative environments, whereas at the personal level the constitutional choice or 'implicit constitution' (Priddat 1992) reflects his/her behavioural disposition. So, for example, at the *social level* the individual agrees to a social environment promulgating and preserving morality as well as at the *personal level* he/she favours a disposition to act according to moral rules. Nonetheless, when the individual is confronted with PD situations – given his/her situational constraints – he/she may be induced not to act according to the moral rules pre-selected at the (social and personal) constitutional level. This suggests that the individual is not a 'pure-rule-follower', that is he/she is committed *only to a certain extent*, where the extension of the commitment maybe depends on the situational opportunity-cost of acting according to the constitutional rule. Hence, deviant behaviour may be imputed either to the strength of the rule (or disposition) or to the individual ability to cope with it, given the situational opportunity-costs. This suggests an inverse relationship between the strength of endogenous constraint/individual rule and the exogenous constraint/social rule: the weaker the former, the stronger the latter in order to preserve the constitutional choice. Then, 'constitution is a kind of investment in long-term-rationality constraining or internalizing the negative externalities of short-term-optimization' (Priddat 1992, p. 69).

'Positional externalities' (Frank 1991) offer one of the possible explanations for these conflicting choices of the individual at the constitutional and situational levels. Sometimes the constitutional norm itself – established at the social level on the basis of everybody's preferences – builds up a specific context which stimulates everybody's incentive to free ride. Should the norm disappear, so does the free riding: that is, the 'positional externalities' generated by the constitutional norm – and the associated free-riding incentive – vanish. Schelling's (1973) helmet example elucidates this point. Hockey players, if they are left to their own devices, almost never wear helmets, even if almost all of them would vote in favour of helmet rules in secret ballots. Actually, not wearing a helmet, on the one hand, increases the probability of winning, but on the other hand, increases the probability of getting hurt. If players evaluate the higher probability of winning more than they value the extra safety, it is rational to free ride by escaping the constitutional rule, thereby not wearing helmets. Yet, when all of them get rid of their helmets, the comparative advantages vanish. The usual incentive structure in the face of public-good financing is here replicated: from the agent's perspective the constitutional norm at the social level is valuable only to the extent the others follow it, thus giving him/her a comparative advantage in free-riding.

Deviations from constitutional rule may be explained also in terms of a different nature or by different components of rationality:

PD rationality versus procedural rationality. The difference here is between the rationality of utility maximisation at the level of each specific choice and the rationality (even from an evolutionary perspective) of an overall utility maximisation by following norms, recipes or procedures for action. Within the moral sphere, the behavioural implications associated with these two postulates of rationality are a case-by-case moral action versus a moral routine. The interaction between these two components of rationality shapes the individual behaviour and hence generates a bias in favour of either adherence to or deviation from a routine.

However, even a 'pure' procedural rationality would call for an innovative behaviour in some circumstances. Otherwise not much difference would exist between the inflexible rule follower and the 'rational fool'. Once recognised as a failure in the current rule-governed path of behaviour (in terms of the rate at which it generates non-preferred outcomes, Vanberg 1989) or a change in the environment (actually, what is 'fit' is always relative to an environmental situation) procedural rationality itself calls for a revision of the rule set.

Although the set of rules is not sticky, we should expect some degree of inertia in their revision in so far as learning takes time and is costly: hence, an optimal balance of innovation would require a correct evaluation of the trade-off between the adjustment costs and the rate of less preferred outcomes.[3]

Then, the rate of deviation from a rule-governed path of behaviour is a function of the environment as well: we could expect a positive relationship between the degree of environmental complexity and the likelihood of a rule-following behaviour. On the other hand, within a dynamic context, the more general rules are, the longer the time span over which they are expected to be operative.

In short, some internal factors (the strength of the rules, the nature of rationality and the degree or speed of the revision process) as well as some external factors (the nature of the environment) push the individual towards 'mixed' behaviour.

Once it is recognised that internal constraints exist and play an important role, a related question is evaluating their rationality. We can suggest that situational case-by-case maximisation belongs to a narrow interpretation of rational behaviour or, as argued earlier, to a PD rationality. But a larger notion of rationality – bounded rationality, procedural rationality,[4] evolutionary rationality – would call for rules.

We do not mean that all behavioural routines or procedures are rational (or efficient), we just maintain that favouring behavioural regularities over situational choices is not necessarily irrational. As argued earlier, sometimes efficiency itself calls for a technology of rules as a behavioural expedient, and in economics efficiency seems a strong argument to support their rationality. We do not deny that in some occasions situational cost-benefit analysis shows a greater efficiency than the rule-following methodology; yet, in some other circumstances the cost-benefit analysis in itself is inefficient: the information-gathering process is costly; in addition, with only bounded rationality, the selection of the relevant information turns out to be difficult, and the causality nexus between action and results is even more complex to assess when uncertainty is pervasive. In all these circumstances, rationality itself selects a routine over a situational cost-benefit analysis.

Moreover, the failure of a routine may depend not on the *technology of rules* but rather on the *type of rules selected* – for example, because of a wrong inference from the learning process used to build up a routine. In other words, what may be wrong is not the methodology of using rules but the type of rules used (where the latter may be evaluated from the rate at which they generate non-preferred outcomes). In this circumstance, it is not a matter of changing the 'method-governed' behaviour but rather the 'rule-governed' behaviour. Once a change in the environment or a failure in the learning process or some other shortcoming in the technology of rule building is recognised, it is just a question of searching for a new 'program' that works better, to speak in Simon's terms (1982) or to search for a new 'constitutional choice', to speak in Vanberg's terms (1988). The adaptive fit relative to the environment creates the proper incentives to search for a higher problem-solving ability: 'while 'errors' and 'mistakes' do not have a systematic place within a rational maximization framework, they play an essential and critical role from an evolutionary perspective' (Vanberg 1989, p. 31).

In conclusion, the performance of some behavioural methodology – that is rules without choice versus choice without rules – is context-dependent, and any assessment of it has to account for the complexity of the choice setting, the agent's competence in dealing with situational choices, and the quality of rules themselves. Evaluation of these aspects may induce people to divorce the concept of rationality from that of case-by-case maximisation.

From this perspective, rules create a bridge between procedural rationality and the more sophisticated notion of expressive rationality. 'People are less certain about their objectives and the environment in which they operate, less autonomous but more active and enquiring, one might say, than the people who are fully described by a set of well defined objectives' (Hargreaves Heap and others 1992, p. 3).

By definitively abandoning the means-end framework of the instrumental (or PD or Nash) rationality, the economic agent evaluates his/her own preferences and ends according to a (normative) criterion on what is worth pursuing.[5] Through this normative assessment, actions – and similarly rules and procedures – reflect the individual's assessment of what is valuable: hence, rules and procedures are not necessarily instrumentally linked to situational choices but rather they reflect an overall idea, a more comprehensive view, of worthiness and goodness (in this respect, then, the Kantian imperative can be thought to belong to the expressive rationality).

The implication is that actions, and specifically rules and procedures, are information-generating devices signalling what individuals regard as worthy and good (Hargreaves Heap 1989): transferring such values from the individual to the social level suggests that, to some extent, conventions, social norms and institutions reflect the expressive rationality of individuals belonging to the same community, their ideals and their moral endowment.

Till now we have assessed that internal constraints exist, that they matter, and that they may be rational. A further question is where they come from. Internal constraints stem from frictions as well as from the evolutionary learning aimed at overcoming them: we mean both environmental and subjective frictions (that is Simon's rationality bounds or Heiner's agent's imperfections). A 'perfect' agent in Heiner's sense (1983) is the one able to maximise in any single circumstance, namely a moment-by-moment optimiser: endowed with frictionless capacities, optimising is his/her best strategy. But for a 'non-perfect' agent, such a strategy turns out to be too demanding: hence, despite its non-optimal results, a 'rule-following' pattern of behaviour remains the best policy. Of course, by no means can moral rules be deduced as the by-product of exogenous as well as internal imperfections. Yet, it is well-known that, from an evolutionary perspective, rules – including the moral ones – are attempts to increase adaptiveness to the environment, given limited subjective capabilities. In other words, natural selection will lead not only to the survival and development of those species that are more adapted to their environment – that is, to the 'survival of the fittest' – but also to greater capacities to react through further adaptation to changes in the environment. Thus, some of the individual's rules come from the learning process which incorporates experiences – one's own past experiences together with the observed ones – and selects them through a mechanism of trial-and-error elimination (Vanberg 1989). Only the most successful experiences become the relevant inputs of the rule-formation process. *Ceteris paribus*, that is to the extent the human being's environment does not evolve in any crucial aspect, such rules tend to be preserved and transmitted: hence, they enter into the genetical background through evolutionary learning. Since 'whatever is successful is likely to appear more often in the future' (Axelrod 1984), also the personal disposition to act according to the technology of constraints is embedded in the genetical transmission, then becoming innate, at least to some extent.

> 'In short, human behaviour is explained not in terms of a reliably forward-looking maximizing calculus, but in terms of a 'backward-looking' reliance on what in the past has been experienced as useful strategies' (Vanberg 1989, p. 35).

In some way this 'genetical' character of rules and constraints as well as the process of trial-and-error elimination which shapes their set are a component of the knowledge-growth process in its evolutionary perspective; '... the growth of our knowledge is the result of a process closely resembling what Darwin called 'natural selection'; that is, *the natural selection of hypotheses*: our knowledge consists, at every moment, of those hypotheses which have shown their (comparative) fitness by surviving so far in their struggle for existence; a competitive struggle which eliminates those hypotheses which are unfit. ...From the amoeba to Einstein, the growth of knowledge is always the same: we try to solve our problems, and to obtain, by a process of elimination, something approaching adequacy in our tentative solutions' (Popper 1972, p. 261).

NOTES

1. From this perspective the use of rules is evaluated as one of the attempts to understand economics along biological or evolutionary lines. A recent discussion on the use of the biological metaphor in economics is in Hodgson (1992).
2. A discussion of these aspects includes the contributions by Buchanan (1975), Heiner (1983), Vanberg (1988), Prelec and Herrnstein (1991).
3. A certain degree of inertia in rule revision can be explained also through an evolutionary perspective: 'In general, there has to be a degree of resistance to change, with small or negligible responses to minor fluctuations in conditions, and stresses have to be quite severe before new developmental adaptations are triggered. Otherwise the organism could be over-reacting to environmental fluctuations with disastrous results' (Hodgson 1989, p. 11).
4. Although bounded rationality and procedural rationality share a crucial feature, that of following rules, they diverge significantly in the motivations inducing agents to follow rules. Procedural rationality exhibits a social dimension in that the same rules are shared by several agents: hence, they function as coordinating and communicating devices and not just as means to overcome agents' short-cut calculating abilities, as in bounded rationality (see Hargreaves Heap 1989).
5. A somewhat similar point is recently discussed by Hausman and McPherson (1993).

PART I
THE STRENGTH OF ENDOGENOUS CONSTRAINTS

1 From endogenous constraints to economic results

In his/her action space – the marketplace, the political arena, the family, etc. – the economic agent is confronted with both exogenous and endogenous constraints. Following Hayek (1964), 'useful institutions which serve the intercourse of men, such as language, morals, law, writing or money…' (p. 5) fall into the first category of constraints. And, of course, the list of institutional or externally given set of constraints can be enlarged to include income, technology, information and so on. So, we can argue, some exogenous constraints derive from a need of coordination – so for example language, writing, money – others arise from a scarcity of resources – so for example income, information, technology, time. As Becker (1993) points out, 'Different constraints are decisive for different situations, but the most fundamental constraint is limited time. Economic and medical progress have greatly increased length of life, but not the physical flow of time itself, which always restricts everyone to 24 hours per day. So while goods and services have expanded enormously in rich countries, the total time available to consume them has not.

Thus wants remain unsatisfied in rich countries as well as in poor ones. For while the growing abundance of goods may reduce the value of additional goods, time becomes more valuable as goods become more abundant' (p. 386).

Endogenous constraints, namely the ones internal to the economic agent, are of different types too: they include the ones belonging to the cognitive sphere, to the emotional sphere, and to the moral sphere. Like most of the exogenous constraints, also some of the latter bind economic agents in their decision-making process.

The individuals' bounded rationality, that is their limited computational and information-processing capabilities, creates a constraint arising out of the nature of the decision-takers themselves, and such a constraint makes possible only a limited degree of rationality. The average (wo)man's limited capability to cope with reality comes from two main sources: uncertainty and complexity of the world. From the former viewpoint, such an internal constraint plays a crucial role when agents have imperfect and incomplete information on their exogenous environment and/or the probability to receive some specific information depends on how many people already have it,[1] when they feel little competence in some specific contexts,[2] when they do not quite know whether or not to believe the information, whenever they do not know which informational inputs are needed in their decision-making process, when they ignore the determinants of other people's choices, and so on. It follows that people's decision-making will be affected by *mistakes* – when they assign a wrong subjective probability distribution to events – by *ambiguity* – when they fail to assign a unique subjective probability distribution, or by *ignorance* – when they have no beliefs at all about the likelihood of events (e.g. Kelsey and Quiggin 1992, Barrett and Pattanaik 1993, Kelsey 1993).[3] From the latter perspective – i.e. the complexity of the world, even when individuals know everything they need for their decision-making – that is, even when the (subjective) uncertainty assumption is dropped – they find life too complicated to compute an optimal strategy.[4] Actually, repeated observations show that quantitative increase in available data does not result necessarily in a corresponding rise in quality of decisions. If data is initially restricted, additional information results in better decisions, but beyond a threshold level processing additional data causes mistakes and confusion (Cadet 1992). Further, the individual may over/underestimate the degree of control he/she exerts on the environment ('control illusion') and also neglect or over-emphasise some effects or objectives of his/her action ('value illusion'). Of course, the individual may be supported by a learning process, but this takes time, is costly and may not be fully successful (for example, situations change): once again the optimising rationality collapses and the individual's bounded capacities become his/her endogenous constraint in the actual decision-taking. *Allowing for uncertainty as well as complexity and in the face of limited capabilities, constraining one's own behaviour by using rules (of thumb) becomes an indispensable method for coping with reality*. The concern, then, is with discovering the most effective rules of thumb, which economise on the scarce resources of the mind.[5] From this perspective, hence, the focus shifts away from the orthodox viewpoint of 'choices within constraints' to 'choices among constraints'. In other words, borrowing an expression by Raiffa (1991), 'Decision trees are made, not borne' (p. 341): on the one hand, they generally involve a high degree of complexity and abstraction; on the other hand, their building up is likely to reflect the individual's as well as environmental imperfections. To the extent decision trees are too complex, imperfect or incomplete, they can be replaced by simpler, 'standard' rules. For example, ambiguity (in the technical sense referred to before) may lead the individual to select as his/her decision rule the maximin criterion or also to privilege the *status quo* (Kelsey and Quiggin 1992, Kelsey 1993).[6]

In addition, emotions as well as other psychological factors may affect the agent's choice-making process, especially under conditions of uncertainty. There is no doubt that the emotional and psychological sphere may significantly affect the economic one by imposing some (internal) constraint to the agent's choices. The degree of anxiety influences the results of his/her economic activity, his/her saving decisions, his/her preferences towards risky assets, etc. After all, risk aversion – and the related economic choices such as the insurance decision – comes from the psychological sphere. Furthermore, strong emotions may affect the allocation of one's energy, constraining or emphasising one's efforts. Posture, the rate of breathing, or the timbre of the voice may be interpreted as clues relating to the counterpart's behavioural disposition that could favour or prevent some economic exchanges. Even the spreading of emotions may affect economic results: for example, panic may affect the performance of financial markets, fashion the purchases of consumption goods, and so on. After all, the 'animal spirits' derive directly from emotions.

This last consideration suggests that the effectiveness of such constraints is not necessarily associated with the rationality requisite: as Arrow (1986) suggests, any economic theory that is linked with reality, as for instance Keynesian theory, is based on hypotheses that differ from that of rationality.

Also the moral code – not to cheat, to reciprocate fair behaviour, to tell the truth, to keep a promise, to respect personal and property rights, or in a phrase, to do the 'right thing' – may create binding constraints on the individual's action. Sometimes moral constraints are even more demanding since they imply a concern for others: in this circumstance, morality also means altruism. Of course, such a distinction is arbitrary and vulnerable to many criticisms: regardless of the boundary between altruism and other moral rules, we might characterise the whole morality sphere as an 'impartial' constraint (Vanberg 1988) in that the individual is induced to pursue an action which is beneficial to other people or to the whole society, rather than to his/her immediate interest (when, of course, social and personal interests diverge). At the extreme, the Kantian imperative induces people to do the 'right thing' regardless of the particular incentive structure associated with specific choice settings.

Turning back to Hayek's argument, he includes among what we have defined as exogenous constraints also morality. The argument requires a further qualification: (i) we have to distinguish between coordination rules and moral rules. Actually, their nature and their behavioural implications largely differ, with the latter involving PD-type situations (Sugden 1986, 1989, Vanberg 1988, Vanberg and Buchanan 1990, Hardin 1993). Coordination rules or conventions – such as road rules, language rules, the use of a general medium of exchange – in some way are self-enforcing since there arise only personal disadvantages to drive on the wrong side of the road or to use a language which other people do not understand: each person wants to follow it just because everyone else does. Hence, no adverse incentive of free-riding arises: personal and social interests largely coincide.[7] Moral rules, conversely, are not self-enforcing: within a social setting, interdependence in group behaviour incorporates both congruence and conflict of interests in such a way that usually there is a strong incentive for pursuing self-interest rather than social interest. Social institutions, then, are required to preserve moral rules across society. (ii) Only when individual moral constraints are translated into an institutional setting aimed at promulgating and preserving moral values, these also become exogenous constraints. Social pressure or some kind of expected sanctions usually affect individuals' behaviour significantly.

We can distinguish different sources of subjective constraints: some of them are 'natural' or innate, so to say. Namely, they are (at least to some extent) beyond the individual's influence, though they emerge within the individual as genetic disposition: so, for example, bounded rationality. In some respect, such constraints are 'given', like the external ones. Some other subjective constraints are 'artificial' in that individuals are able, at least to some extent, to 'manipulate' or even to build such constraints up *ad hoc*, i.e. in order to better cope with the environment and pursue their own goals. As far as morality is concerned, moral rules are partially manipulated in that the learning process plays an important role. For example, past experience, the reward and punishment mechanism the individual faces, parents' investment in human capital of their children,[8] as well as social interactions affect the individual's moral constraint. In this respect, morality is very close to other 'human' endowments which reflect the individual's 'history', investment decisions, previous experience, and so on (Vanberg 1988).

Then, the artificial endogenous constraints may be the outcome of the learning process which modifies what the individual *can* do. That is, the learning process can modify the individuals' 'behavioural technology' (Kliemt 1990). At the end of this transformation process, 'individuals may get locked in with certain habits, traits of character or behavioral dispositions that seem to restrict their strategy space' (p. 75).

Some others of these artificial endogenous constraints derive from the individual's *voluntary restriction* of his/her degrees of freedom.[9] That is, individuals choose to 'chain' themselves to certain behavioural rules that are endogenously determined: they are for example empirical rules such as rules of thumb, routines, procedures, or commitments. Apparently the strategy of devising 'homemade' constraints seems inconsistent with the rationality paradigm; yet, as will be shown later, rationality seems compatible with a voluntary restriction of one's strategy space and even to require it. The rationally self-imposed constraints may be required in several occasions:[10] (i) under uncertainty conditions, (ii) with market failures, (iii) within the strategic interaction either with *other individuals* or with *other selves*[11] (Schelling, 1984b, refers to the strategy of consciously coping with one's own behaviour as 'strategic egonomics' and Ainslie, 1992, as 'picoeconomics').

In binding one's choices, the technology of the internal constraints may operate in two directions (Kliemt 1990): the individual may either alter his/her strategy space by eliminating some available choice through behavioural rules or commitments, and/or he/she may alter the material incentive, namely the payoff associated to some (still) available choice. In the latter case, although not eliminated by the feasible opportunity set, the choice is not any longer attractive. The techniques for self-control used by Ulysses facing the Sirens[12] and by the future mother during the delivery fall into the first class of strategies. As explained by Schelling (1984a), an increasing occurrence of obstetricians is the future mother's request to withhold anesthesia during delivery. Physicians often suggest that a facemask be put next to the patient during the delivery to provide her with it should she need it; yet some of them refuse such an opportunity *a priori*. The interesting aspect is that even an experienced woman – who is able to anticipate both the pain during the delivery and the consequent request of relief through anesthesia – refuses it *ex ante*, that is before the critical time. Actually, she expects to regret afterwards the use of anesthesia (since, for example, she thinks it turns out to be detrimental for the health of both her child and herself). The future mother anticipates a transient period when current preferences change dramatically and are replaced by 'contingent' preferences: so she needs cooperation from the medical team in order not to satisfy the latter ones (which would induce her to ask for anesthesia). She may ratify her choice afterwards by expressing her gratitude that no anesthesia was provided even when requested according to the new, 'contingent' preferences. In both the Ulysses and future mother cases, then, *ex ante* elimination of some available choice requires cooperation from others (the crew and the medical team respectively): although this aspect is not an essential requisite for self-imposing endogenous constraints, it helps in building them up.

The well-known blackmail story by Schelling (1960) and Frank (1988, 1989) belongs to the second category of self-constraining strategies. The frightened kidnapper wants to set his victim free, but is afraid that the latter will go to the police soon after, although, in return for his freedom, the victim gladly promises not to do so: actually, after obtaining his freedom, the victim has no incentive to keep the promise. In other words, he can offer only 'cheap talk': anticipation of that leads the kidnapper to the decision to kill his victim. The way out for the latter is to commit himself an act in the presence of his captor whose disclosure could lead to blackmail: in this way a bond is created between captor and victim. The victim of the blackmail is still free to go to the trial to accuse his captor soon after he has got his freedom, but the shame for his previous act induces him not to pursue that course of action.

Both 'natural' and 'artificial' endogenous constraints may succeed in overcoming PD-like situations faced when market failure occurs (point (ii) above) and strategic interactions emerge (point (iii) above). These constraints modify the players' incentive structure and the emergence of cooperation leads to the highest payoff.[13] In an evolutionary perspective, the long-run success of the cooperative solution may induce individuals to render 'exogenous' their (moral) 'endogenous' constraints through social institutions aimed at promulgating and preserving social norms. As at the individual level, the *social* techniques to constrain people's behaviour may operate in two (complementary) directions: either by eliminating some non-moral option of behaviour from the agents' choice setting or by altering the relevant payoff associated to some non-moral behaviour. Taboos may be regarded as one means operating in the first direction, and social pressure or other social sanctions operate in the second direction.

A particular class of endogenous constraints are the ones arising from belonging to a specific ethnic group. We need to qualify both the nature of such constraints and how they promote economic results.[14] Ethnic membership is grounded on blood and on other physical features as well as on specific preferences and behavioural rules largely reflecting the cultural background of the group. It follows that: (i) to some extent 'membership' is not subject to choice; (ii) there exist some barriers to entry and exit: it is very difficult for an outsider of the community to get the membership as well as for an insider to get rid of it. One straightforward implication is that Tiebout's model (1956), which is an application of the standard perfect competition model, does not apply within a large society populated by strong 'minorities' since inter-community mobility is significantly precluded; (iii) one noteworthy consequence from our perspective is that *blood, behavioural rules and specific preferences can be regarded as endogenous constraints* which link people to (or exclude them from) an ethnic network. Referring to our previous discussion – the source of internal constraints – some of them (blood and other physical characteristics of the ethnic group) are beyond the individual's control, that is they are 'natural' or innate. Some others, the ethnic behavioural rules – and to some extent even preferences – somehow reflect a learning process which shapes what the individual, as a member of the ethnic group, can actually do or wish.

Ethnic constraints influence economic results in several respects:[15] first, by controlling specific limited resources or markets. For example, an ethnic group may enjoy some comparative advantages to get the best jobs; accordingly, it may also affect market mobility. Second, an ethnic membership creates a trust network among the insiders of the group. Within the same group, generally it is easier to communicate with one another and/or to predict the behaviour of the other party. In other words, the need of knowing and of monitoring the other's behaviour is reduced; accordingly, when market imperfections render some potentially profitable exchange either not viable or very costly, the ethnic network becomes a valuable good.

Lower transaction costs and the consequent capability to exploit gains from trade in the marketplace provide the whole ethnic community with some comparative advantages, which may lead it even to market control: in evolutionary terms, exploiting the competitive advantages accruing from membership to some specific group increases the adaptiveness of the group itself, i.e. its survival strength. These arguments provide a rationale for developing and preserving a group identity through barriers: they are grounded on investment in ethnic capital,[16] sanctions against defectors, conflict against outsiders (discrimination and xenophobia), and ethnic norms.

To the extent specific ethnic features produce economic benefits, the ethnic network may be regarded as a public good; conversely, as long as ethnic characteristics preclude or limit economic opportunities, the ethnic network can be thought of as a public bad. Then, the traditional free-rider and externality problems arise: some would like to enjoy the benefits accruing from differentiation without bearing the associated costs for barrier building (e.g. by escaping from contributing in ethnic capital formation); others outside the group cannot be excluded from some positive spillovers stemming from the ethnic group or would join it to enjoy its greater comparative advantages. It can be suggested, then, that there is a positive relationship between the attitude of free riding and/or the size of externalities and the magnitude of barriers: in other words, barriers (built up also through social pressure, xenophobia, racial conflicts and the emergence of nationalism) can be thought of as a mechanism to reduce free-riding and externalities or as an extreme attempt to internalise them.

NOTES

1. This type of what we can label the 'information externalities' is extensively examined by Banerjee (1993) within a particular information-transmission structure, that is the rumour process.
2. See Heath and Tversky (1991).
3. Camerer and Weber (1992) review recent literature on ambiguity in decision-making.
4. This individual's shortcoming is what Dosi and Egidi (1991) call 'knowledge incompleteness'.
5. On this aspect see, for example, Hey (1981, 1982).
6. The preference for the *status quo* can be explained also on the grounds of the competence hypothesis formulated by Heath and Tversky (1991). According to the authors, the agents' willingness to bet on an uncertain event depends not only on the estimated likelihood of that event and the precision of that estimate but also on their general knowledge or understanding of the relevant context. In other terms, even holding

judged probability constant, individuals prefer to bet in a context where they consider themselves knowledgeable or competent rather than in a context where they feel ignorant or uninformed. One of the implications of the competence on decision-making that we suggest here is that people prefer the *status quo* in situations where they feel uncomfortable about what they know relative to what can be known. Accordingly, it can be argued that preference for the *status quo* is inversely related to general knowledge, familiarity and experience. Our suggestion is further reinforced when psychic payoffs – due to credit and blame from the others – are associated with the outcome (Heath and Tversky 1991): if the individual has limited understanding of some specific problem, failure will be attributed to ignorance, whereas success is likely to be attributed to chance. Conversely, if the individual is an 'expert', success is attributable to knowledge, whereas failure to chance. This asymmetric evaluation of success and failure may induce 'unexpert' people to choose the *status quo* (or conventions or generally agreed behaviours).

7. Following Young (1993) 'A convention is a pattern of behavior that is customary, expected, and self-enforcing. Everyone conforms, everyone expects others to conform, and everyone wants to conform given that everyone else conforms...there is a customary and expected behavior, and everyone prefers to follow the behavior expected of him provided that others follow the behavior expected of them. Under these circumstances we say that people follow a convention. A convention is an equilibrium that everyone expects' (p. 57).
8. A series of well-known papers by Becker deal with this aspect. See, for example, Becker (1992, 1993).
9. Also the deliberate restriction of his/her action space is the result of the learning process. Agent's behaviour and his/her preferences are modelled by the reward/punishment system faced within social interactions. Past experience, then, that is past rewards and punishment, is channelled as a relevant input into the learning process of the individual. Such a process, together with the capacity to generalise from what he/she has already faced, allows the individual to discriminate between different situations and to adopt his/her behaviour to the environment accordingly, by means of voluntary self-imposed behavioural constraints. Starting from the evolutionary biology approach to human behaviour and individual preferences, a similar conclusion is reached by Witt (1985): 'Even if a genetic disposition for the one or the other behaviour exists this can hardly emerge without being modified by environmental, group-specific effects due to learning (conditioning) and insight' (p. 384). Recent discussions on this point are in Bergstrom and Stark (1993) as well as in Simon (1993). The last one makes a link between bounded rationality and conditioning from environment: 'Because of bounded rationality, docility contributes to the fitness of human beings in evolutionary competition. By

'docility' I mean *the tendency to depend on suggestions, recommendations, persuasion, and information obtained through social channels as a major basis for choice*. Most of us who restrict our consumption of fats do so, not because our own experience and research has provided convincing evidence that a fatty diet is unhealthy, but because we have been told, on reliable authority, that such a diet is harmful. 'Reliable authority' is a term describing a social system and interpersonal relations within it. In large measure, we do what we do because we have learned from those who surround us... Behaving in this fashion contributes heavily to our fitness because (a) social influences will generally give us advice that is 'for our own good' and (b) the information on which this advice is based is far better than the information we could gather independently. As a consequence, *people exhibit a very large measure of docility*. On average, it contributes to their fitness and hence drives out nondocility in evolutionary competition' (p. 156-7).

10. Many of these arguments are developed in an earlier version of this work (Fiocca 1992b).
11. One way to reconcile these two views of the agent's *inter-personal* and *intra-personal* conflicts is by thinking that even within a setting of multi-agent interactions and interdependent decision-making, to some extent the relevant 'self' is identified by the relationship with the 'others' (Hargreaves Heap 1993): accordingly, we can label it 'positional self'. We can suggest, then, that from this game-theoretical perspective the emerging 'self' (for example the cooperative one vs. the non-cooperative one) is the *consequence of a contingent renewal of an (implicit) contract* among players, that is conditional to the opponents' action. In other words, the nature of the game of the other players generates an externality on the incentive structure of the individual, each time identifying a new, different self. This argument does not apply, however, when people exhibit 'unconditional' behaviour, like the one induced by Kantian motivations.
12. The classical work on the subject is by Strotz (1955-1956); a more recent discussion is by Gauthier (1991).
13. For an analysis of the emergence of a cooperative solution among players with bounded rationality, see Zemel (1989). In his study cooperative behaviour is obtained in a finitely repeated prisoner's dilemma game where the players are equipped with a formal channel of communication which allows them to send messages to each other, concurrently with the actual moves of the game. The relevant aspect of the game is that the communication protocol used does not involve the transfer of any relevant information: it is just there as a device to tire the players. It saturates their limited calculating resources, hence preventing them from engaging in complex strategies which could potentially

undermine cooperation.

14. Recent contributions on this topic include the ones by Wintrobe (1992), Pagano (1992), Hardin (1993), Simon (1993).
15. An extensive analysis of the economic motivations of nationalism is in Pagano (1992).
16. Typically parents invest in the ethnic capital of their children by sending them to ethnic schools, inculcating ethnic customs, etc. expecting in the future to be repaid with support and choices in accordance with their preferences. An extensive discussion on this point is in Wintrobe (1992) and Borjas (1992).

2 Endogenous constraints and uncertainty

As is well-known, the Expected Utility Theory (EUT) relies on numerous testable hypotheses which have been systematically violated in experimental testing. Although the theory is perfectly valid from the formal point of view or from a normative perspective, the axiomatic propositions it entails are too sophisticated to describe real behaviour; rather they represent a stylised, idealised decision-taker, that is an 'economythical' agent unaffected by mistakes, confusion, inconsistency, lapses of memory, particular mental states. Yet, much of these failures of the theory stem from just such psychological factors or mental states which do affect the decision-taker.[1]

Among those, an important element that the expected utility model neglects is the impact on the decision-maker of the 'counterfactual' information: that is, in the EUT what matters are the properties of the prevailing consequence itself the individual experiences and the relation between such a consequence and his/her tastes or preferences. Usually, however, individuals evaluate not only the consequence occurring by itself but also how this consequence stands in relation to other possible consequences which did not occur – either because in the past decision the individual has chosen a certain course of action within the available set or because a certain state of the world failed to occur. In other words, in the individual's judgment a strong comparative element operates such as the comparison of consequences of different decisions under the same state of the world or of the same decision under alternative states of the world: not only are the properties of the consequence experienced relevant *per se* but also their relations to the properties of other consequences that have not occurred. From this comparison, a feeling of regret/rejoice may arise, depending on the properties of the missed alternative consequences.[2] Such a feeling, then, displays a double impact on the individual: it modifies his/her utility function; moreover, anticipation of this feeling modifies the decision-taking. In this respect, therefore, it can be suggested that the consequences which did not occur create an externality - which can be regarded as a special case of 'positional externalities'[3] - where the source of such externalities is the 'location' of the individual within the frame of reference. Anticipation of this externality affects the agent's decision-making. Such a 'location' or 'context' effect is far from odd, although economic theory generally assumes that agents evaluate their welfare on some *absolute* basis.[4] Yet, position with respect to 'things' and 'people' matters, thereby generating externalities in the form of envy, sympathetic concerns, rejoice, regret, etc.[5] In addition, as has been extensively investigated, the frame - which defines the agent's location - plays an important role in decision-making when risky prospects are involved[6] (see below).

Turning back to regret theory, from the individual's point of view, while it may be perfectly rational not to take into account mental states such as regretting and rejoicing in his/her own decision-making process, it is equally rational to recognise the fact that an alternative choice had put him/herself in a preferable/worse situation and take the consequent feeling into account in his/her decision-taking.

Furthermore, a substantial body of experimental evidence documents that violations of the EUT principles derive from the significant restrictions assumed by the theory about individuals' preferences (even the principle of transitivity has been violated in experiments)[7] and about their rationality. When the choice is complex and uncertainty is pervasive the notion of rationality assumed by the EUT seems too demanding in relation to actual individuals' capacities. Mistakes and confusion during the choice-making process under uncertainty may be the major sources of such violations. This happens, for example, in both the well-known '*preference reversal*' (Lichtenstein and Slovic 1971)[8] and the '*framing effect*' (Tversky and Kahneman 1981).[9]

Awareness of the weakness of the axiomatic approach has led research on decision-making to develop in new directions, which are to some extent complementary: having acknowledged phenomena until then unknown (such as the framing effect), economists have attempted to embed them into theory (as in prospect theory). Having noticed that these violations are systematic and that individuals often do not change their preferences even when someone draws their attention to the mistakes they have made in their decision-taking (such as in the 'Allais paradox'), economists have generalised the expected utility theory (as through the generalised EUT by Machina).[10] Or else, they have proposed alternative theories (like regret theory) that could justify such violations also on the grounds of rationality.

In this rapidly changing theoretical framework a central role is taken by a more careful analysis of the psychology of preferences. In this respect, it is well-known that economic theory is traditionally based on two oversimplified hypotheses: under certainty conditions, preferences are 'given' – reflecting the selfish motivations of economic agents; under uncertainty conditions, they are 'given' too – reflecting agents' risk aversion. From the notion of risk aversion introduced in 1783 by Daniel Bernoulli, only recently economic theory has developed a more sophisticated analysis on preference structure.[11] This updated repertoire includes, for example, intrinsic risk attitude,[12] risk-seeking preferences concerning losses, the framing effect, a less intense pleasure of winning a sum compared with the pain of losing the same amount,[13] standard risk aversion,[14] regret aversion, ambiguity aversion,[15] preference for the high-knowledge bet over the matched lottery and preference for the matched lottery over the low-knowledge bet,[16] suspicions about promises of large payoffs,[17] and so on. Moreover, the number of 'paradoxes' that emerged in decision theory – Condorcet's paradox, Arrow's impossibility theorem, Allais's paradox, Ellsberg's paradox – highlights how puzzling are the individuals' preferences. All those are examples indicating that the individual is recognised as exhibiting multiple and more complex preferences, an aspect consequently introduced into the analysis. *In this context an important role is played by self-imposed rules, that is endogenous constraints guiding the decision-taking and/or preventing certain mental states which may affect negatively the optimisation process through confusion and mistakes* (when, of course, the individual can anticipate such psychological factors and their impact on his/her decisions).

Regret theory (Loomes and Sugden 1982, 1983, 1986, 1987), reflecting the optimising behaviour of the regret-averse individual, represents an evolution of EUT, which is 'neutral' with respect to such psychological components.

From the rationality perspective, at least three aspects are worth stressing: (i) the rationality of certain mental states such as regret; (ii) the rationality of embedding them in the decision-taking; (iii) the rationality of self-imposing constraints which guide agents in their decision-taking aimed at optimising, whenever these mental states play an important role.

With respect to point (i), although we can legitimately maintain (following EUT) that it is rational not to experience such mental states, yet we cannot argue either that they are *ir*rational on theoretical grounds. With respect to point (ii), if the individual, on the grounds of past experience, can anticipate such mental states – like regret or rejoice stemming from his/her choice – it is perfectly rational to assume that these mental states contribute to shaping the process of future decision-making, and then to take them into account, just like any other information input used in such a process. It is precisely a feature of rationality that all the relevant information needed to make a choice is gathered and selected.

Moreover, the rationality of an individual who behaves according to the predictions of regret theory may be justified also from another point of view. It may be legitimately assumed that an individual maximises a utility function that is 'modified' in order to account for regret or rejoice. The idea of utility maximisation that is coherent with that of optimising rationality is therefore entirely preserved. This, obviously, does not mean that only the maximisation of a 'modified' utility is rational, but, rather, that there is room for both theories.

Last, concerning point (iii), when some 'atypical' elements such as regret or rejoice may affect the optimisation process, *the fact that individuals select certain rules that bring decision-making towards optimisation may be perfectly coherent with the notion of rationality. The latter underlines the relevance of the rules that govern the behaviour of economic agents.*

A further step in this direction which justifies the relevance of behavioural rules for the regret-averse individual is prospect theory. Like regret theory, this also stresses the relevance of mental states in shaping the decision-taking process. One of the assumptions of the theory is the different degree of regret stemming from different types of behaviour:

> 'The regret associated with a loss that was incurred by an action tends to be more intense than the regret associated with inaction or a missed opportunity. These observations and others of a similar character contribute to the understanding of how people make decisions and to the elucidation of some puzzles of rational choice' (Kahneman and Tversky 1982, p. 136).

They go on to say:

> 'Regret is a special form of frustration in which the event one would change is an action one has either taken or failed to take. A natural extension of the hypothesis we have developed for the analysis of frustration is that regret is felt if one can readily imagine having taken an action that would have led to a more desirable outcome. This interpretation explains the close link between the experience of regret and the availability of choice: actions taken under duress generate little regret. The reluctance to violate standard procedures and to act innovatively can also be an effective defense against subsequent regret because it is easy to imagine doing the conventional thing and more difficult to imagine doing the unconventional one.
>
> A closely related hypothesis is that it is often easier to mentally delete an event from a chain of occurrences than it is to imagine the insertion of an event into the

> chain. Such a difference in imaginability could help to explain the observation that the regret associated with failures to act is often less intense than the regret associated with the failure of an action.' (Kahneman and Tversky 1982, p. 141-142).[18]

Bearing in mind Kahneman-Tversky's point, we could possibly combine regret theory with prospect theory to suggest that the two types of behaviour – 'break the routine versus follow the rules' – determine a different degree of regret stemming from the wrong decision. Actually, the degree of regret is supposed to be bigger or smaller – the size of the loss being equal – when the latter stems from an innovative rather than from a standard behaviour which is grounded on pre-selected rules. For example, if the treatment of a certain disease were to fail, the doctor's feelings – or those of the patient, for all that – would be different, in the sense that he/she would feel a bigger or smaller regret, depending on the fact that the therapy he/she adopted was a new one rather than a traditional one. Or else, a fall in sales determines a different degree of regret for the sales manager (or the owner) depending on whether the sales campaign is the usual one or else it differs from that of the last years. In both cases, if the doctor or the sales manager have used new methods, the chances of losing their jobs could be higher when a negative outcome occurs.[19]

Therefore, in these instances, to adhere to pre-existing rules may be a useful instrument to reduce the size of unpleasant feelings. In the above cases of the therapy or of the sales campaign, these rules come from the environment (doctrine, marketing techniques, etc). However, even voluntary self-restraint of one's domain of action by means of own rules of behaviour may have the same effect. *'External' constraints (habits, conventions, traditions, doctrine) as well as 'internal' ones may equally lead decision-making towards optimisation when one's mental state becomes important in decision-making itself.* In Part II we will show how self-imposed constraints may be important to 'manipulate' certain mental states that affect optimisation under uncertainty. For this purpose, we shall suggest a particular combination between regret and prospect theories.

NOTES

1. Many counter-examples to expected utility behaviour concerning such mental states include contributions by Allais (1953), Tversky (1975), Machina (1981), Loomes and Sugden (1982), McClennen (1983). An extensive discussion about the effects of moods on decision-making is in Pieters and Raaij (1988).
2. A typical example of how the comparison between properties of consequences matters is that if a gain of $10.00 is the result of 90 per cent of success, the total utility experienced *ex-post*, given the individual has won the gamble, will be lower than if it resulted from a 10 per cent chance of success. This is because the individual would have had a lower expectation for the second gamble, so that when he/she discovers his/her success, the utility given by the $10.00 consequence is boosted by a feeling of rejoicing, greater than the boost that success at the first gamble would have given.
3. 'Positional externalities' formulated by Frank (1991) define situations where the individual's utility depends upon comparison with the others. Here this comparison has been extended to alternative states of the world.
4. For example, it is generally assumed that the level of utility depends upon the bundle of goods the individual does personally consume, given his/her feasible opportunity set. Accordingly, utility is not assumed to be related to the amount other people consume of such goods, or to the amount he/she would have consumed had other states of the world prevailed. Similarly, the individual's preference ordering is invariant over changes in the *representation* of the feasible consumption set. Yet, to some extent the frame of reference or relative setting can significantly affect both the individual's utility function and his/her decision-making. For example, the agents' feeling of competence in a given context - i.e. what they know relative to what others know - affects their willingness to bet on an uncertain event (Heath and Tversky 1991). Comparative assessments and 'perspective illusions' in the face of risky prospects are two of the major sources of such a 'positional' bias. (A somewhat similar point is in Kahneman and Varey 1991). A recent analysis on these aspects is in Fiocca (1994).
5. See, for example, Vickrey (1962) and Frank (1985).
6. Under uncertain conditions it has been argued elsewhere (Fiocca 1990a) that uncertainty becomes a veil between reality and individual risk judgments: sometimes this veil causes mistakes and confusion; other times it simply causes another way of reasoning and understanding problems, i.e. another way of looking at the decision-making problem. Accordingly, sometimes the role of position is mistakenly perceived in decision-making as a consequence of confusion and misrepresentation of

environmental messages under uncertainty. Other times the relevance of position is still consistent with a more complex notion of rationality, also under uncertainty. Hence, the link between the relevance of the relative setting and rationality needs a broad notion of rationality – extended to include its evolutionary dimension – and a more complex structure of motivations – to allow for comparative issues. Passing, it should be noted that the role of position has been evaluated even in experiments involving animals – rats as well as insects – rather than human beings as players (see Battalio and others 1985).

7. Such violations have recently been evaluated also from a normative perspective by Anand (1993).

8. The 'preference reversal' phenomenon sheds some light on how subjects make mistakes even in a very simple framework, such as when they are asked to convert a lottery ticket into a certain sum. In the 'P bet-$ bet' game, the individual is confronted with a choice between a pair of gambles and he/she is asked to assess, for each gamble, what is the certainty equivalent, that is the amount of money payment for certain which makes him/her indifferent to taking the gamble. In many answers the preferred gamble was the one involving a lower certainty equivalent. The preference-reversal phenomenon in social contexts (Loomes and Taylor 1992, Irwin and others 1993) involves serious difficulties in determining the certainty-equivalent that (some category of) people are willing (i) to accept as compensation for risky public projects or (ii) to pay for changes in risks involving damages or injury. Both assessments typically involve a trade-off between small probabilities of highly undesirable outcomes ($ bet) and larger probabilities of moderately undesirable outcomes (P bet). If the mispreferred outcome is the former, preference reversal would imply respectively (i) people's willingness to accept a lower subsidy for public projects of $-bet type, and (ii) taxpayers' willingness to contribute with lower amounts in financing a social insurance against $-bet occurrence. These difficulties involved in social decision-making in the presence of risky prospects give rise, then, to a further problem, i.e. how to determine the certainty-equivalent sums actually as subjects involved in choice-making incurred in mistakes and confusion. The alternative solution, namely assessment of the certainty-equivalent by a third party, would imply the usual problem of inter-personal utility comparisons.

9. The essence of 'framing' or 'reference point' effect is that decision-makers facing risky prospects consistently confuse issues of form (that is, certain presentational features of the problems) and substance (that is, the genuine essence of the problem). Depending on the viewing position (that is, on the references adopted and on the general conditions of presenting the issue), consequences are seen differently: in other words, the decision is affected not only by assessments of probability and utility; the overall

apprehension of the set of available elements and the particular environmental tone or hue associated with them systematically influence the decision-taking. A well-known example is a neat illustration of the role of the decision frame: a group of physicians was presented with some probabilistic data about the effectiveness of two alternative treatments of two forms of cancer. Each physician was asked to choose between the two treatments. However, some physicians were presented with the data in the form of 'survival probabilities', while the rest of the group was given exactly the same information, but in a different form, that is 'mortality probabilities'. It was found that 84 per cent of the physicians chose one treatment over the other when 'survival probabilities' were presented, but the percentage fell to 50 when the choice was presented in terms of 'mortality probabilities'. Among others, recent experiments conducted by Cadet (1992), Ritov and others (1993) confirm the importance played by the frame in decision-taking.

10. On the grounds of experimental evidence (concerning a three-color Ellsberg problem), also Slovic and Tversky (1974) argue that agents are often immune to certain kinds of persuasion.
11. This deeper investigation on the psychology of preferences has led economists to study even that of animals within risky contexts through the experimental methodology. Such experiments were aimed at eliciting the animals' risk attitude and at analysing their violations of the EUT axioms – such as those of transitivity and independence – and even at exploring the framing effect (see Battalio and others 1985).
12. See Schoemaker (1993).
13. '...the threat of a loss has a greater impact on a decision than the possibility of an equivalent gain... It is a commonplace that the pleasure of winning a sum of money is much less intense than the pain of losing the same sum. Accordingly people accept a gamble at even odds only when the possible gain from the gamble is substantially larger than the possible loss. For example, you may find that a 50 per cent chance to lose \$100 is unacceptable unless it is combined with an equal chance to win \$200 or more.' (Kahneman and Tversky 1982, p. 136-138).
14. See Kimball (1993).
15. See Segal (1987).
16. See Heath and Tversky (1991).
17. See Bordley and Hazen (1991).
18. More recent discussions on this point are in Samuelson and Zeckhauser (1988) and in Ritov and Baron (1992).
19. We suggest that the *status quo* is a valuable behavioural rule under uncertainty to overcome both regret and lack of competence. Following the competence hypothesis by Heath and Tversky (1991), agents prefer to bet in situations where they feel competent rather than in those where they consider themselves ignorant. Beside the monetary payoffs, the

authors suggest some psychological payoff in the form of credit and blame – associated with the outcome. If the decision-maker has limited understanding of some specific problem, failure will be attributed to ignorance, whereas success is likely to be attributed to chance. Conversely, if the individual is an 'expert', success is attributable to knowledge, whereas failure to chance. Hence, when agents' knowledge is small relative to what can be known, blame aversion should induce them to follow a generally agreed/conventional pattern of behaviour (or the *status quo*). Hence, the *status quo* could be regarded as a good recipe in both cases of regret aversion and blame aversion. Conformity to the *status quo* is, then, a typical example of behavioural rule under uncertainty when psychological factors matter.

3 Endogenous constraints and the market

In many respects, market performance affects morality; in many respects, morality affects market performance. One dimension of this double interaction between market and morality is that the market does not discriminate among (racial, religious, political, economic) groups, that is the market does not segregate; however, the anonymity of individuals relative to the market mechanism tends to 'flatten' group identity and other values which play an important role in the formation/preservation of moral values within society.[1] Moreover, integration and enlargment of markets tend to dampen the force of moral values;[2] on the other hand, the work ethic influences the size of the market (Buchanan 1991) and the impact of the (altruistically-motivated) voluntary sector on market structures may prevent the evolution of markets themselves (Stark 1993). Furthermore, ethical evaluation affects the types of good which can be exchanged in the marketplace – a familiar argument is the one by Titmuss (1971) on human blood; on the other hand the market mechanism, with the transaction and information-gathering costs involved as well as the power position enjoyed by some transactors, creates an asymmetry between the two sides of the market at the expense of either the supplier or the consumer, thus rendering 'unfair', and hence unviable, some exchange. That is, there is an *ethical limitation of the market* as well as a *market limitation of the ethical exchanges*. These reciprocal externalities generated both by the market and morality suggest that individuals are ethically as well economically interdependent.

One implication of these spillover effects is that usually economic systems tend to rely on the existence of moral incentives promoting work motivations beyond the narrow calculation of immediate personal gain. The backwardness of some economies (Weber 1930, Banfield 1958) is largely due to the scarcity of moral resources and the narrow pursuit of self-interest, whereas the extraordinary level of efficiency experienced by others partially reflects a particular behavioural code based on duty, loyalty and goodwill (Sen 1977, 1987). Acknowledgment that 'work is *work with others* and *work for others*' generates a feeling of belonging to a working community, where diligence, industriousness, reliability and fidelity in interpersonal relationships become strategic inputs of the productive process where human work (as a set of skills, technology, know-how) acquires a central role (Centesimus Annus).

From this perspective, the interrelation between morality and economics rests on the interrelation between duties and economic-social consequences. For example, the justification of profit maximisation relies on several arguments such as that of 'forced maximisation' (Alchian 1950, Friedman 1953) – or in evolutionary terms, of 'survival of the fittest'[3] – and that of the role of profits as a relevant means in producing economic efficiency; yet, awareness of this fact must be 'weighted' by the recognition of the trade-off between efficiency and the social losses which may arise from the maximisation paradigm: 'Profit is a regulator of the life of a business, but it is not the only one; *other human and moral factors* must also be considered which, in the long term, are at least equally important for the life of a business' (Centesimus Annus). Another example relates to the behavioural constraints binding managers and administrators who enjoy private, 'inside', information. Usually the 'insider trading' is ruled out on ethical grounds, namely on unfairness; however, beyond this moral assessment there exists an economic assessment, namely the significant costs of monitoring insiders' behaviour, and the consequent waste of resources. Hence, economic rules and regulations as well as moral codes of conduct may play an important role in affecting economic performance.[4]

The aim of common growth within society inspired by one's social commitment and cooperation affects also one's investment decisions. The choice to invest in one market (geographic area, productive sector, etc.) rather than in another one may reflect a private cost-benefit analysis accounting also for moral considerations – such as giving the chance to human and other economic resources to develop and implement their own potentialities. Hence, redistribution goes beyond a mere charitable giving, social security, tax treatment, allowing also for a transfer of real opportunities, of access to the labour and product markets, of knowledge and skill, etc. Also from this standpoint, then, morality affects the performance and the potentialities of both input and output markets.

In addition, preferences for a fair treatment may influence both the behaviour of the firm and the market. When the market structure allows it (especially under monopolistic conditions), enterprises are encouraged to use their 'ultimatum' power (in terms of consumer surplus) at the expense of their customers. In these circumstances public intervention, for example by means of regulation, may be justified precisely by the need to eliminate, or reduce, such a power. In the same way, other factors, like sticky wages together with high unemployment, may be interpreted in such a perspective. Differently from the more 'traditional' theory of implicit contracts (e.g. Azariadis 1975) that explains sticky wages essentially on the grounds of workers' risk aversion, these theories explain sticky wages in terms of fairness. This applies even to temporary jobs, which do not guarantee workers from the risk of future unemployment.[5]

Turning now to goods markets, sticky prices may be explained by consumers' reluctance to make 'unfair' transactions, as for instance when prices rise but costs do not (Okun 1981) '...firms in the sports and entertainment industries offer their customers tickets at standard prices for events that clearly generate excess demand. Popular new models of automobiles may have waiting lists that extend for months. Similarly, manufacturers in a number of industries operate with backlogs in booms and allocate shipments when they obviously could raise prices and reduce the queue.' (p. 170). The same sense of fairness may explain why consumers may consider a price rise to be fair, even when demand is low: '...in practice, observed pricing behavior is a vast distance from...do-it-yourself auctioneering...' (p. 169).

The results of a survey by Kahneman and others (1986b) confirm that market conditions can somehow reflect the 'common idea' of fairness. For instance, sales managers may follow three alternative methods to allocate the tickets for a match when supply is short of demand. They can distribute them: (i) according to the willingness to pay the highest price; (ii) randomly, by means of a lottery; (iii) rationing by queues. According to the survey, by an efficiency criterion the best method would be that of allocating the tickets to those who are willing to pay the highest prices, while the worst one, which determines a loss of resources, turns out to be rationing through queues. Conversely, following the equity criterion, it is the last method that appears to be the best one. On the other hand, as we have seen elsewhere (Fiocca 1991), agents are not always willing to favour the efficient choice versus the ethical one (whenever, of course, these two choices are incompatible). However, even apart from ethical considerations, some conventions within society, such as rationing by queue (Sugden 1989), confirm that many behaviours that are established and generally accepted may reflect rules and criteria that are far from efficient.

As we have just mentioned, the ethical motivation may affect not only market conditions but also the individual firm's choice. This occurs essentially when success in the firm's transactions also depends on customer and staff willingness to 'punish' its unfair behaviour. Therefore, apart from institutional constraints (stemming from law, technology, and so on), profit maximisation is limited by moral considerations. Investing in a firm's reputation, being unwilling to provide 'lemons' and to fully exploit the opportunities provided by market conditions are different aspects of this 'opportunistic' perception of justice that allows the firm to maximise profits in the long-run.

However, not always an 'instrumental' use of morality motivates the firm's fair behaviour. Even if there are no 'external' constraints such as a 'threat' from consumers or the staff, and no regulation from government, a firm may avoid exploiting its 'ultimatum' power. From this point of view, some market failures, like for instance those due to monopolies, may be overcome by genuine moral values that favour a fair allocation of resources.

We may add that a spontaneous adhesion to a moral code may occur even in non-repeated games, like leaving a tip in a restaurant far from home. The experimental investigation by Kahneman and others (1986b) appears to confirm the analogy of results between one-shot games and repeated games:

> 'If the service is satisfactory, how much of a tip do you think most people leave after ordering a meal costing $10 in a restaurant that they visit frequently?
>
> Mean response = $1.28
>
> ...in a restaurant on a trip to another city that they do not expect to visit again?
>
> Mean response = $1.27' (p. 737).

The experimental results show that also the fear of receiving a 'lemon' from a salesman in a far-away town may be unjustified: as was so for the agent in the preceding experiment. Also for the firm the objective function may be adjusted according to its sense of fairness, that does not allow it to exploit fully the profit opportunity available in the market.

> 'A man leaves his car with the mechanic/ A tourist leaves his car at a service station with instructions to replace an expensive part. After the customer/tourist leaves, the mechanic examines the car and discovers that it is not necessary to replace the part; it can be repaired cheaply. The mechanic would make much more money by replacing the part than by repairing it. Assuming the [customer/tourist] cannot be reached, what do you think the mechanic would do in this situation?
>
> Make more money by replacing the part
>
> customer: 60% tourist: 63%
>
> Save the customer money by repairing the part
>
> customer: 40% tourist: 37%' (p. 737).

These results, then, seem to confirm that market decisions are not constrained exclusively by the environment – contracts, regulation, reputation, risk of bankruptcy. 'Implicit' contracts, of a different kind with respect to those traditionally discussed in economic theory, may turn out to be equally binding.

A relevant aspect discussed by Kahneman and others (1986b) is the impact of the 'framing effect' on customer and staff judgement. The influence of this psychological factor is such that, in their judgement of a firm's fairness, economic agents mistake formal aspects with the substance of the matter; consequently, the 'instrumental' use of fairness leads the enterprise to choose, among the available alternative policies, those that, albeit actually meeting the same goals, are 'formally' more respondent to society's preferences and, therefore, to reputation needs. So, for example, people would judge more unfair a firm's policy causing a loss to the other party rather than another one determining a foregone gain of the same amount. From this perspective, also money illusion may be regarded in the light of the framing effect:

> 'A company is making a small profit. It is located in a community experiencing a recession with substantial unemployment but no inflation. There are many workers anxious to work at the company. The company decides to decrease wages and salaries 7% this year.
>
> Acceptable: 38%   Unfair: 62%
>
> ...with substantial unemployment and inflation of 12%... The company decides to increase salaries only 5% this year.
>
> Acceptable 78%   Unfair 22%' (p.731).

Although in both cases the real wage is about the same, the different perspective, namely the different reference point (a wage cut/a nominal growth of wages), has a different psychological impact: a wage cut is regarded as a loss while a nominal growth, even when not adequate to compensate the current inflation rate, is regarded as ethically 'better'.

In all these circumstances, then, it is the 'mixture' between moral constraints and psychological factors which affects agents' choices (firms, customers, employees, etc.).

We suggest that a possible interaction between morality and market may be *over*simplified through the following scheme:

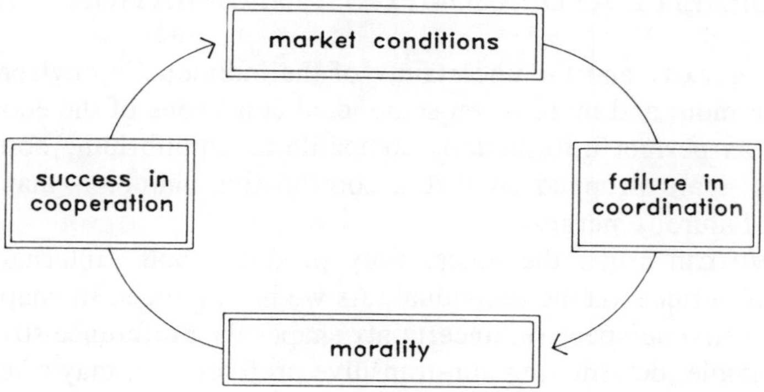

Figure 3.1

In what follows we shall focus on the left-hand side of this interaction in order to analyse how morality together with rationality (we could say *morality as rationality*), through cooperation, may overcome the coordination failure occurring in the market. From this perspective we suggest that (i) rationality *per se* induces the economic agent to do his/her best, subject to his/her constraints, and (ii) what is best depends on the environment: hence, rationality induces to act according to what environment is.

Environment is *complex* (the individual can deal with it only by means of limited capabilities), environment is *uncertain* and it *evolves*. Obviously these three dimensions of the environment closely interact: so, for example, the degree of uncertainty of the environment is positively related to the degree of its complexity, to the rapidity of its changes as well as to the number/probability of states of the world which are going to occur. There emerges accordingly a notion of rationality *conditional* to the environment[6] – *bounded* rationality, *expected-utility* rationality, *evolutionary* rationality – which may lead to the common prediction of cooperation among economic agents.

3.1 MORALITY AND INCOMPLETE INFORMATION

The complexity and the uncertainty of the individual's environment increase more and more when some ideal conditions of the economy – such as perfect information, competition, equilibrium, complete markets – are dropped so that a coordination failure – that is, a market failure, emerges.

We can argue that uncertainty produces both 'internal' and 'external' effects on the individual. As we have noticed in chapter 2, from the first perspective, uncertainty shapes the preference structure (for example, determining non-transitive preferences), may affect the decision process through confusion and mistakes (as, for example, with the framing effect), may generate some particular mental states (like regret).

From the second perspective, the external effects of uncertainty are mainly of an economic nature and typically influence the agents' decision – firms as well as consumers – about the optimal production and the optimal savings respectively. Sheltering one's income from future fluctuations is costly; moreover, some financial instruments, such as insurance, become relevant to reduce or eliminate risk. As is well-known, insurance companies do not always provide their customers with a fair premium in so far as the probability of the negative state of the world is unknown: this happens typically when only one side of the market enjoys useful information.

As is well-known, informational inequalities are one of the major sources preventing the existence of complete markets. Some markets, particularly insurance and futures markets, cannot be perfect and indeed may not exist; consumers may be badly informed about the quality of products and accruing additional information may be very expensive for them, and so on. Hence, the informational bias operates in two opposite directions – with the same likely effect of precluding the existence of some markets: at the expense of either the supplier (when the consumer enjoys useful private information dictating his/her strategic behaviour such as free-riding and moral hazard) or the consumer (allowing his/her exploitation by the seller). So, for example, an individual may be less worried if she buys clothes in her town rather than in another one.[7]

In order to generalise this point, we can argue that as long as the transaction is 'transparent' – in the sense that the characteristics of the goods or services exchanged are readily determined – the exchange relationship is anonymous. It is because the objects of exchange are transparent that the parties to the exchange may be invisible to one another:

> 'I do not know the fruit salesman *personally*, and I have no particular interest in his well-being. *He reciprocates this attitude*... Yet the two of us are able to...transact exchanges efficiently because both parties agree on the property rights relevant to them.' (Buchanan 1975, p. 17, our italics).

However, when there are gains from trade but some aspect of the object of exchange is difficult or costly to monitor, trust becomes a crucial component of the economic transaction: it qualifies the exchange relationship so that the transaction partner is no longer anonymous.[8]

There are a number of reputation mechanisms aimed at building a trust relationship between the two sides of the potential exchange: (i) a market mechanism, via rents; (ii) some moral attitude; (iii) emotional signals; (iv) ethnic features. In the first category it is the market which supplies trust through the price signal while in the other ones it is the individuals that supply trust via some specific attitudes or characteristics. Thus, from this perspective, categories (ii), (iii) and (iv) can be thought of as internal or subjective mechanisms in that they arise from the individuals rather than from their environment.

The first device (e.g. Klein and Leffler 1981, Shapiro 1983) relies on a price premium which provides a firm with a proper incentive structure not to cheat, and so to produce high-quality goods. Hence, the premium has to be at least equal to the gain from cheating, i.e. $p(g_h) - c(g_h) \geq c(g_h) - c(g_l)$, where g_h and g_l are the high-quality and the low-quality goods respectively; $c(\cdot)$ the associated production costs; $p(\cdot)$ the market price. Although the premium gives the buyers a good reason to trust the firm, nevertheless it turns out to be quite expensive from their point of view. Other mechanisms then – the subjective ones – can be either consciously or unconsciously devised to lower reputation costs.

Following the well-known points of Gauthier (1986) and Frank (1987), when some conditions of the stylised economy are dropped, notably competition, the market becomes a 'moral' zone, in that morality prevents strategic behaviour induced by an even distribution of information (such as selling 'lemons' and moral hazard), thereby substituting the missing elements (information), hampering some advantageous exchange. Morality, then, may be included within the range of signals available to individuals to send information to the marketplace, such as the education level (Spence 1974), the purchase of an insurance policy (Rothschild and Stiglitz 1976), the corporation's financial policy (Ross 1977), the bargaining time in a bilateral negotiation (Admati and Perry 1987, Kennan and Wilson 1993), and even the geographical origin of the object of the exchange like the slave's region of origin in the New Orleans Slave Market (Pritchett and Chamberlain 1993). Hence, 'endogenising' ethical preferences is crucial for the market performance ('the market model of morality') as far as they allow otherwise unavailable advantageous exchanges:

> 'In the absence of trust, it would become very costly to arrange for alternative sanctions and guarantees, and many opportunities for mutually beneficial cooperation would have to be foregone...society may proceed by internalization of...norms to the achievement of the desired agreement of an unconscious level.
> There is a whole set of customs and norms which might be similarly interpreted as agreements to improve the efficiency of the economic system...' (Arrow 1971, p. 22).

Among the 'subjective' mechanisms for reputation building, even unconscious behavioural clues can be thought of as commitment devices to the extent they reveal inner dispositions (a discussion is in the next chapter).

Finally, as argued earlier, ethnic membership - grounded on blood and on other physical as well as cultural features - also creates a trust network among the insiders of the group, thus allowing for advantageous exchanges (Wintrobe 1992). Within this ethnic network trust is gained in two ways: reputation and repetition. Of course, these two devices are by no means mutually exclusive: one way to build a reputation is by repetition of the game. However, in this particular context membership gives reputation while repetition just reinforces the latter.

From the standpoint of reputation, within the same group it is generally easier to communicate with one another and/or to predict the behaviour of the other party: accordingly it becomes easier for anyone to assess whether to trust the other.[9] In other terms, the need of knowing and of monitoring the other's behaviour is reduced; accordingly, the transaction costs associated to the potential exchanges decline.

Viewed from the second standpoint of repetition, naturally blood ties different generations and never disappears: hence, blood devises a repeated game with an infinite number of trials, where cheating on the part of one player leads the other (or his/her descendants) to defect in successive rounds, i.e. against the former's descendants. It follows, then, that repetition of the game via descendants reinforces reputation within the group.

As already argued, lower transaction costs and the consequent capability to exploit gains from trade in the marketplace provide the whole ethnic community with some comparative advantages, which may even lead it to control of the market. The argument provides a rationale for developing and preserving a group identity through barriers. However, building ethnic barriers is expensive: the minority faces sunk costs in so far as they are valuable only to that specific ethnic background and, accordingly, they cannot be transferred or sold. Hence, *ceteris paribus*, it might be suggested an inverse relationship between the size of ethnic barriers and the severity of market imperfections. At the extreme, when markets are perfect, we should expect anonymity of transactions; conversely, in some circumstances, market mechanisms exacerbate discrimination.[10]

This consideration enables us to better qualify our previous argument (at the beginning of this chapter): the market does not discriminate among (racial, religious, political, economic) groups – namely, it does not segregate, provided that, *ceteris paribus*, there do not exist market imperfections.

This leads us to a second conclusion: the 'ethic' and the 'ethnic' approaches of the market in the presence of market failures – such as the one originated by asymmetric information – share a common feature: 'endogenising' some specific preferences according to some moral or ethnic code prevailing in the community increases the likelihood of transactions as well as their efficiency. Both approaches, then, provide us with an explanation of some exchanges in the marketplace through non-enforceable contracts or, as labelled by Bowles and Gintis (1993), through 'endogenous enforcement strategies'.

3.2 MORALITY AND EXTERNALITIES

Morality might overcome other types of market failure such as externalities. For both informational bias and externalities, the ethical solution is the 'cheapest' one, when it is available. As suggested earlier, buying antiques may turn out to be 'lemons' and many antique markets would fail to exist unless – as an alternative to some (costly) monitoring activity – society proceeds by endogenising some moral code, based on trust and loyalty, to achieve the desired exchanges in the antique market. Similarly, correction of an externality may be more readily accomplished by means of ethical norms than through other more 'standard' solutions. Actually, the ethical internalisation (for example, via the Kantian code) does not display the 'reciprocity' feature – typically in monetary terms – required by the other solutions:[11] bargaining, trade, political intervention remain outside the ethical solution, with a consequent saving of resources.

Adopting more traditional methods – such as taxation and regulation – to correct the externalities generated, for example, by some resource constraint (Laffont 1975) is costly and may determine additional distortions in the use of economic resources.[12] Yet, the fiscal solution turns out to be necessary in a community of selfish agents: actually, an information campaign by the government to solve the energy problem would fail because of free-riding (anyone would regard as negligible one's own contribution). Conversely, behaviour in conformity to some social code, like the Kantian one, would make the information campaign successful, thus leading society spontaneously to an optimum. Generally speaking, when a moral code is at work within society, even non-economic sacrifices (for example to litter) may achieve important economic goals.

Similarly, in the resource allocation decisions, and notably in the work-leisure choice (Buchanan 1991), the work ethic may be more easily accomplished than any fiscal policy aimed at stimulating labour input. A behavioural adjustment on the part of the workers in accordance with a moral code may determine the desired (Pareto-optimal) increase in the supply of work effort with positive external effects accruing to other parties in the economic system.[13] In other words, supply side economics may work through moral incentives rather than fiscal incentives. Of course, this approach is vulnerable to many criticisms: similarly to Hochman-Rodgers argument (1969), when ethical motivations are not sufficient to provide an optimal level of public good (in this case, the increased labour supply whose benefits affect other parties of the economic system), State intervention is still required to overcome the free-rider problem.[14]

Once the economic and ethical interdependence is recognised – as in the presence of informative asymmetries and spillovers – it may be desirable to invest resources,[15] both at the personal and social level, to build up one's own reputation and to 'expand' a moral code across the community respectively: 'persons rationally will want others to want better wants' (Buchanan 1991, p. 186). Such a moral code requires no cheating – that is, to reciprocate in fair behaviour, to keep one's promises, to tell the truth, to respect personal and property rights. Sometimes, however, the ethical solution for a market failure is particularly demanding – and consequently both the 'individual' and 'social' investments need to be even larger – in that it requires an explicit *altruistic* concern (either genuine or '*ad hoc*') for the welfare of the others: this is the case, for example, of the internalisation of the external effects generated by poverty.

It is noteworthy that if people 'want others to want better wants' they must not be free riders: *vague statements* about the superior economic results accruing from ethical preferences are just 'cheap talk'; in order to induce other people to change preferences, the individual has to invest his/her own resources in the investment – namely he/she must bear the *effective (opportunity-) cost* of the investment. In a public choice perspective, a change of preferences across the community through social investment requires, for example, politicians to spend their own resources in terms of renouncing the exploitation of their positions of power. In other words, only a personal cost may induce other people to sustain the same effort.

Within a large community the free-rider problem is obviously exacerbated. A large society reduces the possible direct incentive of each person to invest privately in promulgating moral norms designed to affect the behaviour of the others; accordingly, he/she will display the incentive to hold back in his/her own contribution. In this circumstance, even if the work ethic is supported by public measures, such as propaganda, the impact on workers' preferences as well as on leisure versus labour decisions may be negligible. The empirical evidence gives mixed results: on the one hand the Japanese experience shows the strength of the work ethic even in very large societies, on the other side the experiences of failure of socialist systems demonstrate that ethical indoctrination produces very weak economic results.

NOTES

1. Friedman (1962) maintains that 'the purchaser of bread does not know whether it was made by a white man, a Negro, by a Christian or a Jew...' (p. 109).
2. Buchanan (1978) maintains that 'This century may be described by developments that drive these two sets of constraints [the external, institutional ones and the internal, moral ones] apart. An increase in population alone reduces the constraining influence of moral rules. Moreover population increase has been accompanied by increasing mobility over space, by the replacement of local by national markets, by the urbanization of society, by the shift of power from state-local to national government, and by the increased politicization of society generally. Add to this the observed erosion of the family, the church, and the law – all of which were stabilizing influences that tended to reinforce moral precepts – and we readily understand why 'Homo economicus' has assumed such a dominant role in modern behavior patterns' (p. 367).
3. More recently, a somewhat similar argument is Williamson's (1975, 1985) suggestion that since hierarchical firms exist, then they have to be both more efficient and most suited to survival.

4. A recent country-study on this topic is in Cullis and others (1992).
5. Experimental evidence of the effects of fairness on the labour market ('the fair wage-effort hypothesis') is recently provided by Fehr and others (1993).
6. A similar approach is in Yaari (1991). In assessing the individual's rationality, Yaari uses the notion of environment to oppose the State of Nature to civil society, and to evaluate the different behavioural implications of individuals' rationality in these two contexts.
7. Yet, even in this one-shot exchange, the probability to get a 'lemon' is less than one (even if being foreign is common knowledge among counterparts). While repetition in a PD situation provides valuable assurance for cooperation (within society conventions may be regarded as the counterpart of repetition in theoretical games), the emergence of a cooperative solution in one-shot situations is not straightforward according to the standard economic theory. Recent attempts trying to reconcile moral preferences and one-shot situations rest on philosophical roots (Gauthier 1991).
8. Trust can be thought of as a public good: a trusting environment facilitates contracts, relationships, business, political dealings, etc. (Hardin 1991). A somewhat similar idea is the work ethic by Buchanan (1991) (see next paragraph).
9. See, among others, Breton and Wintrobe (1982), Hardin (1993).
10. The latter, in turn, may produce a feed-back effect on the market: discrimination breaks the market and precludes market mobility. The direction of causality, then, can go in both directions.
11. Although the 'reciprocity' feature may be present even in the internalisation through genuine ethical motivations (Sugden 1984, 1985) or in strategic cooperative behaviour, as in the Tit-for-Tat supergame.
12. The linkage between government regulation and individuals' preferences is also discussed recently by Frey (1992).
13. Following Buchanan's lines of reasoning, the beneficial spillovers of the individual's higher work efforts derive from labour division and specialisation in production accompanied by exchange or trade. Both circumstances, in turn, enlarge the market.
14. Some other lines of criticism of Buchanan's argument are in Pasour (1990).
15. The investment decision will depend on the present value of its expected returns in terms of the availability and size of the market as well as of the 'quality' of the interactions that will take place.

4 Endogenous constraints and strategies

Earlier a distinction was made between the 'internal' and 'external' impact of uncertainty on the economic agent. A proper investigation into the effects of uncertainty requires also a further examination of the source of uncertainty. From this perspective, it is convenient to distinguish between the uncertain conditions deriving from *nature* – that is, from the occurrence of one of the possible states of the world, which are exogenously given for any individual – and the uncertain conditions stemming from the other agents' decision.[1] In the former case, in his/her decision-making process, the individual plays against nature; conversely, in social interactions, the source of uncertainty is the *behaviour of the other agents* (usually the double assumption of players' rationality as well as rationality as common knowledge[2] is implemented in the analysis): in this circumstance, the individual plays against one or more opponents.[3] In this latter class of games, the individual may attempt to exercise some form of strategic control on the other agent(s), namely to endogenise the other players' behaviour.

Again, in such attempts some self-commitment may become a relevant component of the individual's strategic behaviour. Actually, to bind oneself to some behavioural constraint, such as a commitment, renders credible a threat or a promise, eventually leading to a Pareto-optimal outcome. Obviously, building up one's own reputation – the willingness and the capacity to fulfil a promise – is costly: 'cheap talk' in no way is enough for being trustworthy – that is, it is not a valuable informative signal. Then, allocation of one's own resources in trust formation transforms costless, non-binding cheap talk into a commitment: the cost of commitment (typically a sunk cost) being the price one party has to pay in order to be trusted by the other party. Reputation then may be regarded as a capital asset (like education, training, health, physical exercise and other human inputs): once it is built up by pursuing certain (costly) courses of action, the investor may exploit other courses of action – such opportunities as trade and exchanges – not otherwise viable. In other words, after the investment in reputation, the individual's probability distribution (as assessed by other people) to keep the promise displays a lower variance. In a framework where both players assess a positive probability about their opponent's cooperative attitude, the higher such a probability the higher the rational player's incentive to undertake the investment in reputation[4] (a recent experimental investigation where reputation building and altruism interact is in Andreoni and Miller 1993).

Of course, like any other capital formation process, investment in reputation must be embedded into an intertemporal framework or, in other words, into a repeated game between the same players. If the game has no future (at least as perceived by the players), there is no rationale to bear the cost of the investment. Nonetheless, in the real world, empirical evidence suggests that reputation considerations are involved even in one-shot bargaining encounters; moreover, the cost borne by the investor sometimes outweighs the expected gain. As suggested by Vanberg and Buchanan (1990):

> 'Moralistic aggression may be learned as successful behavior in settings where the initiator and the recipient of the aggression are likely to meet again – where the shadow of the future provides a rationale for incurring the costs of the aggression. There are, however, instances of moralistically aggressive behavior that do not seem to fit such a description, because the aggressor cannot reasonably expect the recipient's future behavior to generate benefits to the aggressor that will outweigh the costs of his punishing

> act. Anger may cause people to reciprocate, that is, to retaliate, against defectors even where the potential payoffs from such behavior are outweighed by the costs incurred' (p. 184).

Similarly to aggression, sometimes even certain predispositions which may be interpreted as irrational can be advantageous in that they contribute to build up a reputation (Frank 1989):

> '...suppose that Jones is *not* a pure rationalist; that if Smith steals his briefcase, he will become outraged, and think nothing of losing a day's earnings in order to see justice done. If Smith knows Jones will be driven by emotion, not reason, he will let the briefcase be. If people *expect* us to respond irrationally to the theft of our property, we will seldom *need* to, because it will not be in their interests to steal it. Being predisposed to respond irrationally serves much better here than being guided only by material self-interest' (p. 6).[5]

Moreover, it is well-known that in ultimatum games the prediction of theory is for the rational bargainer to accept any amount of the stake larger than zero and for the rational proposer to offer an amount just greater than zero. However, when some non-monetary arguments, such as fairness, are introduced in the bargainers' utility functions, both the responder will be prepared to face the cost of rejecting an unfair offer and the proposer to face the cost of offering an amount which he/she judges fair (a discussion of these arguments is in Part III). These moral commitments may turn out to be fruitful to both the bargainers in terms of their reputation. To be known as a person who misses good opportunities for the sake of fairness increases the chance to exploit good opportunities. Obviously enough, fairness can by no means be considered exclusively as a strategic expedient to exploit a non-otherwise viable advantageous transaction; nonetheless the latter can be regarded as a by-product of a 'genuine' behavioural disposition.

In all these cases to be perceived as somebody who is ready to hurt him/herself for the sake of revenge or fairness may be the most effective signal. In this range of (seemingly) irrational but very useful signalling techniques, also unconscious behavioural clues can be interpreted as commitment devices to the extent they reveal inner emotional states. Within an asymmetric-information setting, where 'the art of bargaining... is in large part the art of sending misleading messages' (Frank 1988, p. 165) reputation may be developed even through unconscious mimicry.

As suggested earlier, some 'special' opponents confronting each other in the game may be different components within the same economic agent, linked together by strategic interactions. In these familiar two- or more-selves models, the multiple selves typically arise for two main reasons, both associated with an intertemporal framework:

(i) Preferences evolve over time. Defining an individual through a preference ordering over alternative outcomes, a shift in the ordering – due, for example, to the environment evolution – redefines the individual.[6] With the passage of time and a sequence of states of the world, just like any other 'economic good', the individual experiences a continuous transformation into '*contingent selves*'. Hence, if we recognise that motivations are preference-oriented, each self will choose the most suitable course of action aimed at satisfying its own preferences (that is at maximising its expected utility). As long as we recognise that the evolution of the environment produces an evolution of preferences, accordingly we may distinguish between courses of action favouring present preferences and those ones favouring future preferences. Obviously, the two classes of preferences – and needless to say, the associated choices – are likely to be incompatible.

(ii) Preferences conflict at a single point in time. The conflict – typically between short-run and long-run preferences – is introduced by viewing the individual as an organisation.[7]

Both the cases require a technology of self-control for restructuring of incentives (often with somebody's cooperation).

We can thus highlight two circumstances in which the need for trust calls for some self-constraint technology aimed at developing the right incentives: (a) in the marketplace, when the commodity attributes are not easily observed and the monitoring costs very high: moral constraints may overcome the adverse incentives to 'cheat' which would undermine advantageous exchanges (see paragraph 3.1); (b) towards other selves, when differing preferences are associated to differing selves: self-command techniques may be implemented to fight against the other selves. In this latter case if the 'present' self *trusts* in its ability to defeat the 'future' self, or the 'long-run-oriented' self *trusts* in its ability to defeat the 'short-run-oriented' self, any self-command technique would be redundant. Yet, as long as this 'strategic' courage is not enough, some 'strategic' substitute should be used against the opponent selves.

There are quite a few examples of preference dynamisation within an intertemporal context such as the all-too-familiar one of Ulysses and Sirens and that of the future mother's concern for anesthesia during her delivery (Schelling 1984a. See chapter 1). In both cases, the protagonists anticipate a change in their preferences during the critical time (the view of the Sirens and the delivery) and they rationally seek to prevent, to compel, or to alter their own future behaviour. Through such constraints, in both cases the individual's customary self enjoys a first-mover advantage over his/her future self.

A related question is which of conflicting preferences are the relevant ones: the present or the future ones? Moreover, why would the individual favour the present ones at the expense of the latter? The answers are not straightforward as far as *intra-personal* utility comparisons between present and future selves seem to be as problematic as *inter-personal* utility comparisons. Despite these difficulties, we may suggest two possible arguments which justify the individual's favour for present preferences. One argument is philosophical, so to say, although it is widely used also in the economic literature of multiple-selves models (or disjoint-selves models). The second argument is grounded on the comparison of the discounted costs associated with the short-run and long-run choices.

From the first perspective, the person choosing now and the one choosing in the future are not the same. While they may care about each other and/or engage in exchange, they are fundamentally separate. Ulysses today has different interests from Ulysses tomorrow, and since both of them are rational, that means they are going to choose different things. From the second perspective, the economic agents usually (are thought to) have a near infinite time horizon across all options: the individual, then, only does not pay attention to future selves when the discounted value of what he/she will get in the future is less than what it costs him/her now.

The evolutionary implication of these arguments is that long-run maximisation (survival) requires self-binding rules in order to constrain short-run choices. In a repeated game, this implies a cooperative rather than a Nash strategy: in the short-run the former involves some costs (for example in the first move of the Tit-for-Tat strategy), but it is likely to turn out to be rewarding in the long-run.

It should be stressed, however, that the short-run objective has not necessarily to be considered irrational. Actually, from the perspective of instrumental rationality which emphasises the consistency between means and end, the short-period choice may also be perfectly rational provided that the economic agent selects the most efficient means for the achievement of given (short-run) ends. In other terms, (instrumental) rationality is 'neutral' about the worthiness of ends. However, it is hard to believe that any kind of objective – no matter how bizzarre – must be seen as good – that is, not compromising the rationality of the person pursuing it. In other words, a more demanding notion of rationality requires also a normative assessment of the objectives pursued. This last consideration leads to the more sophisticated notion of expressive rationality (Hargreaves Heap 1989) according to which it is not enough for the individual to be guided by preferences (and accordingly to select his/her ends); preferences (and hence ends) must be 'valuable' (although questions of worth are difficult to answer). Consequently, 'we have a picture of the individual who is groping for what is worthwhile' (Hargreaves Heap 1989, p. 5). From this perspective, then, pursuing immediate gratification – according to the instinctive component of the individual or to his/her short-run preferences – is likely to fail the test of 'normative' or 'expressive' rationality.

The substitution effect within the individual among 'short-run-oriented' and 'long-run-oriented' courses of action by means of self-imposed constraints leads us to analyse a more general feature which endogenous constraints may exhibit, namely their capability to link different domains of the individual's action. This sort of externality generated by self-imposed constraints creates two specific relations among different courses of actions – i.e. substitution versus complementarity[8] – (Ainslie 1992, Elster 1993). According to the former relation, denial of one course of action by imposing self-constraints allows the individual to seek pleasure from another course of action, which would not otherwise be viable, at least to some extent. Within an intertemporal framework, an obvious example already discussed is the denial – via self-imposed rules – of some short-run courses of action to privilege otherwise non-feasible courses of action in the long-run. But even within a static setting, the substitution effect among action domains can be assessed by introducing into the individual's utility function specific arguments, such as the ones relating to health like drinking or smoking. Deliberate restriction imposed on one of the two arguments generates externalities affecting the second one: hence, within his/her feasible set of actions – defined for example by the physician – rules ease the task of finding an optimal mix rather then a corner solution. According to the second type of relation – complementarity among courses of action – it has been suggested by Elster (1993) that rules on either courses of action build blocks, that is generate spillovers, on the other action. So, for example, weightwatchers might find it easier to give up smoking. In other words self-imposed constraints on specific areas create a general habit of doing so elsewhere. From this perspective, then, the spillover effects consist in a generalised manipulation of the incentive structure in all walks of life.

Adopting these lines of reasoning we can find both an inner and wider (i.e. cross-situational) consistency to the individual's behaviour, although we cannot predict *ex-ante* which type of externalities among actions will prevail – i.e. the compensation effect versus the spillover effect. Regardless of the type, when these externalities arise, the obvious advantage for the individual is a greater/easier direct and indirect control over actions in different walks of life.

NOTES

1. Although, of course, the other agents can also be treated as 'part of the nature' and the action of each one as one of the possible (and mutually exclusive) states of the world.

2. An extensive discussion on this point is in Geanakoplos (1992). A recent discussion is also in Cudd (1993).
3. Recently Gradstein and others (1992) have analysed the equilibrium outcome within a context of multi-agent interactions where agents share a common uncertain environment, with the source of uncertainty arising both from the nature and from the others' behaviour.
4. In this case (instrumental) rationality is not any longer common knowledge in so far as both rational players assess a positive probability about the opponent's 'irrational' altruistic concerns.
5. 'Could Colonel Ghadafi and Ayatollah Khomeini have understood this principle better than the cool, rational leaders of Western nations trying to deal with them?' (Dixit and Nalebuff 1991, p. 166).
6. The seminal work on this topic is by Strotz (1955-1956). Important subsequent contributions include Pollak (1968), Hammond (1976), Yaari (1977), Schelling (1984a, 1984b), Gauthier (1991).
7. This approach includes the contributions of Thaler and Shefrin (1981) and Fiocca (1990b).
8. Elster (1993) labels these relations respectively 'compensation effect' and 'spillover effect'. Following the author, if a person follows a certain rule-governed pattern of behaviour P in one sphere of life, let's say X, he/she will not follow P in sphere Y (so rules create what is labelled here as a substitution effect among actions in the two spheres X and Y). Conversely, if the agent follows P in X, accordingly he/she will do so in Y (referred here as a complementary relation between spheres). As suggested by Elster, combination of these two relations produces a zero-sum effect, which becomes relevant in the 'hydraulic model' of the mind.

5 The rationality of endogenous constraints

It can be argued that 'rationality is what rationality does': such a perspective emphasises the *pragmatic component* of rationality.[1] In order to better pursue given ends – namely utility maximisation – as long as rationality requires self-imposed constraints, it is *pragmatically rational* to restrict one's own strategy space by means of self-commitments.

The greater emphasis posed by orthodox economic theory on exogenous constraints compared with the subjective ones is maybe justified by tradition rather than their minor relevance: as repeated observations of experimental designs show, both categories of constraints are important when individuals find themselves in a decision-taking situation. Hence, a proper investigation on decision-taking requires the inclusion also of endogenous constraints in the economic analysis, like any other relevant element which affects agents' decisions. Such attempts are needed in order to better qualify economic theory as well as the notion of rationality.

From this viewpoint, we can legitimately justify the nexus, which apparently sounds odd, between rationality and voluntary restriction of one's own degrees of freedom through rules and commitments. Actually, a widely accepted belief in orthodox economic theory is that a greater availability of choices is better. For example, the individual is better off when he/she is allowed to choose between public provision and private provision of some goods or services; following regret theory, a 'choiceless' utility is lower than that accruing from an action the individual has chosen, and so on. Yet, in several circumstances, a shortage of choices may help individuals and even lead them to a Pareto improvement. In other words, rules without choice may happen to be better than choice without rules. This occurs not only because of the agents' lack of specialisation in many fields or their failure in a deep understanding of their needs and interests, or else because of their bounded rationality impeding them to gather and select properly the relevant information needed in their decision-taking. The advantages arising from a restriction in the range of one's own options are founded also on the 'external' factors, namely the agent's environment, other than 'internal' factors, that is his/her limited capability.

To quote a well-known example, let us consider the insurance market. Because of adverse selection, everyone is better off by the required purchase of insurance reflecting the average risk in the population. Actually, the high-risk persons are better off as far as they can purchase insurance at rates that are lower than the actual risk they face; whereas low-risk people can purchase insurance which turns out to be more advantageous to them than the insurance offered if only high-risk people purchased it. Such a situation highlights that market equilibrium is dominated by a compulsory purchase plan.

Once we have recognised that some *external constraints* may improve the individual's welfare, a further step is to admit that even some *internal constraints* may do the same. As in the case of insurance, as some exogenous constraints may overcome some market failures – such as the externalities generated between low-risk and high-risk people – so 'endogenising' some constraints may achieve the same goal, even yielding a better performance to the extent the latter turns out to be the cheapest solution.

In order to compare the costs associated respectively to the endogenous and the exogenous solutions, several examples can be cited. Let us consider again asymmetric information. The informational gap separating the two sides of the antique market makes the probability of receiving a 'lemon' high, thus precluding some exchange. In a non-repeated game (as for example, in a local market far away from one's own home), control over strategic incentives would require high monitoring costs aimed at protecting the 'weak' side of the market. The likelihood of such transactions, then, seems related to the availability of 'cheap' monitoring means, such as the seller's 'conscience'.

Rationality itself calls for more efficient, that is cheaper, means to reach one's own ends.

Thus, the significant gap between rationality and self-imposed constraints only seems apparent: actually, all the circumstances here considered – uncertainty, market failures, strategic interaction among different selves – share the common requirement of endogenous constraints aimed at optimising (or, at least, at reaching a certain target level of achievement) at the minimum cost. Rules and commitments, then, represent the *endogenous instrument* to overcome external (uncertainty, market failures) as well as internal shortcuts (mental states, conflicting goals). Adoption of such rules is thus explained on the grounds of rationality: optimising rationality, bounded rationality, procedural rationality, and cognitive rationality may all be advocated to justify endogenisation of constraints.

On the other hand, in a world of imperfect and costly information and scarce resources (also those of the mind) the relevance is widely recognised of pragmatic rules (of thumb) guiding the individual to an approximate optimisation, or, at least, to satisfy goals consistent with his/her aspiration level. Although rules of thumb are sensibly different in nature from self-imposed endogenous constraints, to some extent they show that helping oneself through rules and other behavioural constraints is compatible with, or even required by, rationality.

Further, a normative assessment of rationality within the means-end framework requires a deeper investigation of both means and ends. As suggested at the end of chapter 4, a more sophisticated notion of rationality reflects the individual's concern about his/her preferences and aims: in other words, it is not enough for the rational individual to act according to his/her preferences and to check the consistency between means and ends. Preferences must be 'worthy' and, as long as the goals pursued are 'preference-oriented', goals must be 'worthy' accordingly. Thus, preferences and ends deriving from this concern become expressively rational as far as they reflect the agent's ideas about what is worthy, satisfying and pursuing.

Similarly, even when goals are clearly given, the translation of these into actions depends upon whether the context within the optimising process takes place as well as on the pattern of social interdependence. In other words, the correct agent's action may not be straightforward even though there seems to be a strictly dominant strategy: for example, it is well known that in a PD context, where the pattern of social interdependence incorporates both congruence and conflict of interests, the relevant outcome is sub-optimal although it arises from the individual rational strategy. Obviously enough, cooperation would be the most efficient means to best pursue one's own ends: moral constraints, then, would be helpful when social interdependence reflects a PD-like situation. Likewise, in other contexts (uncertainty, market failure, strategies), the 'goodness' of means for given goals would call for specific strategies, such as that of endogenising constraints which serve better the agent's preferences and goals.

From this perspective, rationality may be regarded as a necessary but non-sufficient condition required to reach the best outcome. To show this point, once again we may use the PD context and assume 'common knowledge' as well as the absence of behavioural constraints. More specifically, our assumptions are: (i) rationality as common knowledge; (ii) the dominant (non-cooperative) strategy as common knowledge; (iii) no behavioural commitments on the part of players. The relevant prediction, of course, is a sub-optimal outcome: rationality on the part of each player together with common knowledge of that leads them to a Pareto inefficiency.

Conversely, if we assume that at least one player is induced by a genuinely moral constraint – for example of a Kantian type – to keep his/her promise, and this attitude is common knowledge among players, the outcome of the game would be Pareto-efficient via cooperation.

From this example we may suggest that 'rationality + constraints' (in this case of moral type) is the crucial formula to reach some goals which a Nash rationality would preclude. Accordingly, we can legitimately argue that: (i) not necessarily what is rational (= pursuing the dominant strategy) is always efficient; (ii) efficiency may be achieved with some means other than rationality (= constraints); (iii) hence, assessment about the rationality of specific means to pursue a given end is not always the right approach.

These lines of reasoning lead us to a further step, which is even more drastic: we may suggest that sometimes behaving in the 'right' way – that is, according to a Nash rationality, may turn out to be disadvantageous: in all these circumstances we can talk about 'self-defeating' rationality.

One way to 'rescue' rationality is to enlarge its notion so as to embed it in an evolutionist perspective. Leaving the State of Nature – where individuals are represented by their selfish rationality – in order to reach civil society, rationality itself leaves some room for cooperation or, generally speaking, to self-commitments.[2]

From this viewpoint, it is indeed remarkable that any assessment about rationality must be embedded into the context within which it operates: undoubtedly this wider perspective of rationality complicates the nexus between action and objectives. Then, bearing in mind some of the aspects discussed above, the following scheme can be sketched:

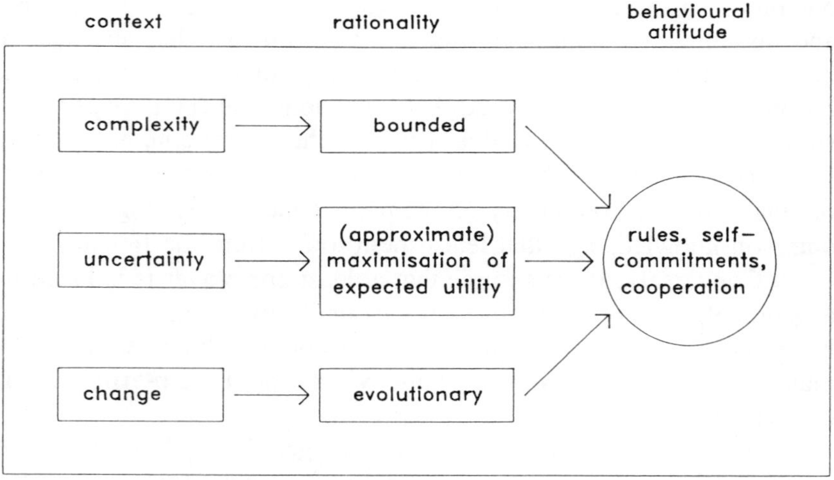

Figure 5.1

Obviously enough, we have already noticed that such different 'contexts' not only are mutually compatible but even complementary to characterise the environment within which the economic agent operates. Specifically, each context emphasises a specific 'component' of rationality. The relevant aspect, which is worth stressing, is that even starting from different perspectives, a common prediction is reached (quite far from the more traditional notion of rationality), that is, the crucial role of rules, self-commitments, and cooperation, where the latter can be regarded as one of the ways in which self-commitment takes form.

Finally, it is generally accepted that although cooperation may be grounded on bounded rationality (quite a few attempts illustrate the relation between these two[3]), it is obviously founded on motivations other than subjective 'frictions'. As Yaari (1991) maintains, civil society - which leaves room and justifies cooperation among agents also from an economic perspective - in no way can be regarded as an 'imperfect' State of Nature, where cooperation has no role to play.

Let us turn now to an even stronger argument by suggesting that sometimes rationality alone is neither a necessary nor a sufficient condition for pursuing in the best way our goals.

5.1 DO ENDOGENOUS CONSTRAINTS NEED TO BE RATIONAL TO BE USEFUL?

As long as rationality does not always succeed in satisfying in the best way agents' preferences, admittedly some other non-rational criterion guiding individual choices may turn out to be even more helpful, mainly because it allows coordination among actors.[4]

Some of these rules arise from habit and social conventions; sometimes they are generated by environmental uncertainty, from imperfect information or from insufficiently strong motivations inducing the pursuing of a different course of action:[5] for this purpose they are usually termed *salient* or *prominent* rules rather than rational choices.[6] Our suggestion is that, in accordance with its nature, the 'salient' strategy is closer to that of rules of thumb rather than to mistakes generated by uncertainty and imperfect information. The 'salient' strategy is a guide arising from experience and established procedures, from conventions as well as common beliefs across society, and so on. Both salient choices and rules of thumb represent the *pragmatic* strategy implemented in decision-taking when some shortages prevail, stemming either from the environment or from the individual's limited capability: nonetheless, the frictions associated with rules of thumb are still compatible with the notion of (bounded) rationality. Further, it is indeed remarkable that to the extent the 'salient' strategy is common knowledge (which is plausible as far as the source of salient choice are often conventions, common beliefs, etc.[7]), it can lead to actors' coordination – in the same fashion of signals – and, hence, to a successful result which rationality could fail to achieve in a strategic setting.[8] For the purpose of our analysis, the implication of such a perspective is that even when the individual constrains him/herself to keep a promise or to tell the truth, not on the grounds of a moral code but simply because he/she cannot find a reason to behave differently, or just because he/she adheres to conventions, and whenever this 'salient' strategy is common knowledge, the latter may lead the individual to achieve his/her ends, precluded to the rational choice.

A large body of empirical evidence in the laboratory confirms the benefits from establishing a convention as a 'signal' to be sent to the other players about one's own behaviour. Even in a genuine 'ultimatum game' an equal division of the stake is often observed, while strategic rationality would predict a biased distribution of resources in favour of the allocator. The post-experimental discussion among players sheds some light on this observed behaviour (see Part III). The equal division is the relevant signal players are willing to send to the opponents about their behaviour (according to a common sense of fairness). In the experimental evidence, then, the 'salient' strategy becomes the best one since it leads players to coordinate their choices.

NOTES

1. A somewhat similar point is in Hey (1993).

2. An extensive discussion on this point is in Yaari (1991).

3. Several kinds of 'friction' have been suggested which might lead to a cooperative behaviour such as 'limited control' (Rosenthal 1981), 'limited information' (Kreps and others 1982, Andreoni and Miller 1993), 'limited implementability' (Rubinstein 1986).

4. Schelling (1960) in particular stresses that some rules guiding human behaviour, despite not being grounded on the rationality requirement, succeed in coordinating actors. For instance, some rules guided by etiquette - which of course can be interpreted as a particular class of conventions - sometimes lead the individuals to choices which do not satisfy even transitivity, usually referred as one of the cornerstones of the rational-choice paradigm. Yet, such rules are still efficient as coordinating mechanism. To show this point we can borrow an example given by Anand (1993) in a somewhat different context: '...imagine that you are at a friend's dinner party and your host is about to offer you some fruit. If you are proffered an orange or small apple, you would rather have the orange, and if the choice is between a large apple and an orange you decide you would rather have the large apple. As it happens your friend is out of oranges and emerges from the kitchen with two apples, one large and one small. How should you choose? Etiquette seems to suggest that one might take the small apple...' (p. 344). Moreover, some rules or conventions *work efficiently* as coordinating mechanism although they are *not intrinsically efficient*. For example, as suggested elsewhere (Fiocca 1991), 'first come-first served' and the 'first on' rules are predominant in allocating resources by enforcing property rights. Some of these conventions, such as the ones mentioned above, are more likely to emerge and/or to survive than others; yet, the efficiency argument is not their point of strength. Actually, rather than enforcing property rights through these rules, other alternative methods (such as lotteries and turnover) may be more efficient inasmuch as they do not imply a kind of race which is a waste of resources, i.e. a deadweight loss. Nonetheless, in several countries and in quite a few public institutions, queueing is a prominent rule to allocate scarce resources. Yet, a more sophisticated notion of rationality may explain a portion of such conventions (Hargreaves Heap 1989). As noticed earlier, expressive rationality requires the agent's inspection about which preferences and consequent actions are valuable: hence, rules, norms, procedures are information-generating means in that they reflect what people regard as valuable and worthy in their life. A common culture within society induces people to share to some extent what is worthy and valuable: thus a portion of social conventions and norms reflects the values prevailing within society in that specific time, so becoming the symbolic language to express them. From this perspective, then, some conventions are regarded as the expressive rationality of society.

5. An extensive discussion on this point is in Sugden (1986, 1991).
6. See, for example, Lewis (1969) and Gilbert (1989). The latter maintains that the salient choice is not the consequence of the individual rationality: 'rational agents as such cannot be expected to do their part in a salient solution to a coordination problem' (p. 73).
7. As Sugden (1986) suggests: 'Once a convention has become established, there is no puzzle about why individuals are attracted to it: each person wants to follow it because everyone else does. It is of no direct concern to any individual whether a different convention would be better for everyone, since no one has the power to change what everyone else does' (p. 46-7).
8. As Schelling (1960) notices, individuals display a great ability in coordinating their behaviour through conventions, and that this ability is somewhat different from their rationality. Following one of Schelling's examples, two individuals, who are not allowed to communicate with each other, are asked to choose between 'heads' or 'tails'. Should they make the same choice, they both are awarded with a prize; otherwise none will get anything. Rationality on the part of both players does not seem helpful: there is not a rational motivation to choose either side as far as the probability of winning is the same (0.50). Yet, among the 42 people belonging to the experiment sample, 36 chose 'heads': hence, selecting 'heads' raises the probability of winning from 0.50 to 0.86. Given this generalised tendency, then, the best strategy turns out to be 'heads'. Conventions, rather than rationality, have led players to the best strategy via coordination of their actions: it is just this coordination capacity that makes conventions successful and hence attractive.

6 The necessity of 'genuine' versus 'instrumental' endogenous constraints

The funny story proposed by Kavka (1983), *The Toxin Puzzle*, recently rediscussed by Sugden (1991), sheds some light in qualifying the *nature* of endogenous constraints needed to achieve the agent's ends. Here the relevant distinction is founded on *genuine* versus *instrumental* constraints, where the latter are built up '*ad hoc*', that is they are outcome-oriented. Admittedly, 'genuine' preferences or constraints may turn out to be fruitful in reaching a preferable outcome, but only incidentally; namely, achievement of this outcome is only their 'by-product'. A typical example concerns the Kantian imperative: as is well-known, this is not outcome-oriented although it may contribute in reaching relevant economic results (see paragraph 3.2).

From this perspective we suggest a further point, focussing again on the relation between rationality and morality: (i) rationality may be instrumental – there does not exist a single notion of rationality – and morality may be 'instrumental'; hence, in this instrumental perspective, morality and rationality may be identified (although, of course, not only instrumental morality is to be regarded as rational); (ii) nonetheless, when morality is implemented in an instrumental fashion, it may fail in reaching the end pursued by rationality itself – that is, optimising. Here, the real matter does not rely on the inconsistency between means and end (that is, on the means-end framework because of the inappropriate means aimed at optimising), but rather on the shortage of some crucial resources (even the moral ones following Hirsch 1976): when the means needed to optimise are genuinely moral values and they fail to exist, the objective may also fail to be achieved accordingly. In other words, in the optimising process the true *nature* of morality is likely to become a crucial input of the process itself.

Incidentally, these considerations draw attention to another aspect of the origin of preferences: as is generally pointed out, every assessment about their rationality must be dismissed. Evolution rather than rationality seems a more promising approach: in an evolutionary perspective nearly everything may find an explanation in terms of survival and reproduction, including preferences: my taste for sweet food goes back to ancestral roots when human beings were eating fruit to survive. Accordingly, even genuinely moral preferences, in this evolutionary perspective, may be regarded as optimising tools for the survival and evolution of society itself.

In *The Toxin Puzzle*, the case is presented of two individuals who on Monday, in order to win one million dollars, are asked to promise that the following day they will drink an unpleasant toxin (whose effects would last only twenty-four hours): such a promise is enough to win the prize, regardless of the fact that they will actually drink the toxin the following day. However, in order to win the prize, the two individuals must be able to convince a team of psychologists that on Tuesday they really intend to drink the toxin, even if the day after they do not intend to actually do that.

Both the individuals, of course, want the prize; however, they go a different route to get it. Following the suggestion of his strategic and forward-looking rationality, on Monday the former, whom we shall label as the 'rational' one, promises to drink the toxin on Tuesday; however, he anticipates that on Tuesday, after having got the prize, he will not keep the promise: actually, his rationality itself suggests to act thus in order to maximise his utility: 'one million dollars is better than one million dollars plus the toxin'. Unfortunately, the rational individual, anticipating his future behaviour, is not able to convince the team of psychologists about his intention to drink the toxin, thus losing the prize. Hence, the 'instrumental' promise was not convincing: the need to keep the promise was not grounded on the genuine need to do the 'right thing', namely not to cheat (when cheating seems to be the most advantageous strategy). The individual has been trapped, then, into his rationality itself.

For the 'genuinely moral' individual, induced for example by the Kantian imperative, having promised is a good reason to keep the promise – that is, to be committed, and this personal attitude would convince the team. The point of the story is not to suggest that the moral individual is irrational;[1] similar to the previous conclusions, we emphasise that sometimes it is the strength of endogenous constraints rather than rationality that leads the individual to successful results.[2]

The above considerations are somewhat similar to Arrow's (1982) criticism on the unlimited rationality paradigm: thanks to their capacities, only rational agents are expected to be rich. But in real life this is not necessarily true and, as in *The Toxin Puzzle*, it happens sometimes that just these capacities turn out to be disadvantageous for the individual: it is the moral individual rather the rational individual who becomes rich.

NOTES

1. For a discussion on the rationality of the Kantian imperative, see Sugden (1991).
2. A similar approach is in Frank (1989): 'Being known to experience certain emotions enables us to make commitments that would otherwise not be credible. The clear irony here is that this ability, which springs from a failure to pursue self-interest, confers genuine advantages... Being predisposed to respond irrationally serves much better...than being guided only by material self-interest.' (p. 6).

PART II
A CASE STUDY: THE EFFECTS OF ENDOGENOUS CONSTRAINTS ON INTERNATIONAL COOPERATION

7 The effects of moral constraints and uncertainty on decision-making about foreign aid policy

The general discussion in the previous part of the work emphasises the relevance of endogenous constraints in determining economic results, and their compatibility with the notion(s) of rationality. As has been pointed out, such constraints originate from areas quite apart from the market – from the cognitive process, from moral preferences, from 'genetic' features, from the emotional sphere, and so on. Nonetheless, they are likely to produce a significant impact on the market itself.

In Nature, interactions generated by reciprocal altruism, even among different species, lead to advantageous exchanges; in its ancestral evolution, reciprocal altruism promotes economic transactions that market imperfections would preclude. The biological selection of reciprocal altruism – in economic terms, the reciprocal advantage of market exchanges – makes stronger such constraints, so as to justify, even from a rational perspective, the existence of self-imposed constraints. It is their success in genetic selection, and – in economics – it is their success in allowing transactions even within non-Walrasian contexts which explains and legitimates their strength.

In this part of the book we shall try to investigate the effects of endogenous constraints on a particular class of economic decision-making, namely on foreign aid policy.[1] For this purpose, we will consider a specific class of endogenous constraints – that is, the moral ones.

To explore the impact of moral constraints on foreign aid, in what follows we propose a new perspective founded on a particular combination between economic theory under uncertainty conditions (essentially regret theory) and economic theory of altruism. We suggest that regret may be a real factor in (at least some) people's decisions; utility produced by actions taken under duress may be increased by a rejoice feeling stemming from a chosen action; the consequences of definite actions or abnormal/unconventional/non-routine actions inspire more anticipated regret (and rejoicing) than 'inactions' or *status quo*/conformity with standard practice. The original Loomes-Sugden's regret model does not make any distinction of the last type. Kahneman and Tversky (1982) make this point much better. Hence, our attempt is to embed K-T perspective into L-S framework applied to the specific altruist's decision-making problem in the choice between different types of philanthropic contributions, and more exactly in the choice of the foreign aid policy that governments pursue.

Through this approach we provide a possible rationale of three aspects characterising the foreign aid policy of industrialised countries in favour of developing countries:

(i) the relevance of a country's own contribution – namely, the importance of playing an 'active' role in the international policy for foreign aid rather than free-riding;

(ii) the relevance of a particular foreign aid policy, according to some rule such as: 'finance exclusively investments, not current expenditure';

(iii) the tendency not to break this rule by extending it both over time and across recipient countries.

In what follows the interactions between the industrialised country (hereafter, IC) and the developing one (hereafter, LDC) are proxied by the interactions between the representative citizen of each country (for example, the representative agent is either a voter or a policymaker of each country); consequently, the whole analysis will be developed in terms of the representative agent's utility function. Further, concerning the preferences of the IC agent, two psychological attitudes are assumed to be relevant in his/her decision-taking about international cooperation: his/her altruistic attitude[2] as well as his/her regret aversion.

It is noteworthy that the regret perspective turns out to be appropriate in decision-making analyses where the psychological elements (regret, rejoice, or in general particular moods of the decision-maker) matter a great deal in the final decision. When we deal with institutions or countries' decision-making, regret theory seems less appropriate. Nonetheless, since we have proxied the industrial country through its representative citizen and the decision-making in philanthropic contributions through his/her decision-making, regret theory still seems a suitable perspective. The approach seems equally legitimate if we consider the citizen's utility function from the politician's point of view – namely, according to the latter's perception of the citizen's utility function,[3] instead of directly using the utility function of the representative citizen. In both cases, in fact, the decision-making process involves important subjective, psychological elements.

7.1 ALTRUISM AND REGRET AVERSION

The interpretation of the first aspect (point (i) above) of our analysis is grounded on the distinction suggested by Arrow (1975) about the *different possible attitudes of the altruist*: '(1) The welfare of each individual will depend both on his own satisfaction and on satisfactions obtained by others... (2) The welfare of each individual depends not only on the utilities of himself and others but also on his contributions to the utilities of others...' (p. 17). In both cases, there exists an interdependence between the utility of different subjects, namely a 'philanthropic' externality, but what distinguishes the two classes of philanthropic attitudes is the individual's desire to contribute in the second case. In other words, in order to internalise the externalities generated by the interdependent utilities between donor and donee, in the first case the philanthropic individual derives utility from seeing someone else's satisfaction increased, irrespective of whom has contributed to do so; in the second case, this is not enough as far as the internalisation of philanthropic externalities requires also one's own donation. There are several implications of these two versions of philanthropy, and notably the former is consistent both with free-riding in voluntary contributing for others welfare, and with crowding-out of one's own contribution by a social policy aimed at increasing social welfare. Conversely, in the second class of philanthropy, the individual's contribution is valuable *per se*: this implies that the altruist's satisfaction requires an 'active' role in voluntary contributing for the welfare of others.

Translating point (2) of Arrow's argument in our framework of foreign aid, we assess that internalisation of interdependent 'utilities' between (the representative citizens of the two) countries requires that the industrial country plays an active role in international foreign aid policy. The relevance of one's own contribution can be emphasised on several and somewhat more traditional grounds such as the Kantian motive to give, the desire of reciprocating (for example, Sugden 1984, 1985), the desire to obtain a joint-supply (for example, Posnett and Sandler 1986), the social pressure exerted on the potential donor, etc.

In what follows we propose a new perspective for interpreting altruistic contributions: following the lines of regret theory, the altruist's overall utility may be increased by the rejoice feeling stemming from the outcome (higher poor people's welfare) of the action he/she has selected (contributing).

From this perspective, we recall the modified utility function[4]

$$m_{ij}^{k} = c_{ij} + R\,(c_{ij} - c_{kj}) \tag{1}$$

where:

m_{ij}^{k} = 'modified' utility function;

c_{ij} = 'choiceless' utility;

R(.) = regret/rejoice function, with $R<0$ for regret and $R>0$ for rejoice.

According to our interpretation, eq. (1) represents the (modified) *utility function of the altruist*. Through the argument c_{ij}, he/she experiences a 'choiceless' utility accruing from the poor people's increased welfare, although he/she has not contributed: actually, for the altruist, the others' welfare is a public good, entering into his/her utility function even without his/her own contribution.

Moreover, according to the standard notion of public good, the altruist cannot be excluded from these benefits, that is from the pleasure he/she derives from the others' welfare.

Bearing in mind these features of philanthropic giving, the interpretation of the choiceless utility in this particular context relies on the *non-excludibility from the benefits stemming from a public good*. Because of the non-excludibility of philanthropy as a public good, the consequence of the other people's coontributions – the external benefits generated by the increased welfare of poor countries – is somewhat imposed on him/herself. In a representative democracy, for example, the altruist does not go to the poll to vote in favour of the candidate/platform/political party supporting international aid or he/she escapes taxation through which foreign aid is financed: nonetheless, the agent experiences the (positive) consequences of others' contributions. Hence, this particular interpretation of regret theory, and notably our lines of reasoning underlined by the choiceless utility, seems consistent with the first point of the Arrowian hypothesis (free-riding in philanthropic giving even on the part of the altruist).

However, through the second component of the modified utility function, $R(c_{ij}-c_{kj})$, the altruist may augment his/her utility (with respect to the 'choiceless' situation) according to a rejoice feeling stemming from a chosen action (contributing, according to the second point of Arrow's hypotheses). Comparing the utility originated from cooperation (c_{ij}) with that deriving from no cooperation (c_{kj}), the individual will rejoice whenever he/she has chosen the most successful alternative (contributing).

7.2 WHEN COOPERATION PRODUCES REJOICE

At this stage of our analysis a major aspect should be emphasised. With respect to the 'choiceless' situation, the economic agent may augment his/her utility according to a rejoice feeling stemming from his/her own contribution. This happens provided that two conditions hold:

(1) The decision-maker must be able to perceive *a nexus between his/her own contribution and the final outcome* (namely the others'

increased welfare). This nexus fails to exist or, however, is not properly perceived within a large community, where each one's contribution represents only a negligible portion which does not remarkably affect the size of total voluntary transfers.

It is well known that in voluntary giving one's personal contribution within a small community of donors is likely to have a significant impact on the final outcome (that is, on the total amount of contributions or on the others' welfare increase, if we assign a positive relation between the two variables). In this case, the individual's contribution does affect the final outcome (the overall size of the voluntary transfers) via example or imitative behaviour, social pressure, ethical considerations, group identity, etc. Usually such elements are taken into account in people's decision-making especially in small communities where the prevailing face-to-face relations make social control operative, stimulate imitation, reinforce the moral values of individuals, develop a group identity or, in other terms, make fund-raising more efficient.

In our analysis a small community is assumed: precisely, the 'small community' of the leading industrial countries or, better, that one of their representative citizens. Much as in a oligopolistic situation, where the action of each decision-maker affects the others' action (the production decision) as well as the final outcome (the whole production available), here the decision of any single country affects the final outcome – namely, the size of voluntary contributions – both through the influence on the other industrial countries' decision and one's own contribution (which constitutes a significant portion of the overall benefits available). In this way the nexus between one's own action and the final outcome exists and it is clearly perceived.

(2) In addition, the decision-maker has to be sure that his/her own contribution is used successfully, so as to effectively increase the others' welfare; otherwise, *the best course of action would have been free-riding*. If this is the case, the value of R $(c_{ij}-c_{kj})$ would be negative and *ex-post* comparison of the two choices available *ex-ante* would induce the decision-maker to regret his/her contribution.

Conditions (1) and (2) highlight some features of our analysis. First, the altruistic attitude is 'outcome-oriented': the decision-maker takes into account the close relation between his/her action and the associated consequence. Second, the altruist decision-maker, who *is willing to contribute but is also regret averse*, has to minimise the probability that a negative state of the world would occur, consisting in a waste of resources devoted to philanthropic giving. It follows that some devices of *behavioural rules* can be thought in order to manipulate *ex-ante* the occurrence of the regrettable outcome.[5]

A waste of the donor's economic resources may derive from: (a) an inefficient fund-raising implying that resources are not transferred on a 'dollar for dollar' basis (the well-known idea of the leaky bucket); (b) an inadequate contribution from the other industrialised countries, which makes insufficient and thereby useless one's own contribution; (c) a modification in the incentive structure of the donee, leading him/her to behave inefficiently (the well-known moral-hazard problem); (d) the latter's failure to cope with an efficient allocation of the transferred funds (even when a strategic behaviour is absent).

When the source of inefficiency comes from the donors' side, as in case (b), *ex-ante* manipulation of the probability of a regrettable outcome can rely on an assurance scheme.[6] For example, the potential contributor announces to the (representative citizens of the) other industrial countries his/her willingness to make a voluntary transfer, and before making the actual donation he/she observes the others' responses: the potential donor will contribute only provided the others will do the same. Therefore, recent attempts by the leading industrial nations to design and jointly implement specific economic policies can be regarded as a relevant assurance mechanism preventing a waste of resources, thereby enabling them to perform harmonious national policies. Through this assurance scheme, policy coordination can in principle make each participating nation better off than if it chose to operate in isolation although, as empirical evidence suggests, finding coordination rules when the effects of policies are uncertain turns out to be difficult.

On the other hand, the waste of transferred resources may derive from an inefficient behaviour, whether strategic or not, of the donee, as in cases (c) and (d): it may be the case that the recipient country uses foreign resources for current expenditure whilst their efficient allocation would require investments aimed at stimulating economic growth. Hence, *ex ante manipulation of the outcome may induce wealthy countries to adopt specific rules in order to deliberately restrict the range of options available to them in foreign aid*. For example, the industrial country decides on a resource redistribution exclusively devoted to investment spending (rather than current expenditure). The prevailing rule in foreign aid policy, then, would be: 'finance exclusively investments, not current expenditure' (see point (ii) at the beginning of this chapter).

From this paternalistic perspective, the donor's voluntary self-restriction of the available range of actions by means of behavioural rules reflects his/her belief that he/she is the best subject entitled to understand the social-economic needs of the donee as well as the link between needs and resources.[7]

Provided that such mechanisms - and notably rules - are successfully formulated, for the altruist regret-averse decision-taker his/her own contribution plays a crucial role in increasing his/her utility.

As we have discussed earlier (see chapter 4 of Part I), these *ex-ante* self-commitments limiting the degree of one's own freedom may be the solution to the strategic interactions among agents - in our context, among the representative citizens of the two countries. This perspective suggests a link between the regret and the Samaritan's dilemma (Buchanan 1975) approaches. In the former, these behavioural rules are adopted to minimise the probability of regret, and in the latter to pursue an optimal long-run strategy. In both cases rules matter as long as psychological, subjective elements matter.

7.3 STRATEGIC INTERACTIONS IN INTERNATIONAL COOPERATION

As is well known,[8] the Samaritan's dilemma arises whenever the extension of aid increases the number of situations requiring it, because of the modification of the incentive structure aid causes on the recipient (moral hazard). By means of his/her strategic behaviour, the latter induces the donor to give a larger support than he/she would be willing to do if he/she had the possibility to precommit him/herself adopting rules for personal choices.[9]

Bringing the dilemma to an international level, it has been shown (for example Bauer 1976) that government programmes to promote economic development instead are likely to retard the political and economic changes necessary to promote economic growth.

Here, the interactions between the representative citizens of the two countries are recasted within a strategic-game setting, where the IC agent is motivated by an altruistic concern towards the other and the latter by moral hazard. The more capable (or the more talented or the more lucky) IC citizen is moved by the miserable conditions of the latter who, in turn, may rely on the other's good feelings. Consequently, the representative citizen of the LDC may regard the other as a sort of insurance against the adverse states of the world, thereby taking a morally hazardous course of action (that is, a waste of the economic resources transferred). Specifically, the recipient country may decide to use foreign aid for current expenditure, whereas an efficient allocation of resources, aimed at stimulating the economic growth of the country, would basically require new investments.

Hence, the representative agent of the IC could experience two alternative courses of action:

(a) he/she may behave charitably. Actually, he/she belongs to a compassionate (affluent) society and his/her attitude reflects this type of society: therefore, his/her values, culture, and preference structure are such that he/she may be seriously injured by watching the representative agent of the LDC suffer (or starve, or be affected by a bad calamity). Hence, although aware that the LDC's interest calls for investment expenditure, he/she transfers resources aimed at immediate gratification of the unlucky country through current expenditure.[10]

(b) Alternatively, although it is painful, he/she may behave noncharitably, deciding to transfer resources exclusively for investments. In this way, the IC decision-maker exercises a strategic control over the latter, preventing a morally hazardous behaviour. When the altruistic concern of the IC agent is common knowledge, vague threats to cut off voluntary contributions if the recipient country fails to invest will be only non-binding, costless cheap talk, thereby remaining ineffective. In order to make convincing such threats, that is to transform the cheap talk into a reliable commitment, some devices are to be thought out:[11]

— the wealthy country may delegate the decision power in particular choice situations to an agent (the World Bank, for example) who is instructed to act in accordance with the strategic norms that are selected in advance. The agency device serves two objectives simultaneously. Firstly, the representative citizen of the LDC is more likely to believe that the delegated agent will behave in accordance with instructions. Secondly, by delegating the action to the agent, the representative citizen of the IC will not subject him/herself to the anguish of situational response which may account for a large share of the anticipated utility loss;

— the representative citizen of the IC may adopt *ex-ante* personal behavioural rules. In this way he/she avoids the (short-run) cost of facing the dilemma about the policy to pursue on a case-by-case basis. According to the long-run objective, this rule may be: 'finance only investment of poor countries and not their current expenditure'. Such a rule may be defined *'optimal' from several perspectives*: first, it allows the donor to pursue the *foreign policy which is assessed to be the best one for the welfare of the recipient country*; second it *minimises the utility loss of the representative citizen of the industrial country* (avoiding situational dilemmas); accordingly *its adoption is perfectly consistent with the citizen's rationality*.

We can notice, then, that both the interpretations of regret theory (notably, *ex-ante* manipulation of the probability of the regrettable outcome) and the Samaritan's dilemma reach the same conclusion, that is the relevance of self-imposed constraints to limit cooperation into specific spending categories.

7.4 GENERALISING A BEHAVIOURAL RULE IN COOPERATION

Until now we have proposed a theoretical justification to assess the relevance of one's own contribution (paragraph 7.1) and of some behavioural rule on which foreign aid policy relies (paragraphs 7.2 and 7.3). The following analysis attempts to justify why, once it is chosen, the donor government tends not to break such a rule, thereby extending its policy over time and towards all poor countries (point (iii) at the beginning of this chapter). Also this aspect will be mainly explained through regret theory, by proposing a particular interpretation of the regret-rejoice function R(.) (in eq. 1) and of prospect theory.

Earlier in the analysis (paragraph 7.2) we have assumed that the decision-maker can manipulate *ex-ante* the probability of a regrettable outcome, an aspect not considered by the original formulation of regret theory. In addition, we now assume that the decision-maker can minimise the *ex-post* regret stemming from an *ex-ante* wrong decision, an aspect not considered by the original regret theory either. In our context, where regret aversion influences decision-making in international aid, repetition and innovation of the individual behaviour display an important psychological impact. As noticed before (chapter 2 of Part I), this aspect has been pointed out, among the first ones, by Kahneman and Tversky (1982) and in our analysis it is embedded in regret theory through the regret-rejoice function R(.).

The impact of the nature of the action – 'repetition versus innovation' – in the regret-averse agent's decisions about foreign aid can be investigated by assuming a greater regret associated to a (wrong) innovative behaviour than the one stemming from a (wrong) standard procedure. The general idea can be summarised as follows: dealing with diversity usually is very distressing. Hence, nobody would want to be the person who has broken the rule, that is a standard procedure, when the result of such a change turns out to be negative. This is a strong argument in national and international policy, but it may also be important for decision-making on a personal level, as quite a few examples may illustrate. As suggested earlier (chapter 2 of Part I), if the result of a medical therapy in treating a certain illness is negative, the physician's (and indeed the patient's) perception about the result may change significantly depending on whether the physician has followed the traditional or an innovative therapy. Similarly, a sales decline may be perceived with different degrees of regret by the sales manager (and shareholders) depending on whether the manager used the old rather than a new advertisement agency for the seasonal sale campaign. In both cases, the responsibility of the action is more deeply perceived in an innovative action rather than in a standard procedure. In other words, we would expect more damage in the career of the politician, doctor, manager if the negative results derive from his/her innovative behaviour rather than from an established practice.

A further example may help illustrating this prediction in foreign aid. Assume two (representative citizens of two) industrial countries are following a routine behaviour. For the first one, country A, the ruling policy is that of financing mainly/exclusively investment expenditure in a developing country; conversely the second one, country B, follows a different pattern, financing mainly or exclusively current expenditure of the same country. So, for example, the former transfers $5 billion per year for investment, while the other transfers the same amount for current expenditure. At a given point in time, however, country A breaks this standard behaviour and decides to finance the current expenditure of the recipient country by the same amount of $5 billion. Later on the resources transferred to the developing country turn out to be completely wasted because of their inefficient allocation.

Although the two giving countries, A and B, remain in an *identical objective financial position* – consisting in a waste of $5 billion which could have been used in more profitable ways – *their subjective position may not*, since they may feel different degrees of regret – country A experiencing a greater regret than country B. Such a difference depends on the responsibility of the country's action: actually the losses incurred by country B derive from a '*status quo*', that is continuing to finance current expenditure rather than to finance investment expenditure; the losses incurred by country A derive from an *innovative behaviour*, that is changing policy to finance current expenditure rather than investment expenditure. According to the theory (eqs. (3) and (3') below), the representative citizen (and indeed the politician) of country A feels more upset than that of country B (regardless of their *objective* financial positions) because the former feels responsible for his/her innovative behaviour. For example, the politician of country A becomes more liable to attacks from the opposition than his/her colleague of country B.

The implication of the above discussion for foreign aid is quite straightforward when we postulate that, once a ruling policy has been chosen, this becomes the 'standard procedure': that is, the 'routine behaviour' is to finance investment expenditure rather than current expenditure. In this case following the rule 'finance only investment of poor countries and not their current expenditure' can reduce regret in case of a financial loss.

In order to formalise the above argument, let us introduce the different-regret assumption within the modified utility function as follows:

$$m_{ij}^{k} = c_{ij} + R_1(c_{ij}-c_{kj}) \qquad (2)$$

$$m_{ij}^{k} = c_{ij} + R_2(c_{ij}-c_{kj}) \qquad (2')$$

where:

$R_1(c_{ij}-c_{kj}) = R_1(x)$ *if* A_i *is the 'status quo' action* (3)

$R_2(c_{ij}-c_{kj}) = R_2(x)$ *if* A_i *is the 'innovative' action* (3')

The utility function, then, is *'adjusted' for both regret* (according to the LS's formulation) and the *nature of the action.*

In the case of regret, that is if $X<0$, we obtain:

$$|R_1(X)|<|R_2(X)| \qquad (4)$$

namely, regret stemming from actions adhering to rules and established procedures is going to be lower compared to that associated to an innovative behaviour: in the former case, the (negative) impact of regret on the utility turns out to be smaller.[12] In the preceding example, $R_2(.)$ is the function pertaining to country A, who has broken the routine.

In the present analysis, therefore, self-imposed behavioural constraints play a double role in the decision-making process:

— they minimise *ex-ante* the probability of the regrettable outcome occurring: the prevailing rule assumed in this context is financing solely investment spending;

— they minimise *ex-post* regret stemming from the wrong action: devising pre-commitments, such as that of financing investment spending, assumes a *spatial* as well as a *temporal* dimension.

Recasting the foreign aid policy within a theoretical framework where uncertainty, particular states of the mind, and moral constraints play a remarkable role, suggests two distinguishing features of the technique of voluntary self-imposed constraints: as argued in Part I, they are compatible and in some instances even required by an optimisation strategy, when the latter is affected by both 'external' and 'internal' (or subjective) frictions. Moreover, such a technique favours a bias towards the *status quo* and a resistence to reform. One implication of political economy is that governments often fail to adopt policies that economists consider to be efficiency-enhancing. The proposed explanation here is the 'non-neutrality' of the political choice (following a routine/breaking the *status quo*) whenever a failure is likely to emerge.

NOTES

1. An earlier analysis of this specific decision-making context is in Fiocca (1992b).
2. We do not address the question whether donations arise from a 'genuine' or an 'as if' altruism. From this latter perspective, policymakers have long recognised that the welfare of their economies is tied to the welfare of the world economy. Because goods, services, capital, and even labour are mobile internationally, economic policies in one country invariably have spillover effects on others. Having decided they can no longer ignore these global effects, and hoping to build a more stable world economy, governments have made many attempts to coordinate their economic policies also through foreign aid.
3. We do not address the question about the 'quality' of the information possessed by the politician on the citizen's preferences. Whatever they are, what really matters here is that such a representation affects the politician's decision-making about foreign aid policy: in particular, his action will reflect a genuine or 'as if' regret aversion of the citizen, depending on the goodness of preferences' representation/information.

4. We recall very briefly the main assumptions of regret theory. First, the individual chooses over a set of actions [A_1, A_2,..., A_n] (rather than among risky prospects as in EUT). Each action is an n-tuple of consequences, one consequence for each state of the world. When a certain state of the world is revealed, the individual compares his/her actual situation with the one he/she would have been in, had he/she made different choices in the past. Comparison between 'actual' and 'potential' consequences, and indeed between 'actual' and 'potential' actions within the available set, produces either a pleasant sensation of rejoice or a painful sensation of regret, as the individual realises that a different choice would have led to a better or a worse situation respectively. Hence, the utility/disutility accruing from the actual consequence is 'modified' by a sensation of pleasure or regret arising from that comparison. In other terms, the psychological experience of rejoice/regret associated with having a certain consequence will depend not only on the nature of that consequence but also on that of the others.
The key elements of the theory, then, are that (i) individuals experience particular feelings such as regret/rejoice; (ii) the consequence of his/her action does not generate (dis)utility *per se*; rather the latter is 'modified' by regret/rejoice; (iii) the individuals' attitude to compare different outcomes, including the potential ones, violates the axiom of independence of irrelevant alternatives (which is one of the cornerstones of EUT).
Let us assume n (mutually exclusive) states of the world with the associated (objective or subjective) probabilities, and a pairwise action [A_i, A_k]. The choice an individual faces is either to accept A_i and simultaneously reject A_k, or else to accept A_k and simultaneosly reject A_i. Following the authors' notation, the consequence of choosing A_i if the jth state occurs is denoted by x_{ij}; the probability of the jth state occurring is p_j (obviously, $0 \leq p_j \leq 1$ and $p_1 + p_2 + \ldots + p_n = 1$); c_{ij} is the utility stemming from x_{ij} and c_{kj} that deriving from x_{kj}.
For any individual there exists a 'choiceless' utility, c_{ij}, which the individual would derive if the consequence were experienced other than as a result of choice, for example, if the consequence were imposed in some way. Suppose he/she contemplates accepting A_i (and rejecting A_k): should the j_{th} state occur, he/she will experience x_{ij} (and simultaneously miss out on x_{kj}). Thus, in addition to the choiceless utility c_{ij}, he/she may also derive some increment or decrement of utility due to rejoicing or regret: an increment if $c_{ij} > c_{kj}$, whilst a decrement if $c_{ij} < c_{kj}$. Individuals, then, are assumed to make a double assessment: (i) they evaluate the outcome x_{ij} *per se*, and accordingly will experience a given satisfaction; (ii) they compare x_{ij} and x_{kj}.
It follows that the expected utility function is 'modified' for the regret/rejoice sensation (according to eq. (1)), where m_{ij}^{k} is the utility

from selecting *ex-ante* A_i (and rejecting A_k), as the jth state occurs. The difference between m_{ij}^k and c_{ij} derives from the regret/rejoice which is embedded into the regret/rejoice function R(.). If:

$$c_{ij} - c_{kj} > 0\ ,\ \ R(.) > 0 \ \ \Rightarrow\ \ m_{ij}^{k} > c_{ij}\ ;$$
$$c_{ij} - c_{kj} < 0\ ,\ \ R(.) < 0 \ \ \Rightarrow\ \ m_{ij}^{k} < c_{ij}\ ;$$
$$c_{ij} - c_{kj} = 0\ ,\ \ R(.) = 0 \ \ \Rightarrow\ \ m_{ij}^{k} = c_{ij}\ ;$$
$$c_{ij} - c_{kj} = \xi\ ,\ \ R(\xi) = 0 \forall \xi \ \ \Rightarrow\ \ m_{ij}^{k} = c_{ij} \ \ \Rightarrow\ \ \textit{regret}$$

theory leads to the same conclusions of EUT.

Also, $\partial m_{ij}^k/\partial c_{kj} < 0$ which denotes the impact of regret: the better the missed opportunity, the bigger the regret.

The optimising objective together with the regret-aversion assumption leads to maximisation of the following expected 'modified' utility:

$$E_i^k = \sum_{j=1}^{n} p_j m_i^k$$

which is the weighted sum of utility accruing from action A_i associated with the mutually exclusive states of the world.

5. It is noteworthy that *ex-ante* manipulation of the probability associated to an adverse state of the world is not considered in Loomes-Sugden's regret theory; this is a further hypothesis introduced in this specific context.
6. A well-known analysis of the assurance mechanism within the context of voluntary transfers is in Vickrey (1962); a more recent discussion of the assurance problem grounded on experimental evidence is in Isaac and others (1989).
7. This 'paternalistic' approach may be criticised on the grounds that the donee can make the best judgement about an efficient use of transfers. If this applies, for the regret averse decision-maker manipulating *ex-ante* the negative outcome may imply just the opposite strategy of not restricting the donee's degree of freedom in using transfers. The point here resembles the traditional debate on welfare expenditure.
8. See, for example, Buchanan (1975). A number of examples are also in Wagner (1989).
9. A discussion on the inefficiencies arising from the Samaritan's type of altruism is, for example, in Bernheim and Stark (1988) and Lindbeck and Weibull (1988).
10. We should argue that in this game context there are no problems of *information* and *rationality* (which would affect the *information-gathering capability*, the *calculating abilities of the individual*, would create *confusion, mistakes, illusion*, etc.). The source of the problem – which makes a (wo)man a Samaritan – is another one: it is the individual weakness which produces the 'dilemma' and its solution. Such a

weakness is embedded in the individual intertemporal utility function, affects the size of the (subjective) discount rate and, through the dilemma, the choice between short- and long-run utility maximisation. Hence, the source of this dilemma and of the final outcome is the nature of the individual's utility itself rather than his/her irrationality (whatever the notion/aspects of rationality we consider: consistency between objectives and choices, individual information-gathering and computing abilities, consistency between information and beliefs, and so on). Therefore, even though the Samaritan fully (and correctly) discounts the effects of his/her current action on future choice settings, he/she might still find it too painful to behave strategically. Hence, as we suggested earlier, rationality alone may not be enough for optimising and some additional constraints are required.

11. It should be noted that in such an instance one's commitment to act in a given way is considered trustworthy not on the basis of one's willingness to bear the costs associated with that behaviour, but rather on one's ability to reduce those costs in order to make the behaviour 'painless' and therefore more likely.

12. Similarly, in case of rejoice, that is $R(X) > 0$, the circumstance that:

$$|R_1(\cdot)| < |R_2(\cdot)| \qquad (4')$$

will imply that the rejoice arising from the '*status quo*' is smaller than the one stemming from innovation.

PART III EXPERIMENTAL EVIDENCE: ENDOGENOUS CONSTRAINTS IN THE LAB

8 Fairness as an endogenous constraint

In the marketplace as well as in other bargaining situations, economic agents take advantage of the 'ultimatum' power they enjoy or, conversely, they are exploited by the 'ultimatum' aspect of their exchanges. So, for example, in some market environments (notably in monopolistic conditions) the profit-seeking firm tries to exploit its ultimatum power at the expense of consumers: the traditional argument for government intervention in the market is avoidance of such an ultimatum which is measured by the consumer surplus. Similarly, also outside the market, utility-maximising agents engage in bargaining whose outcome, in accordance with the game theoretic prediction, would be accepted by all parties although they are left with a final wealth distribution which is 'unfair'.

Yet, many attempts have been devoted to enrich the widespread understanding of economic agents by means of more realistic behavioural assumptions. One way to proceed in this direction is recognising that some endogenous constraints – that is, some non-monetary motivations such as fairness, play a significant role in determining the nature of the outcome stemming from economic actors' interactions (see chapter 3 of Part I). The main economic implication of such moral constraints is that firms behave 'fairly' even in the absence of incentives such as the promise of future customs or the threat of regulation. Similarly, people may be willing to give up some mutually advantageous bargaining in order to reach fairer splits of the final wealth. Also according to experimental evidence, individuals refrain from unfair proposals and/or are ready to punish 'unfair' individuals, even bearing some cost for this.

Similarly to the case that we have labelled elsewhere as 'self-interest theories of philanthropy' versus 'altruistic theories of philanthropy' (Fiocca 1990a), it is also difficult to distinguish the boundary between a *genuine* and an *opportunistic* taste for fairness. So, for example, profit-seeking firms would attach some value to fairness to the extent that not being fair towards customers would imply a good deal of fruitful transactions being foregone. As maintained by Okun (1981), the readiness on the part of customers to resist unfair transactions, such as price increases which are not associated to cost increases, may lead to the failure of some markets to clear.[1] Similarly, the fair outcome of an ultimatum game could be explained by the proposer's fear (quite often justified) that the recipient may refuse a negligible positive offer.

Then, we should recognise that optimising with multiple (and sometimes conflicting) motivations - money, fairness, fear, etc. - is much more complex than optimising by means of an overall criterion - self-utility maximisation. Moreover, a 'non-game theory' attitude on the part of individuals may be just the result of a bounded rationality: people may not understand the theory or else need some time to learn games(wo)manship. In this case, then, fairness is likely to be just an 'incidental' outcome.[2]

8.1 THE EXPERIMENTAL RESULTS ON FAIRNESS: AN OVERVIEW

A main distinction among bargaining games can be drawn between (i) a one-period game, which is a genuine ultimatum game and (ii) a multi-period game, which is a sequential bargaining with offers and counter-offers across periods.

The ultimatum aspect of the 'easy' games, such as the one performed experimentally first by Guth and others (1982), is that the recipient can only accept the allocator's proposal or, alternatively, choose the conflict leading both players to get nothing. The authors divide their sample of graduate students in economics into two groups of equal size. All subjects in one of the two subgroups are assigned the role of player 1, namely the proposer, who always has the first move. They are informed in advance that their opponent, the responder, would be chosen randomly from the other subgroup. The games differ only with respect to the stake *c* to be divided within each couple (the size of the cake to be distributed varies between DM 4 and DM 10). Player 1 can propose to distribute that amount any way he/she prefers just by filling a form assessing: 'I demand DM *x*'. The recipient can either accept, hence getting (*c*-*x*), or reject the offer. The experiment is run twice, the second time with the same subjects but one week later: this gives the possibility to compare the results obtained from 'unexperienced' people (playing in the first week) and from 'experienced' people (playing later on). In both cases, especially for the first sample, experimental data were quite inconsistent with the game theoretic predictions: most allocators offered more than a token payment and many offered an equal split. In the first experiment the modal offer (7 out of 21 cases) was an equal division, the mean offer was .37*c*, and only two participants asked for the whole cake, namely the amount roughly consistent with the equilibrium prediction. Also refusals were very rare (only 2 out of 21 cases). In the replication of the experiment, the experienced people's decision behaviour was slightly different: the average offer was only .32, and only two players proposed an equal division; the greater frequency of conflicts (5 out of 21 cases) even in the face of some positive offers, was the consequence of more 'greedy' experienced proposers together with the responders' willingness to resist unfair allocations.

In a multi-period game, a sub-game-perfect equilibrium can be found through a backward induction. Let's consider the simplest case of a two-period game with an alternating-offer structure (e.g. Binmore and others 1985, Bolton 1991). In the first round a certain stake *c* has to be divided between proposer and responder: if the latter accepts the allocator's proposal, the stake is divided accordingly. If an agreement is not reached, the game moves towards a second period where subjects play a reverse role, that is the previous proposer becomes the responder and vice versa, and the stake is reduced by some discount factor δ ($0<\delta<1$): that is, due to delay, it turns out to be only δc. If also this second period ends in disagreement, both players will receive nothing. Hence, reasoning by backward induction, in the first period the proposer's reservation offer is δc, thus claiming for him/herself the amount $(c - \delta c)$.

The idea underlying the discount factor in sequential bargaining games is that the length of time to reach an agreement is costly, as for instance in industrial relations where agreements between trade unions imply a loss of working hours as well as other additional costs. Similarly, players are usually increasingly penalised as they move towards a successive period in the attempt to reach an agreement.

An important feature of sequential bargaining games is that what happens in a certain period (for example, the potential amount to be divided, the exact role played by each subject) partially depends on what happened in the previous period(s) and, in turn, the future outcome(s) will depend on what happens now: from this respect, these games differ from a genuine (single-period) ultimatum game where the role played by each subject and the amount to be divided are usually purely random. As has been noticed, this can be considered a weakness of one-period games: '.... the one-stage ultimatum game is a rather special case, from which it is dangerous to draw general conclusions. In the ultimatum game, the first player might be dissuaded from making an opening demand at, or close to, the 'optimum' level, because his opponent would then incur a negligible cost in making an 'irrational' rejection. In the two-stage game, these considerations are postponed to the second stage, and so their impact is attenuated' (Binmore and others 1985, p. 1180).

In quite a few of these studies, the length of time, that is the number of periods, is recognised as a crucial variable. Actually, as it is pointed out by Guth and others (1982), 'subjects do not anticipate future decisions in the way which characterizes the individually rational decision behavior in ultimatum bargaining games. Players tend to neglect that there is a last stage which is so important for the normative solution. Thus it is more than doubtful whether the special structure of ultimatum bargaining games will be fully recognized if the bargaining process is more complicated in the sense that the number of stages is very large' (p. 370).

The degree of experience that subjects acquire during the game has also been evaluated. Data from experiments in both one-period and multi-period games seem to contradict the theory, even when a learning hypothesis is introduced. While we should expect that people with experience would play strategically, empirical evidence (for example Guth and others 1982) shows that people either with experience or without experience do not approach their strategic equilibrium. Thus, as Guth and others suggest, 'Independent of the game form, subjects often rely on what they consider a fair or justified result' (p. 384). Kahneman and others (1988) try to analyse players' motivations in more depth: will the proposer behave in accordance with his/her taste for fairness even when his/her proposal cannot be rejected? Data show that although offers made by the allocators cannot be rejected by the responders, offers are still generous: 76 per cent of the sample distributed the stake evenly.

Experimental results obtained by Guth and others (1982) induce the authors to maintain that game theory is 'of little help in explaining ultimatum bargaining behavior' (p. 385). Binmore and others revise Guth and others experimental design also by adding a second period to the bargaining game. The game was played twice: in the second game subjects behaved more in accordance with game theory, inducing the authors to conclude that 'subjects, faced with a new problem, simply choose 'equal division' as an obvious and 'acceptable' compromise ...we suspect, on the basis of the present experiments, that such considerations are easily displaced by calculations of strategic advantage, once players fully appreciate the structure of the game' (p. 1180).

Neelin and others (1988) run different multi-period games, with differing numbers of periods: the argument is that the outcomes of varying-period games can be compared in order to avoid conclusions that are specific to a particular length of the game. In particular, they conduct an experiment in which subjects play four times a 5-period game with all the payoffs increased by $15. The results do not change significantly: there was no evidence of the effects of experience, as far as the observed offers differed from those predicted in the direction of the strategic equilibrium over the four rounds.

Ochs and Roth (OR) (1989) assumed a fixed amount of

resources to be divided between players, 100 'chips', with differing cash values whose size depends on (i) the period in which an agreement is reached; (ii) the bargaining position (in the role of proposer or responder) of the individuals. The authors build a complex experimental design allowing for eight scenarios generated by different combinations of two discount rates (4.4, 6.4, 6.6, 4.6) and two different lengths of time (a two-period and a three-period game). In addition, each player participates in ten consecutive bargaining rounds[3] with all parameters held constant, that is with the same scenario but with a different opponent. Hence, the experiment design, through repetition, allows the observation of the strategy of experienced players. The results of their experiments induce the authors to maintain that the high frequency of disadvantageous counterproposals proves that there are non-monetary arguments in the bargainers' utility function.

Partially on the same lines of reasoning as OR's study, Bolton (1991) runs a two-period experiment with alternating-offers. Similarly to the previous one, the pie is a fixed amount of resources with differing cash values depending on the relevant time discount factors. A crucial treatment variable of the experiment is the subject's experience: some of the games are played only by subjects who have no previous experience with bargaining experiments. A relevant assumption of the model is that bargainers make their decisions as if they were negotiating over both 'absolute' and 'relative' money. The former is measured by cash, and, according to the standard theory, the player's utility is measured by the amount of money earned. Through the comparison of absolute measures, relative money allows for some distributional evaluation as an argument of the bargainer's utility function. The comparison model, as referred by the author, shows that people display both strategic and fair attitudes. Specifically, 'obtaining fairness does not appear to be a moral imperative: subjects consider the pecuniary price and have varying reservation values' (p. 1128).

Moreover, as it has been shown by Guth and others (1991), in a multi-period ultimatum bargaining with an increasing cake, fairness can be used in an 'instrumental' way, that is to promote efficient results (a larger cake). From this perspective, the structure of the game can be regarded as a sequential PD game, where the emerging cooperation promotes efficient results. In the game, two subjects alternate in being the proposer. Each is entitled to declare whether his/her demand is an ultimatum or rather he/she prefers to continue bargaining for a larger cake in the next period (provided that his/her proposal is not accepted and that the specific period is not the final one). So the interesting feature of the game structure is its double nature: depending on the proposer's decision it can be regarded either as a genuine ultimatum game or as a multi-period bargaining game. Obviously, by postponing the agreement, players can divide a larger size of earnings. Thus, while the perfect equilibrium prediction leads to an immediate acceptance of the ultimatum assigning most of the cake to the proposer, efficiency requires to postpone the agreement in order to enjoy an increasing cake. On the other hand, since the proposer can declare his/her offer as an ultimatum, delaying the agreement through a rejection of the other's proposal may be very risky.

The main hypotheses tested through the experimental design are the following: whether subjects behave according to the game theoretical pattern (namely they exploit their ultimatum power and claim nearly all the cake for themselves); whether efficiency generates fairness (namely people reach the last round so attaining the largest cake); whether continued bargaining promotes fair allocation (namely whether equal splitting is observed in the latest rounds); whether the degree of fairness depends on the profitability of cooperation (namely on the size of the cake). Moreover, since each subject plays the same game twice in the same role but with a different partner, the experimental design allows to investigate also the effect of experience. The results are mainly on the lines of previous experiments in that genuine gamesmenship is rarely observed (only 13 of the 51 proposers used their ultimatum power in the first period of the game and none asked for nearly the whole cake). On the other hand, only a few observations support an equal splitting decision. Moreover, 27 games out of 54 reach the final period. Altogether these data validate neither gamesmanship nor efficiency as the dominant feature of players' interactions.

Further, data support the hypothesis of an 'instrumental' use of fairness in that the degree of cooperation increases with its profitability: the proportion of ultimatum decisions for the second period is 44 per cent while in the third one it declines, being only 20 per cent. In addition, such a proportion is 42 per cent for Δc = DM 3 and only 21 per cent for a strong increase of the cake, namely Δc = DM 10.

Also the prediction of the increasing degree of fairness through time seems to be supported by the experimental results: actually, a significant decrease in the average relative demand across rounds is observed. Finally, although in the repetition of the game a number of players played less – some stopped short of the second and the third round – the authors suggest that this circumstance cannot be regarded to support the intuition according to which learning induces strategic behaviour. In fact, the average relative demands were nearly the same in the first and in the second plays, rather than more greedy in the second one.

Altogether the experiment produces 'mixed' results: the observed behaviour seems neither consistent with the game theoretical predictions – even when the normative solution is easy to calculate and quite obvious – nor with an efficiency criterion which would encourage the postponement of agreement.

On the grounds of the experimental results we have briefly overviewed,[4] the general conclusion is that non-monetary motivations matter and, accordingly, subjects seem to behave more like 'fair(wo)men' than 'games(wo)men', often reaching an equal division of the final wealth. Yet, as has been shown (Shogren 1989), such a result turns out to be reversed in experimental designs where fairness is defined in the context of loyalty. When the agent plays as a member of a team, rather than on his/her own as in most bargaining experiments,[5] he/she shifts his/her taste for fairness from his/her opponent to his/her team, that is the bargainer will be fair only to the group with whom his/her loyalty lies. Then, in this special context of loyalty, experimental evidence seems more consistent with game theoretical predictions.

OR's experiment is the starting point of our experimental design, as far as both share the common aims of exploring whether the bargainers' utility is accurately measured by their monetary payoffs and of investigating the effects of experience. Yet, our study differs from that by OR in many respects:

— OR's multiperiod framework leaves some room for bargaining (through the discount rate δ and the alternation of roles between allocator and responder). Put in a slightly different way, in OR's experimental design, what happens now (the role of the players and the cash value to be divided) depends on the past and will affect also the future bargain. Hence, in some way the nature of the game (the sequence) affects the outcome. Instead, our experiment has the nature of an ultimatum, without any possibility of a counter-offer: the proposal may be rejected with the cost for both players of getting nothing. Hence, the different nature of the game affects the degree of punishment of the greedy opponent. In OR's bargaining sequence the penalty turns out to be less severe depending on the discount rate and the period in which the agreement (if any) is reached;

— rather than a fixed amount of resources (with different cash values), we consider four alternative stakes to be randomly selected;

— in OR's experiment the learning hypothesis is tested just through repetition of the game against different, anonymous opponents. In the present experiment, experience is tested not only by repetition but also through the two alternative variants of incomplete/complete information.

NOTES

1. An extensive analysis of this point is in Kahneman and others (1986a, 1986b).
2. Binmore and others (1985) suggest that experience is sufficient to turn 'fairmen' into perfect-equilibrium 'gamesmen'. Similarly, Neelin and others (1988) assess that when perfect equilibrium predicts inaccurately it is because bargainers fail to develop a backward induction.
3. Players were told that at the end of the game one of the ten rounds would be randomly selected, and that they would be paid on the basis of the outcome of that specific round.
4. Extensive surveys are, for example, in Thaler (1988), Roth (1988) and Guth-Tietz (1990).
5. As suggested by Shogren (1989), 'Each bargainer is an island with no loyalty other than to himself or perhaps the world...An individual's loyalty can range from his own ego to a world view of a collective brotherhood of man. Realistically, the majority of individuals will have

a threshold of loyalty which separates the fairman from the gamesman in each of us. Explaining this threshold will improve the correspondence between theory and observed phenomena' (p. 319-20).

9 Building a new experiment: are people games(wo)men or fair(wo)men?

Our work tries to raise questions rather than to give answers (unless very tentative ones). The main questions envisaged in our experiment[1] are the following:

(i) do people display non-monetary arguments in their utility function? and, if so:

(ii) how do the increasing monetary opportunities stemming from the environment affect non-monetary arguments?

(iii) how does the learning process/experience affect these non-monetary arguments?

Put in a slightly different way, question (i) concerns the sense of fairness of subjects; question (ii) is related to the possible trade-off between the taste for fairness and pragmatic opportunities; question (iii) concerns the interactions between fairness and strategies.

In order to highlight some behavioural interactions among agents we have implemented an experimental methodology in the lab.

a. Question (i): the taste for fairness

Also on the grounds of experimental economics, a now established literature emphasises the relevance of non-monetary arguments in people's utility function. Quite a few of these experiments concerning individuals' non-selfish attitude are along the lines of the free-rider idea: actually, the free-rider problem is strictly associated to the expansion of the voluntary sector. As suggested elsewhere, the goods and services provided by the voluntary sector are to a large extent public goods; once this is recognised, the free-rider problem emerges since anyone could enjoy the benefits stemming from the voluntary sector without bearing the associated costs (Fiocca 1990a).

Although the free-rider approach is very interesting, it is not the only one available to test non-selfish and cooperative attitudes of agents. As suggested, another appealing idea is exploring agents' sense of fairness.

Assuming the bargainer's utility is measured exclusively by the monetary payoff, that is by the amount of the stake, in one-period bargaining games the theory predicts that there exists a perfect and unique equilibrium where the allocator makes an offer approaching zero, while the recipient accepts all positive offers (Rubinstein 1982). As is well-known, the ultimatum aspect of this one-shot game is that the responder can only accept the allocator's proposal or, alternatively, choose the conflict – that is, refuse the amount, in which case both receive nothing. In this simple ultimatum game, rationality on the part of both players requires that, if c (>0) is the whole stake to be divided between the two parties, the allocator will claim for him/herself the amount Ec (where E is a positive real number such that 0<E<1), leaving the minimal positive amount (1-E)c to the other; conversely, the rational responder would always prefer the alternative which yields more for him/herself (that is, (1-E)c>0, where the sign > denotes 'is preferred to'). However, allowing also for some non-monetary concerns, such as fairness, we may assume E to be some function of both monetary and non-monetary arguments of the players' utility function, defined on the domain [0,1]. Then:

$$E = E(M,F) \tag{5}$$

where M is the monetary argument in the player's utility, and F denotes the non-monetary argument, which may be identified with the player's taste for fairness. Of course:

$$\partial E/\partial M > 0 \tag{6}$$

The derivative's sign concerning F is less obvious. When fairness exists among players, there will be a *reservation level* E^* corresponding to a certain value, F^*, of the non-monetary argument such that: $E^* = E(F^*)$. Above or below E^* the players – in their different roles of allocator and responder – will either reject or accept the offer. More specifically, for both proposer and responder, there exists a certain E^* such that, when $E > E^*$:

$$\partial E/\partial F < 0 \tag{7}$$

and when $E < E^*$:

$$\partial E/\partial F > 0 \tag{8}$$

Actually, from the *proposer's point of view*, an excessively high value of E could induce either the refusal from the (fair) responder or anyway could affect the proposer's taste for fairness. Similarly, from the *responder's point of view*, excessively high values of E (that is, excessively low values of $1\text{-}E$) would appear too 'insulting' to be accepted according to his/her sense of fairness. Actually, he/she may feel insulted by a 'greedy' proposal and accordingly would reject a positive offer, thus contradicting the theory prediction. This is represented in expression (7) for both players. Also, excessively low values of E would not be proposed or accepted when both parties are fair, as shown by expression (8).

Then, according to this simple representation, the values of E desired by *both* players could show the following pattern with respect to people's fairness:

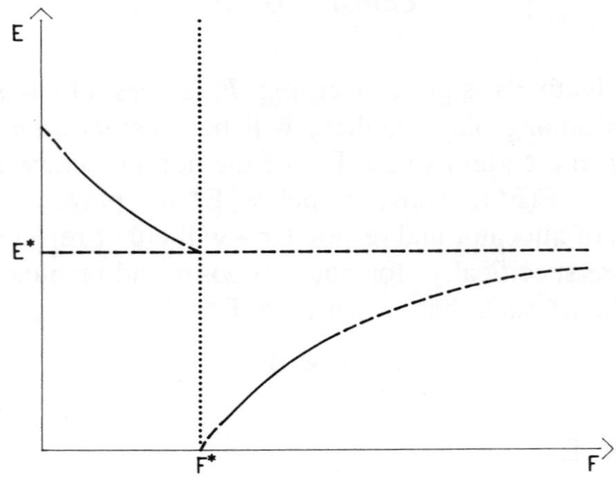

Figure 9.1

with a discontinuity point at F*.

The above discussion assumes, for simplicity of notation, that E^*, that is the reservation level, is the same for both proposer and responder. Of course, this might not be the case, being E^* determined by the individual's *subjective* taste for fairness (and money).[2] Accordingly, there will exist two different functions $E^P = E^P(M,F)$ and $E^R = E^R(M,F)$ for the player in his/her role respectively of proposer and responder.

Finally, the perfect equilibrium prediction (*PEP*) of game theory, mentioned at the beginning of this discussion, would imply the following expression for E:

$$E = E(M,\bar{F}) \tag{9}$$

because in that case people have only monetary arguments in their utility function, which implies that F is fixed at some value $\bar{F}$ or, eventually, it is equal to zero. Hence:

$$\partial E/\partial F = 0 \tag{10}$$

in the PEP case.

As mentioned above, when we assume that the individual has an ideal of fairness, he/she may wish to 'punish' the too greedy counterpart even if this means bearing some costs for him/herself, which in a genuine ultimatum game would imply that both parties will receive nothing. This opportunity-cost of fairness is what we call the '*price of fairness*' (the counterpart being the '*risk of greed*').

Such an opportunity-cost is assumed to be positively related to the size of the cake to be shared: hence, an interesting point worth exploring is the impact of an increasing opportunity-cost of fairness on the outcome of the game. So, for example, if in sharing a pie the proponent offers to give the other only a negligible part of the pie, the latter may refuse – even if, being rational, she knows that a handful of crumbs is better than nothing. If her refusal implies that also her opponent will not receive the pie at all, this means that the former prefers to punish the other (accordingly bearing the cost of receiving nothing) rather than to receive a little piece of pie: hence, some non-monetary argument – that we call her sense of fairness – seems to prevail in some circumstances. But in which ones? This leads us to turn to the second question.

b. **Question (ii): fairness versus fear**

When the *pragmatic* opportunities stemming from the environment increase, how do people deal with such opportunities? If, for example, Irene offers Margherita not just a handful of crumbs but 1/5 or 2/5 of the pie, will Margherita still punish her greedy mate? Obviously enough, the opportunity-cost of Margherita's sense of fairness – that is, the price of her fairness, is increasing: 2/5 of the pie is much better than nothing.

In other words, do people preserve *genuinely* their need of fairness or, rather, are they '*bribed*' by such opportunities, making a 'compromise' between fairness and money? How much pie should Irene offer to Margherita to satisfy her need of fairness? How many slices are enough to tempt her on merely 'pragmatic' grounds?

c. **Question (iii): experience**

Even assuming people having only monetary arguments in their utility function, it may be the case that players do not approach the game-theoretic solution (PEP) since they are confused or they do not have a deep understanding of game theory. Should this be the case, we would expect experience to affect people's behaviour towards the game theoretical prediction. Nonetheless, if this strategic outcome does not occur even among experienced people, we might assume that people display preferences for what they consider a fair allocation.

All the considerations in points (*i*), (*ii*), (*iii*) are the bulk of our experimental design. It consists of a 2-person, one-shot game representing a genuine ultimatum game.

Four increasing amounts of money – representing the increasing 'price of fairness'/'risk of greed' – are proposed to be divided within each couple of players (in the experimental design named respectively *Proposer* and *Responder*). In particular, we also include situations with a high amount of c, namely c = £ 60.

The learning hypothesis is tested in two different ways:[3]

1. through repetition of the one-shot game: the 'sharing decision' is repeated in 8 successive rounds, in each of which both the amount to divide and the pairing of players are equally likely to be (randomly) selected.
2. through two alternative scenarios: with incomplete and complete information, respectively.

Before describing and analysing in more detail the new experiment (chapter 10), we develop a further discussion of point (ii) – that is, fairness versus fear (paragraph 9.1), and we summarise our main predictions (paragraph 9.2). Finally, the results and the test statistics are reported (chapter 11). (An appendix is also provided for further details of the experiment).

9.1 MORE ABOUT THE PRICE OF FAIRNESS AND THE RISK OF BEING GREEDY

The one-shot game, coupled with the punishment mechanism (that is, getting nothing at the end of the game), would involve a lot of uncertainty about the final outcome. Actually, when the player commits him/herself *ex-ante*, acting '*as if*' he/she was the Proposer or the Responder (see chapter 10 for more details of our experimental design), he/she ignores the decision of the other and eventually each individual is paid (if any) on the basis of playing just once.

Now, as mentioned earlier, the individual may care little to be paid at all when the amount to be divided turns out to be not very significant: the fairness argument prevailing versus the monetary one. Yet, he/she would not take the risk of missing a good opportunity to earn a significant amount of money as the sum to be divided increases. In the presence of four amounts of money, as the ones assumed in our experimental design (c_1 = £ 5, c_2 = £ 10, c_3 = £ 25, c_4 = £ 60), what is likely to happen is that as c_i (i = 1, 2, 3, 4) increases, the recipient is prepared to accept a smaller and smaller percentage – that is, a more and more unfair share of the sum. In other words, we should expect a relation between the size of the stake c and the corresponding share $(1-E^R)c$ that the recipient is willing to keep for him/herself, which is increasing at a decreasing rate. Graphically:

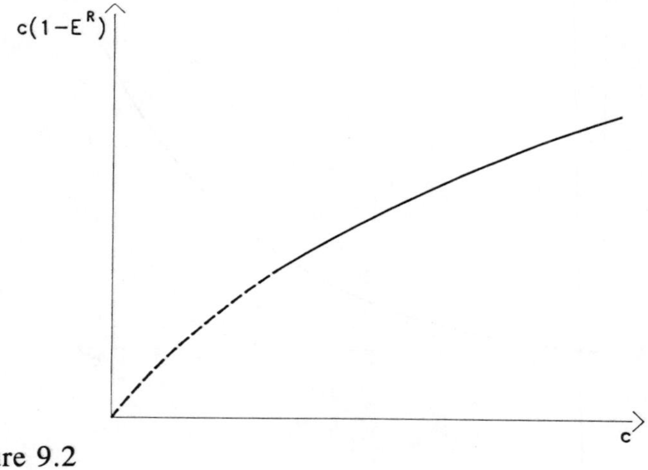

Figure 9.2

This means that the Responder's function E^R can be now expressed as follows:

$$E^R = E^R(M,F,c) \tag{11}$$

where

$$\partial c(1-E^R)/\partial c > 0 \tag{12}$$

and

$$\partial^2 c(1-E^R)/\partial c^2 < 0 \tag{13}$$

The size of the stake c is therefore entering the function E^R as a new argument.

Similarly, as c increases, also the Proposer may be prepared to keep a smaller and smaller percentage of the stake, namely to tolerate a more unfair/greedy behaviour of the Responder, in the fear of having nothing. In this case, the amount $(1\text{-}E^P)c$ that the Proposer is willing to leave to the Responder will be an increasing function of the stake size c, at an increasing rate:

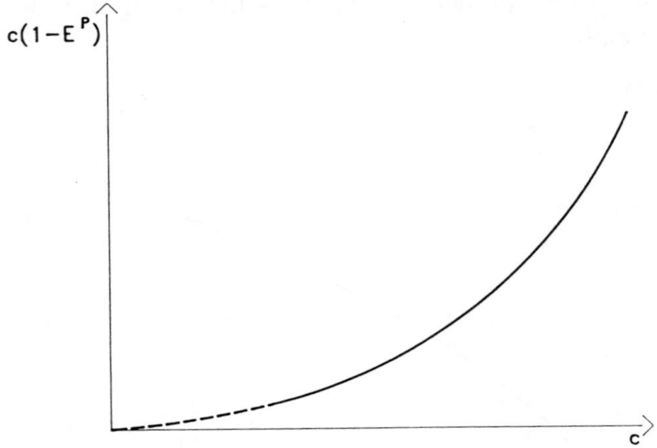

Figure 9.3

Hence, c will enter again the Proposer's function E^P as follows:

$$E^P = E^P(M,F,c) \tag{14}$$

where

$$\partial c(1-E^P)/\partial c > 0 \tag{15}$$

and

$$\partial^2 c(1-E^P)/\partial c^2 > 0 \tag{16}$$

in this case. So in both (13) and (16), the player's fear is captured by the sign of the second derivative.

In both cases, we could observe unfair allocations (either in favour of the Proposer or in favour of the Responder). Hence, as the monetary opportunities from the environment increase, the individual's risk aversion may increase accordingly. In this case, fairness strictly interacts with fear, and it becomes difficult to separate the two motivations – namely, the non-monetary and the monetary arguments of the actor's utility function. Such interactions give rise to a *trade-off* between fairness and fear (or risk aversion) as c_i increases, unless the individual's sense of fairness is particularly strong (in the same fashion as the Kantian principle).

In other words, if there were no interference of risk aversion with fairness, so that only the arguments M (money) and F (fairness) would determine the pattern of the functions E^R and E^P, then the functions represented in Figures 9.2 and 9.3 would be simply linear increasing functions in the size of the stake. That is, we assume that both M and F make $c(1-E^R)$ and $c(1-E^P)$ increasing functions of c, while the role of risk aversion is represented by c as an argument of E^R and E^P, and by its influence on the sign of the second derivatives. Therefore, according to our discussion, fear – or risk aversion – should be able to influence the outcome of the game determining a number of conflicts between partners that declines with the size of the stake.

9.2 SUMMARISING OUR MAIN PREDICTIONS

According to the above discussion, the main predictions which we would like to test through the experiment are the following:
(i) '*games(wo)manship*': if people display non-monetary arguments, we shall not obtain the PEP – according to which Proposers only make offers close to zero while Responders accept all positive offers;
(ii) '*fairness versus fear*': individuals' sharing decisions may be affected by the size of the cake;
(iii) '*experience promotes games(wo)manship*': if people exhibit only monetary arguments in their utility function, inexperienced people (that is people in the first rounds of the game and/or playing the first variant of the game implying no information) would not act strategically. Conversely, experienced people would act according to the PEP.

If this strategic outcome does not occur even among experienced people, so that their behaviour turns out to be inconsistent with the standard theory, we might assume that individuals prefer what they consider a fair allocation.

NOTES

1. An earlier version of this experiment is in Fiocca (1992a).
2. A possible explanation of the fact that E* is the same for the two players is to assume that both prefer equal divisions (to the extent that an equal splitting is regarded as a "common sense" of fairness among players).
3. Obviously, the effects of experience may be evaluated in other ways such as by assuming a different number of periods between games in different experiments (and sometimes even within the same experiment) or by asking the same subjects to repeat the same experiment after a length of time (for example, one week in Guth and others 1982).

10 The experimental design

During the experiment, players interact via linked microcomputers.

The experiment consists of a 2-person simple ultimatum game (which is repeated for 8 rounds), with four alternative amounts of money (£ 5, £ 10, £ 25, £ 60) to be divided between the two agents. During the game, in each round just one of these four amounts will be randomly selected. Then, at the end of the 8 rounds, the actual amount to be distributed between the two players will be selected again at random among the ones that occurred in the past 8 rounds, with each of the 8 rounds being equally likely to be selected.

At the beginning of each round, every participant is asked to divide the four alternative amounts of money '*as if*' he/she was the Proposer (P) or the Responder (R). Thus, for each of the four amounts proposed, the agent has to decide his/her *reservation payoff* below which he/she will not accept the sum if he/she will turn out to be the Responder, and the *reservation giving* above which he/she will not give the sum if he/she turns out to be the Proposer during the game.

Hence, every one decides his/her own reservation sum *ex-ante* – that is, before knowing (i) whether he/she will be the actual Proposer or Responder during the game (the chance to be P or R is equally likely), and (ii) which amount will be effectively selected (each amount is equally likely to be selected). The following screen will then appear on the terminal:

Table 10.1

AS PROPOSER		
Amount to be divided	To me	To Responder
5.0	?	
10.0		
25.0		
60.0		
AS RESPONDER		
Amount to be divided	The least amount I would accept.	
5.0		
10.0		
25.0		
60.0		
Please type in your chosen values at the cursor and press ENTER.		

After this step, for *each round*:
(i) the random pairing is made, and it is randomly selected which member of the pairing turns out to be the Proposer or the Responder. At no stage does anyone know the identity of the person with whom he/she is paired;
(ii) the amount of money to be divided for that round will be randomly selected;
(iii) then, the computer screen will show whether the person has been selected to be the Proposer or the Responder; it also shows the amount of money selected and whether the proposal is *accepted* or *rejected* (see tables below).

Table 10.2

> THE TOTAL AMOUNT TO BE DIVIDED IN THIS ROUND IS 5.0
>
> This round you are a PROPOSER. When the amount to be divided is 5.0 you proposed keeping 3.0 and offering the RESPONDER 2.0.
>
> You have been paired with a responder who will not accept less than 1.0.
>
> Since what you are offering is not less than 1.0 your proposal is ACCEPTED, i.e. this round you get 3.0 and the RESPONDER gets 2.0.

Table 10.3

> THE TOTAL AMOUNT TO BE DIVIDED IN THIS ROUND IS 5.0
>
> This round you are a PROPOSER. When the amount to be divided is 5.0 you proposed keeping 5.0 and offering the RESPONDER 0.0.
>
> You have been paired with a responder who will not accept less than 5.0.
>
> Since what you are offering is less than 5.0 your proposal is REJECTED so for this round you and the responder both get 0.

Table 10.4

> THE TOTAL AMOUNT TO BE DIVIDED IN THIS ROUND IS 5.0
>
> This round you are a RESPONDER. When the amount to be divided is 5.0 you said that the least you would accept would be 1.0.
>
> You have been paired with a proposer who proposes to keep 3.0 and offer you 2.0.
>
> Since what you are being offered is not less than 1.0 you ACCEPT the proposal, i.e. this round the PROPOSER gets 3.0 and you get 2.0.

Table 10.5

THE TOTAL AMOUNT TO BE DIVIDED IN THIS ROUND IS 5.0
This round you are a RESPONDER. When the amount to be divided is 5.0 you said that the least you would accept would be 5.0.
You have been paired with a proposer who proposes to keep 2.0 and offer you 3.0.
Since what you are being offered is less than 5.0 you REJECT the proposal. So for this round you and the proposer both get 0.

At the end of the eight rounds, the single round to be chosen for payment will be selected *randomly* from the eight rounds subjects have played previously. The computer screen will show again the results of that particular round, that is the amount to be divided in that round, how it was divided between paired players, and whether the offer was accepted or rejected.

(i) If it was *ACCEPTED*, each person in the pair will receive the share decided and payment will be made.

(ii) If it was *REJECTED*, both members of the pair receive zero.

So, for example:

Table 10.6

This round you are a RESPONDER. When the amount to be divided is 5.0 you said that the least you would accept would be 5.0.
You have been paired with a proposer who proposes to keep 5.0 and offer you 0.0.
Since what you are being offered is less than 5.0 you REJECT the proposal. So for this round you and the proposer both get 0.

Hence, the outcome of the game, namely the exact amount of

payment accruing to the two individuals, depends on the *interaction* between the offer of the Proposer and the response of the Receiver at that specific round which has been randomly selected at the end of the 8 rounds. If the Receiver has been offered, in correspondence of that amount, a share which he/she judges unfair, that is below his/her reservation payoff, he/she rejects the proposal, so that both the Proposer and the Responder will not receive anything.

Therefore, behind the game there is a crucial mechanism to punish the (exceedingly) unfair partner: the Proposer has the opportunity to punish the Responder if the latter is too greedy – namely, if his/her reservation payoff is too high to match the Proposer's offer; and vice versa for the Responder. This punishment mechanism may be regarded as a means of social control to preserve fairness within the community.

As mentioned earlier, in order to better test the learning hypothesis, this repeated game is played according to two variants:
(i) *incomplete information*. In this variant, at the end of every round, each participant will be told only what happened to him/her: he/she will be given *no information* about the choices made by the other participants and their results. Hence, what the other players do in each round is not recorded on the screen of his/her terminal. Therefore, subjects learn exclusively from their own experience.
(ii) *complete information*. In this variant, at the end of each round, information about what happened to *all* the other pairs (but not their identity)[1] will appear on the screen of each person's terminal (see Table 10.7 below). Therefore, subjects enjoy additional information useful for future decisions just by observing what the other players do.

Table 10.7

Pair	total	Proposer offer	Responder minimum	Result	Division
?? /??	5.00	2.00	1.00	ACCEPTANCE	3.00 / 2.00
?? /??	5.00	4.00	5.00	REJECTION	0.0 / 0.0
?? /??	5.00	1.00	1.00	ACCEPTANCE	4.00 / 1.00
?? /??	5.00	1.00	3.00	REJECTION	0.0 / 0.0
?? /??	5.00	1.00	4.00	REJECTION	0.0 / 0.0

Trying to explore the effects of experience through a full-information framework raises another problem: in his/her decision-making each player may be affected by the decisions of the other players (whose behaviour is displayed on the terminal screen).

We should notice that the influence of the others' behaviour on one's own decision-making is an aspect of true life, and notably of the voluntary sector: it is well-known that the threat of social pressure is a relevant cost (a substitute of legal threat): for example loss of friends, influence, prestige, social acquaintance, etc. Another good example provided by Ireland and Johnson (1970) is that often one of the first instructions given to a young politician is to engage in charitable activities. Thus, 'building a reputation' generally plays a relevant role in non-selfish decision-making, although, when such forces are at work, it is difficult to distinguish between genuine and 'as if' non-selfish preferences (such as fairness in our study).

The same kind of interactions may arise also in lab: for example, regardless of his/her genuine ideal of fairness, in deciding his/her reservation payoff, the Responder may be influenced by the other Responders' decisions. Of course, we cannot exclude the other way round: regardless of the others' decisions, the Responder will ask a reservation share in accordance with his/her principle of fairness, if it is strong enough. Hence, in the experiment, after some rounds, 'implicit' or 'informal' collusion may arise among subjects playing the same role (for example, Responders) in order to 'build a reputation' – that is, to send a 'signal' to the opponents. Similar strategic 'signals' may be sent to the Responders on the basis of some collusive agreements, with the result of manipulating the reservation offer.

We should stress that, although the problem of 'building a reputation' may be quite remote in our experimental design, as we used a random number generator for pairing people in each round, nonetheless we used two other additional devices to avoid the problem: (i) by preserving anonymity even in the complete-information scenario. Actually, as Table 10.7 above shows for the second variant, it is not shown on the terminal screen who the pairs are (actually they are replaced by ??/??); (ii) by not allowing the game to last long enough to create 'reputation building'. Hence, our 8 rounds may represent a 'compromise' between the need for players *to get experience* and *the tendency to strategically build a reputation* (although, of course, we are aware that the choice of 8 rounds is our subjective, and hence arbitrary, evaluation). Therefore, as is often the case in experimental designs, a trade-off arises: through repetition and full information we gain the benefit of exploring the learning hypothesis in more depth, but at the expense of generating possible strategic behaviours such as the one described above. Actually, despite our devices, we cannot be sure of controlling for such a phenomenon during the experiment (in particular see the data of the last session in appendix B).

10.1 METHODS

One hundred students (plus reserves) were recruited from both undergraduate and graduate classes at the University of York. They received an invitation sheet in their colleges (see appendix 1), which told them that since the experiment offered them the chance to earn a substantial amount of money, they were strongly advised to pick up an instruction sheet when they signed up for the experiment (the instructions are presented in appendix 2). They were also told that ten participants were required for each of the ten sessions and that the experiment would require an even number of players; if for any reason an odd number of people arrived, the last person would not take part at the experiment but would be paid 2 pounds for turning up.

Each subject participated in only one session of the experiment, but they were not told in advance which variant (no information/full information) they would. At the first session of the first day (the starting time of the experiment was 9.30 a.m.) only seven people (out of ten) arrived, so that only 3 couples took part in the experiment (warning: running experiments at 9.30 a.m. on Friday may be risky). Participants were assembled in the Experimental Economics room of the University and randomly assigned code numbers which determined the terminal number. A computer program was written to select randomly the pairing for each round as well as who was to be the Proposer and who the Responder. So the chances of each player of meeting a specific subject as his/her opponent were rather low.

Players were asked not to talk during the experiment with all players being seated at desks which were far enough from each other to exclude verbal communication. Attempts to exchange messages during the experiment were not observed. Subjects took their task very seriously and were concentrated during the whole experiment. Most wrote down his/her game 'history' on a sheet of paper and (in the complete-information variant) did the same with that of the others. Each participant could see all the others and hence had full guarantee that the experiment was conducted according to the instruction rules.

Following the instructions, two practice rounds were played. In each round of the session, every subject played with another participant without knowing who he/she was playing with in any given round. All subjects knew that they would be playing with a different opponent from round to round during the session. Before every round, a participant was chosen randomly to select a French card which would determine one of the four alternative amounts to be divided for that round (club = £ 5, diamond = £ 10, heart = £ 25, spade = £ 60): such values were previously written on a blackboard so that every one could easily check them, and the specific value selected was read aloud. At the conclusion of each session, a participant was chosen randomly to roll a dice in order to select one of the previous 8 rounds for the immediate cash payment of the earnings.

NOTES

1. Actually, in the first column of the screen, which is supposed to show the pairing, only question marks appear, in order to preserve the anonymity of couples (see table 10.7).

11 The experimental results

The interpretation of the results obtained in our experiment is proposed throughout the following Tables 11.1 to 11.19 and Figures 11.1 to 11.10. The commentary to such tables and figures will follow in structure paragraph 9.2, where our main predictions are summarised – namely (i) '*games(wo)manship*' (hereafter called GM for simplicity); (ii) '*fairness versus fear*' (hereafter FF); (iii) '*experience promotes games(wo)manship*' (hereafter EX). Our purpose is to check whether these predictions are fully consistent – or not – with the data provided by the experiment.

(i) We start by considering GM. First of all, Tables 11.1 and 11.2 show, for both variant 1 (incomplete information) and variant 2 (complete information), the values (in pounds) of the Proposers' and Responders' divisions – respectively P and R in the tables – which were *effectively* played in every round by each of the 5 couples of students taking part in the sessions. That is, P is the amount that each Proposer in every couple wants to keep for him/herself while R is the amount that each Responder in every couple is willing to accept (for him/herself).

The column labelled 'cake size' in Tables 11.1 and 11.2 corresponds to the amount of money drawn by card in each specific round. At the bottom of each sessions' data we specify the round number randomly chosen for rewarding the participants. Finally, at the bottom of the tables we also provide information concerning the number of rejections and the number of 'fifty-fifty' splits of the cake in all the 5 sessions of each experiment's variant.

In fact, the number of fifty-fifty splits of the cake size drawn is a first, rough indicator of the existence of fairness among players – that is, of some typically non-monetary argument in their utility function, which is a necessary premise to specify our GM prediction. From Tables 11.1 and 11.2 (where the asterisk sign * indicates the couples' offers P,R rejected) we can easily see that the number of equal splits, though not very high in absolute terms, is significantly higher in the full information variant of the experiment (18.5 per cent versus 3.5 per cent). Also, in variant 2 the number of rejected offers is much lower than in variant 1 (6.5 per cent versus 12.5 per cent). We can suggest that fairness, as far as it is proxied by equal shares of the cake and/or by rejections of (unfair) offers, not only generally exists, but also seems to be favoured by the availability of full information to players (a point which will be discussed further in commentary to the EX prediction). Also, for both variants of the experiment, the number of fifty-fifty splits tends to concentrate in the final rounds of each session, suggesting that experience – in the sense of more 'practice' – stimulates the taste for fairness among players. With respect to this point, it was particularly in the last session of variant 2 that our attention was captured by the very high number of equal divisions. So, at the very end of the game of that particular session, we asked participants to write down the motivation inducing them to decide for an equal split (see appendix 3 for more details on the answers). This post-experimental information revealed that most players either *tried to signal some fairness norm* by choosing an equal split or *feared to receive nothing*, or both. Hence, conventions or 'common sense' of fairness (fifty-fifty splits) turn out to be an *important means of coordination* between agents, leading to a positive outcome. However, we will develop this point in more detail in our commentary to the FF prediction. For the time being, we can conclude by noticing that the particular cake size drawn, whether high or low, does not seem to have any special role in fairness, at least according to Tables 11.1 and 11.2 (again, this point will be discussed later in the commentary to the GM prediction).

Some more information concerning the existence of fairness is provided in Table 11.3, where the columns labelled P and R now represent the mean across persons of the P and R values played by each of the 5 couples (and reported in Tables 11.1 and 11.2). In other words, the P and R values presented in Table 11.3 are simply the sum of each (five) P and R values (of Tables 11.1 and 11.2) divided by the number of couples - that is, divided by 5 (except in the first session). In Table 11.3, RP and RR denote what we may call the *mean reservation values* chosen by the participants. That is, the reader will remember (from chapter 10) that, *before* playing each round of each session, players were asked to choose, for each of the (four) possible cake sizes of the experiment, their 'ideal' divisions, both as Proposers (RP) and Responders (RR). Such values are shown, as we will see later, in Tables A and B of appendix B, where we also report the mean across persons (that is the sum of the RP,RR values reported in Tables A and B, divided by 10, which is the number of persons per session). Then, the mean RP,RR values presented in Table 11.3 are only the mean reservation divisions RP,RR corresponding to the specific cake size that was (randomly) drawn in each round of the experiment. In other words, the values RP and RR (for both variants) in Table 11.3 coincide exactly with what we called cE^{*P} and $c(1\text{-}E^{*R})$ respectively in section 9.a. (recall also Figures 9.2 and 9.3), where $E^{*P,R}$ is, as we know, the 'reservation share' of the cake c which is considered fair by Proposers and/or Responders. In chapter 9, we assumed for simplicity that E* was unique for both Proposers and Responders. Here, of course, this is not the case. So, it is more appropriate to label the reservation shares E^{*P} and E^{*R}, and to label the corresponding absolute levels $cE^{*P}=RP$ and $c(1\text{-}E^{*R})=RR$ respectively, where RP and RR are of course the mean reservation divisions calculated across the persons taking part in the experiment. For readers' interest, the complete set of RP and RR values is given in Tables A and B of appendix B, as previously mentioned (Table A concerns variant 1 and Table B variant 2). In addition to the mean values corresponding to the cakes *effectively* drawn in the experiment, this set includes the *ex ante* information concerning the single RP,RR values chosen person by person, round by round and cake size by cake size in each variant, as well as the modal value of RP,RR per

Table 11.1

Experiment's results, variant 1 (incomplete information)

SESSION 1 Proposals (P) and responses (R) of couples (* = rejection)

Round Number	Cake Size	Couple 1 P	Couple 1 R	Couple 2 P	Couple 2 R	Couple 3 P	Couple 3 R	Couple 4 P	Couple 4 R	Couple 5 P	Couple 5 R
1	60.00	35.00*	30.00*	32.00	25.00	35.00	10.00	0.00	0.00	0.00	0.00
2	25.00	14.00	5.00	13.00	9.50	12.00*	22.50*	0.00	0.00	0.00	0.00
3	25.00	12.50	1.00	13.00	10.00	12.50	10.00	0.00	0.00	0.00	0.00
4	5.00	3.00	1.00	3.00	0.10	2.50	1.00	0.00	0.00	0.00	0.00
5	5.00	3.00	0.50	1.00	2.00	2.50	0.10	0.00	0.00	0.00	0.00
6	25.00	14.00	2.00	12.00	1.00	13.50	10.00	0.00	0.00	0.00	0.00
7	5.00	3.20	0.50	2.50	0.50	2.50	1.00	0.00	0.00	0.00	0.00
8	60.00	32.00	10.00	31.00	0.10	30.00	10.00	0.00	0.00	0.00	0.00
Round number 5 was randomly selected for payoff at end of session 1											
SESSION 2											
1	60.00	30.00	25.00	30.00	20.00	40.00	0.00	43.00	10.00	35.00	20.00
2	60.00	30.00	25.00	36.00*	27.00*	35.00*	30.00*	40.00*	23.00*	47.50	0.00
3	5.00	3.00	1.00	3.00	2.00	4.00*	2.00*	2.50	1.00	3.00	1.00
4	25.00	12.50	8.00	15.00*	12.00*	15.80*	10.00*	13.00	1.00	20.00*	10.00*
5	5.00	2.50	1.00	2.50	1.00	2.50	1.00	3.00	1.00	3.00	2.00
6	25.00	12.50	11.00	12.50	4.00	15.00	8.00	16.90*	9.80*	15.00*	12.00*
7	60.00	30.00	30.00	36.00	20.00	33.00	15.00	35.00	20.00	35.60	20.00
8	5.00	2.50	1.00	3.50	1.00	3.00	0.00	2.00	1.00	3.00*	2.50*
Round number 8 was randomly selected for payoff at end of session 2											
SESSION 3											
1	10.00	5.40	4.00	6.00	4.00	5.00	5.00	5.00	4.50	6.20	3.00
2	5.00	2.50	2.20	2.50	2.30	3.00	1.00	3.00	1.50	2.50	2.00
3	5.00	2.50	2.50	2.20	2.00	3.00	2.00	2.70	1.00	2.50	2.00
4	25.00	12.50	6.00	13.00	9.00	12.50	10.00	13.20	10.00	12.50	11.00
5	25.00	12.50	8.00	12.50	6.70	15.00*	12.00*	14.00	11.00	14.10	7.00
6	5.00	3.00	1.50	2.00	2.00	2.50	2.00	2.50	2.30	3.00	2.00
7	60.00	22.00	15.00	30.00	13.90	30.00	5.00	30.00	20.00	35.50	20.00
8	25.00	12.50	10.00	12.50	9.00	12.50	11.00	12.50	4.00	13.00	0.10
Round number 8 was randomly selected for payoff at end of session 3											
SESSION 4											
1	25.00	12.50	10.00	12.50	1.00	13.00	10.00	13.00*	12.50*	18.00	5.00
2	10.00	6.50	1.00	5.00	4.00	5.00	4.00	5.00	4.00	7.00*	4.00*
3	10.00	6.50*	4.00*	5.00	3.00	5.00	4.00	5.00	4.50	5.00	1.00
4	10.00	6.00*	5.00*	6.00	3.00	5.00	1.00	5.00	4.00	6.00*	5.00*
5	25.00	14.00*	12.50*	12.50	10.00	13.00*	12.50*	16.00*	12.00*	12.50	10.00
6	10.00	5.50*	4.50*	5.00	4.00	5.00	4.00	6.00	1.00	5.00	4.00
7	60.00	32.00	20.00	35.00*	29.00*	30.00	19.00	30.00	30.00	31.00	20.00
8	10.00	5.00	4.00	5.00	1.00	5.00	4.50	6.50*	5.00*	5.00	4.00
Round number 5 was randomly selected for payoff at end of session 4											
SESSION 5											
1	10.00	8.00	2.00	5.00	1.00	6.00	0.00	5.00	1.00	5.00	1.00
2	5.00	2.50	1.00	2.50	0.00	3.50	1.00	2.50	1.00	3.50	1.00
3	25.00	20.00	5.00	12.50	12.50	0.00	10.00	20.00	1.00	15.00	1.00
4	5.00	4.00	1.00	2.50	1.00	2.40	0.50	3.00	1.00	2.50	2.50
5	25.00	20.00	12.50	12.50	5.00	12.50	5.00	12.30	1.00	20.00	1.00
6	60.00	30.00	10.00	29.60	1.00	35.00*	27.00*	30.00	30.00	30.00	10.00
7	5.00	3.00	0.50	2.50	1.00	2.50	1.00	3.00	0.00	2.50	1.00
8	10.00	5.00	2.00	4.90	2.00	5.00	1.00	5.00	1.00	5.00	3.00

Round number 1 was randomly selected for payoff at end of session 5
25 rejections (12.5%) and 7 fifty-fifty splittings (3.5%) out of 200 offers

Table 11.2

Experiment's results, variant 2 (complete information)

SESSION 1 Proposals (P) and responses (R) of couples (* = rejection)

Round Number	Cake Size	Couple 1 P	Couple 1 R	Couple 2 P	Couple 2 R	Couple 3 P	Couple 3 R	Couple 4 P	Couple 4 R	Couple 5 P	Couple 5 R
1	5.00	2.00	2.00	3.00	1.00	2.00	1.00	2.50	1.50	3.00	1.00
2	25.00	12.50	9.00	12.50	11.00	15.00	10.00	12.50	6.00	15.00	8.00
3	10.00	5.00	4.00	5.00	3.00	4.00	2.50	6.00*	4.50*	5.50	4.00
4	10.00	4.00	5.00	5.50	1.00	6.00	2.00	4.50	4.00	4.00	3.00
5	10.00	5.00	4.00	5.00*	6.00*	4.00	3.00	5.50	4.00	6.50	3.50
6	10.00	5.00	3.00	5.00	4.00	5.00	3.00	4.00	3.50	5.00	4.50
7	5.00	2.50	1.50	2.50	2.00	2.50	2.00	2.50	2.50	2.00	1.50
8	60.00	30.00	15.00	30.00	10.00	25.00	20.00	30.00	20.00	25.00	15.00

Round number 2 was randomly selected for payoff at end of session 1

SESSION 2

Round Number	Cake Size	Couple 1 P	Couple 1 R	Couple 2 P	Couple 2 R	Couple 3 P	Couple 3 R	Couple 4 P	Couple 4 R	Couple 5 P	Couple 5 R
1	5.00	2.50	0.00	3.00	2.00	2.50	2.50	2.10	0.10	2.50	1.00
2	25.00	13.00	0.10	17.00*	25.00*	12.50	5.00	12.50	0.00	16.00	5.00
3	10.00	6.00	0.00	6.00	2.00	5.00	3.00	8.00	0.00	5.50	0.10
4	5.00	4.00	1.00	2.50	1.50	2.50	1.00	4.70*	0.50*	3.50*	2.50*
5	25.00	20.00	5.00	15.00	7.00	12.50	5.00	12.50	10.00	18.00*	8.00*
6	5.00	4.00	0.00	3.00	2.00	2.50	2.00	2.50	1.50	4.30	0.00
7	10.00	7.00	2.00	6.00	3.00	6.50*	4.00*	5.00	0.00	5.00	4.00
8	5.00	3.00	1.50	3.00	0.00	4.40	0.00	3.00	2.00	3.00	2.00

Round number 5 was randomly selected for payoff at end of session 2

SESSION 3

Round Number	Cake Size	Couple 1 P	Couple 1 R	Couple 2 P	Couple 2 R	Couple 3 P	Couple 3 R	Couple 4 P	Couple 4 R	Couple 5 P	Couple 5 R
1	25.00	12.50	9.90	15.00*	11.00*	15.00	5.00	13.80	1.00	12.50	7.00
2	5.00	2.50	0.00	2.50	1.90	3.20	1.00	2.50	1.00	2.50	2.00
3	25.00	13.90	0.00	12.50	12.00	15.00	10.00	13.90*	12.00*	12.50	1.00
4	10.00	5.00	4.00	5.00	0.00	5.00	5.00	7.00	3.00	5.60	0.00
5	25.00	12.50	2.00	15.00	0.00	12.20	5.00	12.50	1.00	12.50	1.00
6	25.00	12.50	10.00	14.90	5.00	15.00	0.00	12.50	2.00	12.50	12.20
7	5.00	3.00	2.00	2.50	1.00	2.50	0.00	2.50	1.00	2.50	1.00
8	10.00	8.00	2.00	5.00	0.00	6.00	1.00	6.90	0.00	5.00	4.50

Round number 6 was randomly selected for payoff at end of session 3

SESSION 4

Round Number	Cake Size	Couple 1 P	Couple 1 R	Couple 2 P	Couple 2 R	Couple 3 P	Couple 3 R	Couple 4 P	Couple 4 R	Couple 5 P	Couple 5 R
1	25.00	13.00	10.00	12.50	10.00	15.00	5.00	12.50	9.50	12.00	10.00
2	10.00	5.00	3.00	6.00	1.00	7.00	3.00	5.00	4.00	5.00	4.00
3	25.00	13.00	10.00	15.00*	12.50*	13.00	12.00	17.00*	10.00*	13.00	10.00
4	10.00	5.00	4.00	5.50*	5.00*	6.00	1.00	5.00	1.00	6.00	4.00
5	25.00	13.00	10.00	12.50	10.00	15.00	10.00	13.00	1.00	13.00	1.00
6	60.00	30.00	1.00	35.00	15.00	30.00	1.00	33.80	20.00	30.00	15.00
7	60.00	30.00	1.00	40.00	20.00	35.00	15.00	31.00	1.00	30.00	15.00
8	5.00	2.50	1.00	3.00	1.00	3.00	2.00	2.50	1.00	2.50	1.50

Round number 1 was randomly selected for payoff at end of session 4

SESSION 5

Round Number	Cake Size	Couple 1 P	Couple 1 R	Couple 2 P	Couple 2 R	Couple 3 P	Couple 3 R	Couple 4 P	Couple 4 R	Couple 5 P	Couple 5 R
1	5.00	2.50	2.50	2.50	2.00	3.20*	2.00*	2.50	2.50	2.50	2.00
2	25.00	12.50	12.50	12.50	12.50	12.50	12.50	12.50	12.50	15.00	1.00
3	5.00	2.50	2.50	2.50	2.50	2.50	2.50	2.50	2.50	2.50	2.50
4	60.00	30.00	30.00	30.00	20.00	30.00	30.00	30.00	30.00	30.00	30.00
5	10.00	5.00	5.00	5.00	5.00	5.00	5.00	5.00	5.00	5.00	5.00
6	25.00	12.50	12.50	12.50	12.50	12.50	12.50	12.50	12.50	12.50	12.50
7	60.00	30.00	30.00	30.00	25.00	30.00	30.00	30.00	30.00	30.00	30.00
8	25.00	12.50	12.50	12.50	0.10	12.50	12.50	12.50	12.50	12.50	12.50

Round number 1 was randomly selected for payoff at end of session 5
13 rejections (6.5%) and 37 fifty-fifty splittings (18.5%) out of 200 offers

session (indicating the single values selected with the highest frequency). Anyway, Table 11.3 clearly shows that the P,RP and R,RR values are very close in absolute terms to one another, suggesting a tight relationship between the offers effectively played P,R and some 'fair' reservation offers RP,RR on average across players. This is in line with the results of OR's study (p.377), who were approximating the 'fair' reservation offers by the median over the P,R values played. Here we can do better since in our experiment we recorded directly the RP,RR reservation offers of every player for each possible cake size without having to approximate them in any way.

Such a relationship (between P,R and RP,RR) is also proved in Tables 11.4-11.5 (for variant 1) and Tables 11.6-11.7 (for variant 2). These tables summarise the results of the ordinary least squares (hereafter and in the tables LS) regression of the P,R mean values on the corresponding mean reservation values RP,RR (as reported in Table 11.3) and on a constant of regression labelled C in the tables (not to be confused with the cake size also labelled c in chapters 8 and 9). The number of observations of each series P,R,RP,RR is 40 because in each variant of the experiment there are 5 sessions of 8 rounds each, so that all mean values P,R,RP, and RR can be considered as a 'time series' of 40 observations throughout each variant of the experiment. Of course, the inclusion of the constant is justified by goodness of fit considerations, and by the willingness to summarise into the constant the influence on R,P of all possible omitted variables, apart from RP, RR.

Let us start then by commenting on Tables 11.4 and 11.5, which report the regressions' results for variant 1 (incomplete information). Both show a strong, positive relationship between values played and reservation values (RP and RR present positive coefficients, each individually significant, as the t-statistics values show for both regressions). In particular, the column labelled '2 Tail sig.' in the tables shows also the probability of individual non-significance of RP,RR in a two-tailed asymptotic test, which is always rejected (that is, such a probability is always near, or equal, to zero). The high R-squared values show a good global fit of the equations; the high Durbin Watson test values indicate the absence of first order autocorrelation (that is, with respect to the preceding

Table 11.3

Mean proposals and responses (P, R) played in the experiment and corresponding mean reservation values (RP, RR)

SESSION 1

Round Number	Cake Size	VARIANT 1 (incomplete info.) P	R	RP	RR	Cake Size	VARIANT 2 (complete info.) P	R	RP	RR
1	60.00	34.00	21.66	32.17	17.50	5.00	2.50	1.30	2.45	1.55
2	25.00	13.00	12.33	13.08	9.67	25.00	13.50	8.80	13.15	8.20
3	25.00	12.66	7.00	13.00	7.00	10.00	5.10	3.60	5.15	3.15
4	5.00	2.83	0.70	2.42	1.18	10.00	4.80	3.00	5.05	3.25
5	5.00	2.16	0.86	2.42	0.90	10.00	5.20	4.10	4.80	3.30
6	25.00	13.16	4.33	13.08	5.50	10.00	4.80	3.60	4.85	3.25
7	5.00	2.73	0.66	2.78	1.00	5.00	2.40	1.90	2.50	1.70
8	60.00	31.00	6.70	34.67	10.02	60.00	28.00	16.00	30.90	17.10
SESSION 2										
1	60.00	35.60	15.00	33.90	19.06	5.00	2.52	1.12	2.56	1.24
2	60.00	37.60	21.00	35.55	16.95	25.00	14.20	7.02	13.60	6.86
3	5.00	3.10	1.40	3.00	1.30	10.00	6.10	1.02	6.10	1.96
4	25.00	15.26	8.20	14.53	8.45	5.00	3.44	1.30	3.17	0.99
5	5.00	2.70	1.20	2.82	1.45	25.00	15.60	7.00	14.87	5.51
6	25.00	14.38	8.96	14.44	8.05	5.00	3.26	1.10	3.13	1.01
7	60.00	33.92	21.00	34.96	18.07	10.00	5.90	2.60	5.97	2.31
8	5.00	2.80	1.10	2.86	1.30	5.00	3.28	1.10	3.19	0.86
SESSION 3										
1	10.00	5.52	4.10	5.21	3.90	25.00	13.76	6.78	13.44	8.00
2	5.00	2.70	1.80	2.64	1.95	5.00	2.64	1.18	2.76	1.44
3	5.00	2.58	1.90	2.61	2.08	25.00	13.56	7.00	13.33	5.79
4	25.00	12.74	9.20	13.00	10.04	10.00	5.52	2.40	5.56	2.28
5	25.00	13.62	9.14	13.00	9.62	25.00	12.94	1.80	12.91	4.70
6	5.00	2.60	1.96	2.66	2.03	25.00	13.48	5.84	13.21	4.42
7	60.00	29.50	14.78	31.45	18.99	5.00	2.60	1.00	2.70	1.30
8	25.00	12.60	6.82	12.50	6.56	10.00	6.18	1.50	5.78	1.95
SESSION 4										
1	25.00	13.80	7.70	13.60	7.50	25.00	13.00	8.90	13.25	8.25
2	10.00	5.70	3.40	5.55	3.60	10.00	5.60	3.00	5.35	3.35
3	10.00	5.30	3.30	5.45	3.65	25.00	14.20	10.90	13.80	8.65
4	10.00	5.60	3.60	5.55	3.45	10.00	5.50	3.00	5.40	2.85
5	25.00	13.60	11.40	13.55	8.80	25.00	13.30	6.40	13.05	6.15
6	10.00	5.30	3.50	5.25	3.65	60.00	31.76	10.40	31.88	10.10
7	60.00	31.60	23.60	33.30	19.70	60.00	33.20	10.40	31.90	9.60
8	10.00	5.30	3.70	5.25	3.55	5.00	2.70	1.30	2.75	1.25
SESSION 5										
1	10.00	5.80	1.00	5.30	2.00	5.00	2.64	2.20	2.52	2.11
2	5.00	2.90	0.80	2.84	0.95	25.00	13.00	10.20	12.70	9.81
3	25.00	13.50	5.90	15.32	4.50	5.00	2.50	2.50	2.50	2.21
4	5.00	2.88	1.20	2.89	1.10	60.00	30.00	28.00	30.00	26.01
5	25.00	15.46	4.90	14.47	4.15	10.00	5.00	5.00	5.00	4.51
6	5.00	30.92	15.60	34.16	9.10	25.00	12.50	12.50	12.50	11.26
7	25.00	2.70	0.70	2.89	1.10	60.00	30.00	29.00	30.00	26.51
8	10.00	4.98	1.80	5.67	1.70	25.00	12.50	10.02	12.50	10.76

Table 11.4

LS // Dependent Variable is P

Number of observations: 40

VARIABLE	COEFFICIENT	STD. ERROR	T-STAT.	2-TAIL SIG.
C	0.1704930	0.2574349	0.6622761	0.512
RP	0.9752647	0.0150510	64.797424	0.000

R-squared	0.991031	Mean of dependent var	12.60317
Adjusted R-squared	0.990795	S.D. of dependent var	11.31406
S.E. of regression	1.085517	Sum of squared resid	44.77715
Durbin-Watson stat	1.972841	F-statistic	4198.706

Table 11.5

LS // Dependent Variable is R

Number of observations: 40

VARIABLE	COEFFICIENT	STD. ERROR	T-STAT.	2-TAIL SIG.
C	-0.1551873	0.4821275	-0.3218802	0.749
RR	1.0730232	0.0552833	19.409530	0.000

R-squared	0.908374	Mean of dependent var	6.848167
Adjusted R-squared	0.905963	S.D. of dependent var	6.595136
S.E. of regression	2.022430	Sum of squared resid	155.4284
Durbin-Watson stat	1.727831	F-statistic	376.7299

round's values played, which would make no sense here since we know that different people take part in each session). All other tests presented in the tables are well known in econometric practice. In particular, the global standard error of regression is always reasonably low with respect to the mean value of the dependent variable, and the F-statistic is significantly high. The same conclusions can be made exactly for Tables 11.6 and 11.7 below, which show the regressions' results for variant 2 (full information). In fact, for both variants 1 and 2 – that is, regardless of information,

Table 11.6

LS // Dependent Variable is P

Number of observations: 40

VARIABLE	COEFFICIENT	STD. ERROR	T-STAT.	2-TAIL SIG.
C	0.1559380	0.1366216	1.1413860	0.261
RP	0.9909004	0.0099909	99.180239	0.000

R-squared	0.996152	Mean of dependent var	10.46700
Adjusted R-squared	0.996051	S.D. of dependent var	8.920592
S.E. of regression	0.560614	Sum of squared resid	11.94293
Durbin-Watson stat	1.954220	F-statistic	9836.720

Table 11.7

LS // Dependent Variable is R

Number of observations: 40

VARIABLE	COEFFICIENT	STD. ERROR	T-STAT.	2-TAIL SIG.
C	-0.1366741	0.1981831	-0.6896356	0.495
RR	1.0668661	0.0237161	44.984907	0.000

R-squared	0.981568	Mean of dependent var	6.144500
Adjusted R-squared	0.981083	S.D. of dependent var	6.467288
S.E. of regression	0.889504	Sum of squared resid	30.06626
Durbin-Watson stat	2.308094	F-statistic	2023.642

such regressions prove that in our experiment the offers played rise with the size of the reservation offer (as the positive sign on RP,RR's coefficients shows) and do not deviate significantly from it. This summarises a clear role for fairness, which is even more strongly confirmed by Tables 11.8-11.9 (for variant 1) and Tables 11.10-11.11 (for variant 2). Such tables present the results of the LS regression of the mean offers P,R on the cake size drawn. Again, in all the tables the statistic fit of the equations is very satisfactory, as suggested by the R-squared and the other global tests' values, while

Table 11.8

LS // Dependent Variable is P

Number of observations: 40

VARIABLE	COEFFICIENT	STD. ERROR	T-STAT.	2-TAIL SIG.
C	1.0650451	1.2072330	0.8822200	0.383
CAKESIZE	0.5214970	0.0411514	12.672658	0.000

R-squared	0.808657	Mean of dependent var	12.60317
Adjusted R-squared	0.803622	S.D. of dependent var	11.31406
S.E. of regression	5.013778	Sum of squared resid	955.2428
Durbin-Watson stat	2.475023	F-statistic	160.5963

Table 11.9

LS // Dependent Variable is R

Number of observations: 40

VARIABLE	COEFFICIENT	STD. ERROR	T-STAT.	2-TAIL SIG.
C	0.6347133	0.8954877	0.7087907	0.483
CAKESIZE	0.2808340	0.0305248	9.2001972	0.000

R-squared	0.690159	Mean of dependent var	6.848167
Adjusted R-squared	0.682005	S.D. of dependent var	6.595136
S.E. of regression	3.719063	Sum of squared resid	525.5944
Durbin-Watson stat	2.144812	F-statistic	84.64363

the coefficient of the cake size variable is always individually significant and positive. This means that the mean offers P,R increase with the cake size – that is, that fairness intervenes heavily in the outcome of the games: in this respect, we may immediately recall expressions (12) and (15) in paragraph 9.1, which postulated a positive first derivative sign of the Proposer and Responder's offer sizes with respect to the cake size. The positive derivative meant that an increasing amount of money required increasing mean offers in order to be considered 'fair' by players and to avoid rejection from

Table 11.10

LS // Dependent Variable is P

Number of observations: 40

VARIABLE	COEFFICIENT	STD. ERROR	T-STAT.	2-TAIL SIG.
C	0.4296175	0.2153678	1.9948089	0.053
CAKESIZE	0.5082219	0.0082138	61.874118	0.000

R-squared	0.990172	Mean of dependent var	10.46700
Adjusted R-squared	0.989913	S.D. of dependent var	8.920592
S.E. of regression	0.895926	Sum of squared resid	30.50198
Durbin-Watson stat	1.340637	F-statistic	3828.406

Table 11.11

LS // Dependent Variable is R

Number of observations: 40

VARIABLE	COEFFICIENT	STD. ERROR	T-STAT.	2-TAIL SIG.
C	-0.0988821	0.8200814	-0.1205760	0.905
CAKESIZE	0.3161206	0.0312767	10.107231	0.000

R-squared	0.728874	Mean of dependent var	6.144500
Adjusted R-squared	0.721739	S.D. of dependent var	6.467288
S.E. of regression	3.411524	Sum of squared resid	442.2629
Durbin-Watson stat	1.011596	F-statistic	102.1561

the counterpart. Also, Tables 11.10-11.11 confirm that the cake size is important in indicating the players' taste for fairness: a point which the reader may remember was not obvious when only the number of equal splits and/or rejections was examined as an indicator of fairness. Therefore, again, the existence of non-monetary arguments (fairness) in the players' utility function is a hypothesis which is fully consistent with our experiment's data, as indeed the analysis of Tables 11.1 to 11.11 has shown up to now.

However, if fairness exists, as it does according to our data, in order to provide a full and consistent acceptance - or rejection - of our whole GM prediction we must examine whether the existence of fairness implies also that the PEP (perfect equilibrium prediction) will not hold. This could not be inferred from Tables 11.1 to 11.11, but really only from the following Figures 11.1-11.4, concerning variant 1, and Figures 11.5-11.8, concerning variant 2. As can be seen, these figures display on the horizontal axes the mean RP,RR values chosen for each given cake size (that is not only for the cake sizes randomly drawn – see also Tables A and B in the appendix), while the rounds and sessions of each experiment's variant are reported on the horizontal axes. Therefore, a sort of 'time pattern' of mean reservation offers can be analysed (bearing in mind, however, that different people take part in each session). Let us start, then, by variant 1 (with incomplete information), namely by commenting on Figures 11.1 to 11.4. The first remark that can be made is that in all of the four tables the values 5-RP, 10-RP, 25-RP, 60-RP

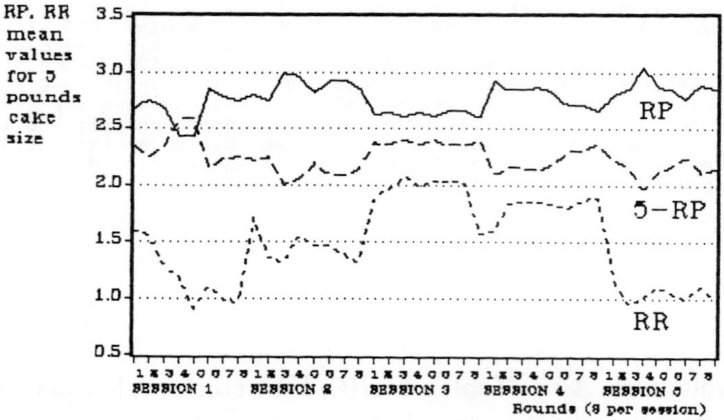

Figure 11.1

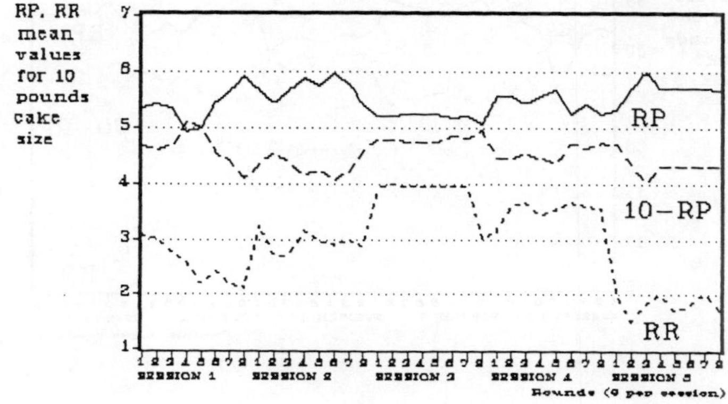

Figure 11.2

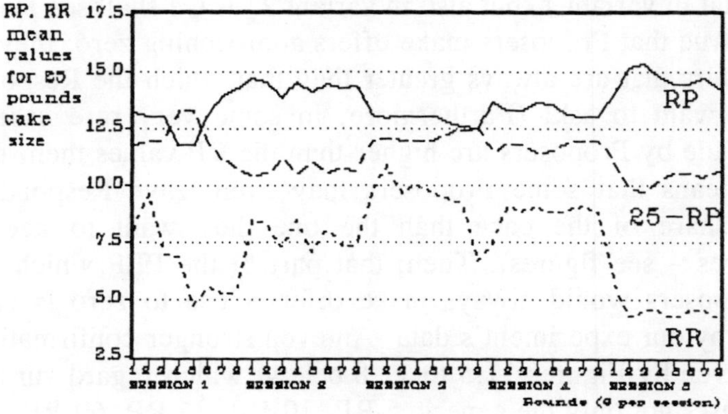

Figure 11.3

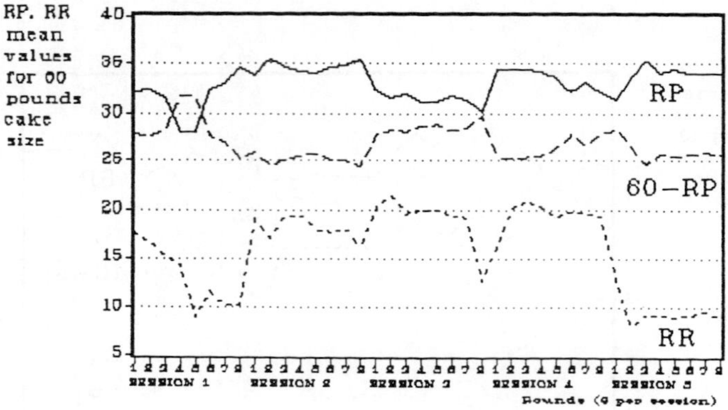

Figure 11.4

– representing the difference between each possible cake size and the reservation proposal – that is, the amount that Proposers are willing to leave to Responders, are always lying above the RR values. This means that in variant 1 (but also in variant 2, as we shall see later on) it is not true that Proposers make offers approaching zero: they even make offers that are always greater than that which the Responders possibly want to ask! (Furthermore, in some very rare cases the offers made by Proposers are higher than the RP values themselves, which means that some Proposers may even leave Responders a greater share of the cake than the one they want to keep for themselves – see figures). Then, that part of the PEP which states that Proposers would always make offers close to zero is clearly rejected by our experiment's data. An even stronger confirmation of this is given by Figures 11.5 to 11.8 below, which regard variant 2: in this case, not only the generic 5-RP, 10-RP, 25-RP, 60-RP values always lie well above the RR values' pattern, but also – and quite frequently – they are actually equal to the RP values themselves! (see figures). This means that there are a good number of rounds in which, even on average (recall that mean values are plotted on the figures), the reservation values RP that Proposers want to keep for themselves are exactly equal to the values they accept to leave to the Responders (and again, in some very rare cases, what is left to the Responder is even more than what the Proposer wants to keep for him/herself – see figures). This again goes against the PEP and shows furthermore that in variant 2 – when complete information concerning all other players is available – fairness in the sense of 'intentional' fifty-fifty split of any possible cake size is stimulated (though Figures 11.7 and 11.8 show, with respect to Figures 11.5 and 11.6, that this phenomenon happens a little bit less frequently when higher cake sizes are involved). On the other hand, and this time for both variants of the experiment – that is, for all Figures 11.1 to 11.8, the RR values tend to be quite low, suggesting that the second part of the PEP, which states that Responders would tend to accept all positive offers, is generally true as far as our experiment's data are concerned. The reader may remember that this latter point was also more or less proved by the relatively low number of rejections occurring in the whole experiment (recall Tables 11.1 and 11.2).

We could, then, conclude the commentary of the data concerning our GM prediction as follows: first, a non-monetary argument in the players' utility function, identifiable with their sense of fairness, generally exists; particularly, fairness seems to be stronger when full information is available to players. Second, the existence of fairness does not imply, according to our data, that Proposers will act in the PEP manner – that is, Proposers do not make offers approaching zero in the experiment. However, Responders still tend to conform to the PEP, because they accept quite generally all positive offers. Then, globally, our GM prediction – which states that if fairness exists, then players will deviate from the PEP – is not rejected by the experiment's data. Knowing this, we can now turn to test our second prediction, namely the FF one.

ii) The FF prediction, as we know, regards the role of fear versus fairness in the players' decisions. Recalling paragraph 9.1, we assumed that 'fear' – that is, 'greedy' considerations, would push Proposers to leave more and more of the cake to Responders as its size increases, in the fear of rejection, which would of course imply earning nothing. Therefore, as Figure 9.3 has clearly shown, we

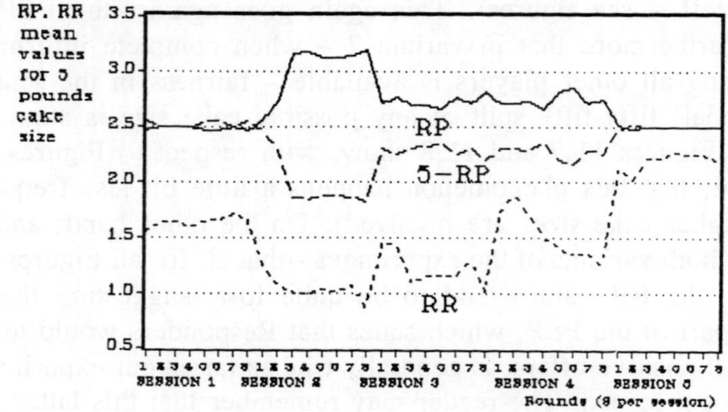

Figure 11.5

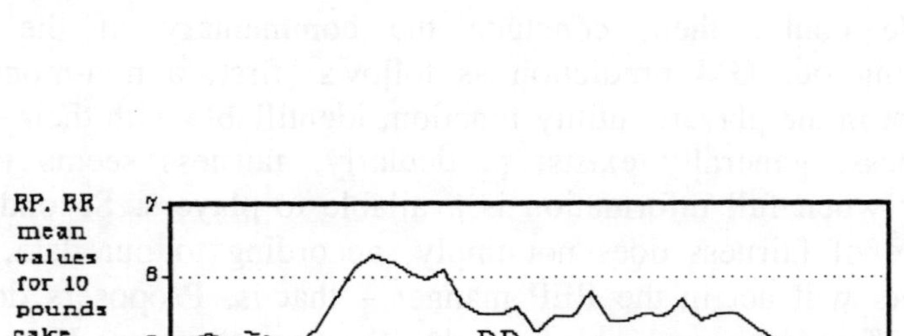

Figure 11.6

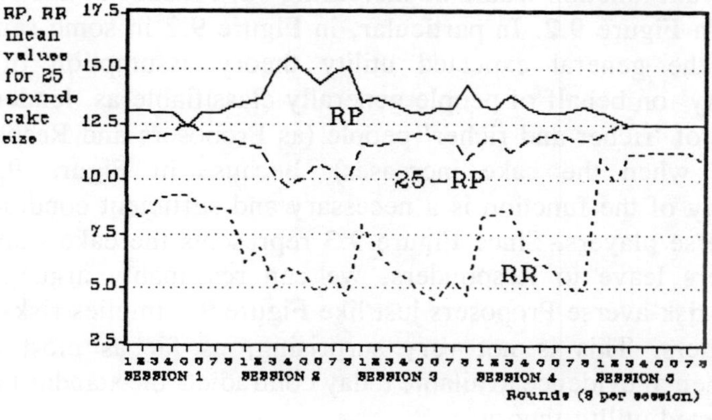

Figure 11.7

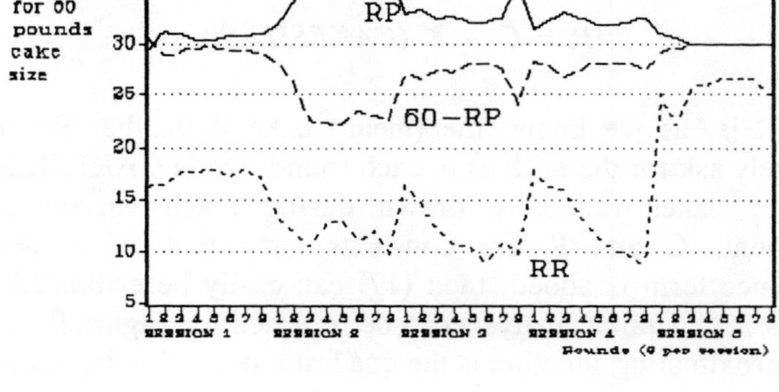

Figure 11.8

could imagine a convex increasing function representing the pattern of the cake share that Proposers leave to Responders in function of the cake size itself. On the other hand, fear would push Responders to keep less and less of an increasing cake size, so that the pattern of the relevant function would be increasing but concave in this case, as shown in Figure 9.2. In particular, in Figure 9.2 in some sense we denied the general expected utility theory assumption of 'risk neutrality' on behalf of people generally classifiable as 'lenders', or anyway of 'richer and richer' people (as Proposers and Responders become when the cake increases), because in Figure 9.2 the concavity of the function is a necessary and sufficient condition for risk-averse players. Since Figure 9.3 represents the cake share that Proposers leave to Responders, we can reasonably argue that it implies risk-averse Proposers just like Figure 9.2 implies risk-averse Responders. This is not very surprising, as far as most of the experimental evidence available today contradicts the standard results of expected utility theory.

Now, will the patterns assumed in Figures 9.2 and 9.3 be consistent with our experiment's data? In other words, will fear interfere with fairness, so that a precise relationship will exist between offers/demands played and the cake size? A first way of checking this FF prediction is to run simple regressions based on equations that represent correctly the patterns of Figures 9.2 and 9.3. Then, it is evident that the simplest function approximating Figure 2 is the square root function – that is, in our case:

$$R = C + K\ (CAKESIZE)^{1/2} \qquad (17)$$

where R is, as we know, the (mean) cake share that Responders effectively ask for themselves in each round, while CAKESIZE is the series of cakes randomly drawn during (each variant of) the experiment. C and K are constants such that, if a stochastic disturbance term is added, then (17) can easily be estimated by LS regression. A similar analysis can be repeated for Figure 9.3, whose best approximating function is the quadratic one – that is, in our case:

$$CMINUSP = C + K\,(CAKESIZE)^2 \qquad (18)$$

again easily estimable by LS, and where the dependent variable is now CMINUSP = CAKESIZE - P (being P the mean proposal played out in each round). The results of the LS estimation of equations (18) and (17) are presented respectively in Tables 11.12-11.13 (for variant 1) and Tables 11.14-11.15 (for variant 2). All regressions are satisfactory from a goodness-of-fit point of view,

Table 11.12

LS // Dependent Variable is CMINUSP

Number of observations: 40

VARIABLE	COEFFICIENT	STD. ERROR	T-STAT.	2-TAIL SIG.
C	3.7117427	1.1270834	3.2932280	0.002
CSQUARED	0.0067510	0.0007280	9.2738404	0.000

R-squared	0.693559	Mean of dependent var	9.521833
Adjusted R-squared	0.685494	S.D. of dependent var	10.56614
S.E. of regression	5.925575	Sum of squared resid	1334.273
Durbin-Watson stat	2.665828	F-statistic	86.00412

Table 11.13

LS // Dependent Variable is R

Number of observations: 40

VARIABLE	COEFFICIENT	STD. ERROR	T-STAT.	2-TAIL SIG.
C	-4.7997792	1.4960487	-3.2083042	0.003
CROOT	2.7190557	0.3180564	8.5489748	0.000

R-squared	0.657920	Mean of dependent var	6.848167
Adjusted R-squared	0.648917	S.D. of dependent var	6.595136
S.E. of regression	3.907765	Sum of squared resid	580.2838
Durbin-Watson stat	2.353859	F-statistic	73.08497

Table 11.14

LS // Dependent Variable is CMINUSP

Number of observations: 40

VARIABLE	COEFFICIENT	STD. ERROR	T-STAT.	2-TAIL SIG.
C	4.2619741	0.4059968	10.497555	0.000
CSQUARED	0.0073033	0.0003069	23.795817	0.000

R-squared	0.937111	Mean of dependent var	9.283000
Adjusted R-squared	0.935456	S.D. of dependent var	8.634845
S.E. of regression	2.193723	Sum of squared resid	182.8720
Durbin-Watson stat	2.315443	F-statistic	566.2409

Table 11.15

LS // Dependent Variable is R

Number of observations: 40

VARIABLE	COEFFICIENT	STD. ERROR	T-STAT.	2-TAIL SIG.
C	-6.2554495	1.4084890	-4.4412484	0.000
CROOT	3.0408497	0.3169348	9.5945598	0.000

R-squared	0.707817	Mean of dependent var	6.144500
Adjusted R-squared	0.700128	S.D. of dependent var	6.467288
S.E. of regression	3.541523	Sum of squared resid	476.6105
Durbin-Watson stat	1.222868	F-statistic	92.05558

as the R-squared and other global tests' values confirm. The regressions are satisfactory also from the point of view of the individual significance of the CSQUARED = $(\text{CAKESIZE})^2$ and CROOT = $(\text{CAKESIZE})^{1/2}$ regressors, as the t-statistic and 2 Tail-sig. values confirm, especially for Tables 11.12 and 11.14 (namely, those concerning the Proposers' risk aversion). Also, the regressors' coefficient sign is always positive, as expected since the functions ought to be increasing in the cake size. Therefore, we can reasonably argue that, assuming square root and quadratic 'cake share' functions respectively for Responders and Proposers, there exists in our data a positive role for fear among players, which seems to be a bit stronger for the Proposers than for the Responders, although certainly significant for both. Fear is confirmed by all Figures 11.1 to 11.8 previously examined: looking at each figure, and starting from the ones relative to the smallest cake size (£5) up to the biggest one (£60), we can see that the difference between the values 5-RP, 10-RP, 25-RP, 60-RP and the values RR plotted in the figures tends to widen as the cake size grows (that is, it shifts from 5 to 10 to 25 and finally to 60 pounds). On the other hand, the difference between the same values 5-RP, 10-RP, 25-RP, 60-RP and the values RP tends to remain constant across the different figures (or even equal to zero in Tables 11.1 to 11.4, concerning the complete information variant, which, as we know, shows also a higher degree of fairness among participants). Anyway, the pattern described in Tables 10.4 to 11.4 certainly means that Proposers leave to Responders more and more of the cake size if this is big, for fear of receiving nothing if a refusal occurs. So, at least in relative terms, there is a certain 'greed' among players, though not in absolute terms. This is because, as a last remark, we must say that no Proposers and/or Responders taking part in each session ever asked for the whole cake (or for very high shares of it anyway).

Finally, as we mentioned earlier, in session 5 of variant 2 there were a big number of equal splits of the cake, so that participants were asked to write down their motivations for such a choice. Those motivations (reported in appendix 3) show a big role of fairness in players' decisions, but also of fear: this explains why, sometimes, in Figures 11.1 to 11.8 the pattern of RP and the pattern of the cake sizes minus RP were exactly equal. Of course, however, in these figures the impact of fairness and the impact of fear were not always easy to isolate from one another.

Generally speaking, our FF prediction thus appears to be fully consistent with the experiment's data. We have tried to verify whether, at a very aggregate level, our whole dataset concerning the two variants could represent anything like Figures 9.2 and 9.3, using, this time, the reservation offers rather than the offers effectively played (as in Tables 11.11-11.14 above). This would allow us to have a really complete test of our FF prediction. Such a (further) test could only be made graphically: actually, it would not make much sense to regress (mean) reservation values on a cake size variable which was drawn only a good deal of time after the reservation levels were selected by players alone (that is without playing anybody else but only by choosing some sort of acceptance level both as Proposer and Responder). So, more precisely, we have considered all the mean reservation offers RP, RR reported in Table 11.3 for both variants 1 and 2; we summed up all the RP values for variant 1, and we divided the result by 40 (that is by the total number of rounds in variant 1). The same procedure was repeated for the RR values of variant 1, and for the RP and RR values of variant 2 (which also has 40 rounds): in this way, we obtained four numbers (the 'aggregate' RP, RR's of variant 1 and the 'aggregate' RP, RR's of variant 2) that might be reasonably termed as 'means of means' of all the reservation offers across each variant. Successively, those four values were plotted against the four possible cake sizes (that is 5, 10, 25 and 60 pounds) in Figure 11.9 (for variant 1) and Figure 11.10 (for variant 2) below, in order to obtain a pattern of the (aggregate) reservation response - denoted RR in the figures - and of the difference between the cake size and the (aggregate) reservation proposal - denoted C-RP in the figures - in function of the cake size itself. In other words, both Figures 11.9 and 11.10 represent the pattern of reservation divisions of the cake. As can be seen, both

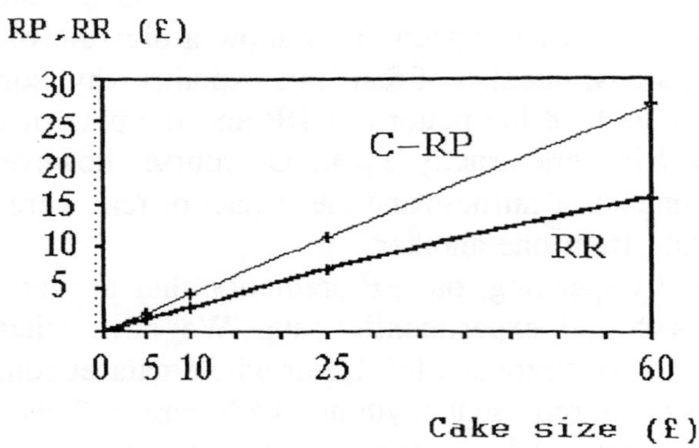

Figure 11.9

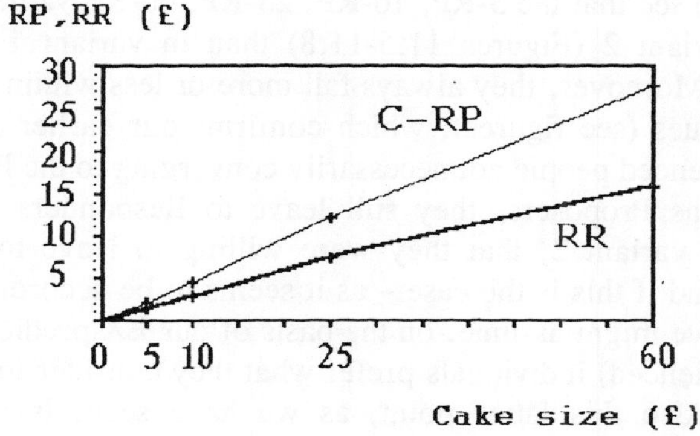

Figure 11.10

figures show that C-RP grows with the cake size much faster than RR: taking into account the very small range of possible cake sizes (only four), we can nevertheless say that also Figures 11.9-11.10 support the existence of risk aversion in one-shot games like the ones proposed in our experiment. This means that our FF prediction is fully consistent with all our experimental data.

Then, the role of full information about players in the framework of GM and FF still remains to be investigated in somewhat more detail, and this is done here below.

(iii) In the preceding analysis we have often seen that the complete information variant of the experiment (variant 2) always presented a higher 'degree of fairness', so as to speak, with respect to variant 1. This could be inferred just by looking at the (high) number of equal splits of the cake, at the (low) number of rejected offers, and at the portions of equality between the mean reservation proposal patterns RP and the cake sizes minus RP patterns in Figures 11.5-11.8. From these indications, we can already say that it will generally not be true, at least in our experiment, that more 'experienced' people (that is those playing in variant 2, with full information about their counterparts) will always act according to the PEP. In other words, experienced people do not tend to make offers close to zero as Proposers, although they might still tend to accept all (fair) positive offers as Responders. Recalling again Figures 11.1 to 11.8, it is immediate to see that the 5-RP, 10-RP, 25-RP, 60-RP values are not lower in variant 2 (Figures 11.5-11.8) than in variant 1 (Figures 11.1-11.4). Moreover, they always fall more or less within the same range of values (see figures), which confirms our earlier statement about experienced people not necessarily converging to the PEP. This is because, as Proposers, they still leave to Responders the same amounts, in variant 2, that they were willing to leave to them in variant 1. And if this is the case – as it seems to be according to our data – then we might assume, on the basis of our EX prediction, that (more experienced) individuals prefer what they consider to be a fair allocation. Also this latter point, as we have seen, is until now confirmed by the data.

However, there is indeed an even more precise and definitive way to check the consistency of the EX prediction with our data: that consists of setting up, only for variant 2's data of course, the four LS regressions presented in Tables 11.16 to 11.19 below: as the reader may see, the regressions of Tables 11.16-11.19 are identical to those already presented in Tables 11.10-11.11 and 11.14-11.15 (also concerning only variant 2), except for the additional regressors – either P or R, depending on the regressand being R or P. Such

Table 11.16

LS // Dependent Variable is P

Number of observations: 40

VARIABLE	COEFFICIENT	STD. ERROR	T-STAT.	2-TAIL SIG.
C	0.4194430	0.2008466	2.0883748	0.044
CAKESIZE	0.5407494	0.0147082	36.765189	0.000
R	-0.1028960	0.0397221	-2.5903941	0.014

R-squared	0.991681	Mean of dependent var	10.46700
Adjusted R-squared	0.991231	S.D. of dependent var	8.920592
S.E. of regression	0.835359	Sum of squared resid	25.81948
Durbin-Watson stat	1.618230	F-statistic	2205.200

Table 11.17

LS // Dependent Variable is R

Number of observations: 40

VARIABLE	COEFFICIENT	STD. ERROR	T-STAT.	2-TAIL SIG.
C	0.5420810	0.8036802	0.6744983	0.504
CAKESIZE	1.0743566	0.2941598	3.6522894	0.001
P	-1.4919388	0.5759505	-2.5903941	0.014

R-squared	0.770496	Mean of dependent var	6.144500
Adjusted R-squared	0.758090	S.D. of dependent var	6.467288
S.E. of regression	3.180894	Sum of squared resid	374.3692
Durbin-Watson stat	1.289190	F-statistic	62.10847

Table 11.18

LS // Dependent Variable is CMINUSP

Number of observations: 40

VARIABLE	COEFFICIENT	STD. ERROR	T-STAT.	2-TAIL SIG.
C	3.3454044	0.4245619	7.8796633	0.000
CSQUARED	0.0058662	0.0004617	12.706314	0.000
R	0.3099622	0.0817048	3.7936831	0.001

R-squared	0.954723	Mean of dependent var	9.283000
Adjusted R-squared	0.952275	S.D. of dependent var	8.634845
S.E. of regression	1.886365	Sum of squared resid	131.6598
Durbin-Watson stat	2.342272	F-statistic	390.0943

additional regressors represent, of course, the role of full information on the players' decisions as Proposers (so that R appears as an additional regressor in Tables 11.16 and 11.18) and as Responders (so that P appears as an additional regressor in Tables 11.17 and 11.19). Needless to say, the global statistical fit as well as the individual significance of all regressors is satisfactory in all the tables; the interesting point concerns rather the sign of the additional (or, we might say, 'informational') regressor's coefficient sign, which

Table 11.19

LS // Dependent Variable is R

Number of observations: 40

VARIABLE	COEFFICIENT	STD. ERROR	T-STAT.	2-TAIL SIG.
C	-5.8452145	3.6702820	-1.5925791	0.120
CROOT	2.8296987	1.7698427	1.5988420	0.118
P	0.0430682	0.3550004	0.1213186	0.904

R-squared	0.707933	Mean of dependent var	6.144500
Adjusted R-squared	0.692146	S.D. of dependent var	6.467288
S.E. of regression	3.588348	Sum of squared resid	476.4210
Durbin-Watson stat	1.200071	F-statistic	44.84172

is negative in Tables 11.16-11.17, as opposed to Tables 11.18-11.19, where it is positive. This means that in Tables 11.16-11.17 the additional or informational regressor, representing the counterpart's decision, induces the players to reduce the amount of the cake that they want to keep for themselves, either as Proposers (Table 11.16) or as Responders (Table 11.17). In other words, 'the more he/she wants, the less I will have to ask for myself' might be the strategy of each player in this case. However, it is very important to bear in mind that the informational regressor presents a negative sign only when the cake size increases at a constant rate, that is only when only CAKESIZE is included as a regressor in Tables 11.16-11.17. If CAKESIZE increases at an increasing rate (as in Table 10.5, where its squared value is included as a regressor) or at a decreasing rate (as in Table 11.19, where its square root value is included as a regressor) then the informational regressor presents always a positive sign. In this case, the players' strategy might be 'but the more and more he/she wants, the more and more I will have to be careful, and adjust accordingly the size of my own requests', which implies a positive sign for the informational variable. Put in a simpler way, Tables 11.16-11.17 show that complete information stimulates fairness, but Tables 11.18-11.19 show that it stimulates also fear, especially for the Proposers. It appears as if the data of variant 2 were amplifying the validity of our previous predictions GM and FF. From a strictly econometric point of view, such a conclusion is confirmed by attempting a Lagrange Multiplier F-type test: first, we test the model assumed in Table 11.10 (which will be our null hypothesis, or restricted version of the model, without informational regressor) against the model assumed in Table 11.16 (which will be our alternative hypothesis, or unrestricted version of the model, with informational regressor). Then an absolutely identical procedure is repeated by testing Table 11.11 against Table 11.17, Table 11.14 against Table 11.18 and finally Table 11.15 against Table 11.19. As is known, the formula used for the F-test in these cases is the following:

$$F = (R^2(H_1) - R^2(H_0))\ ((n-k-s)/s)/(1 - R^2(H_1)) \sim F(s,n-k-s) \tag{19}$$

where H_0 denotes the null hypothesis, H_1 the alternative one, R^2, of course the R-squared value, n the total number of observations in the regression (n=40 in our case), k the number of regressors in the restricted version of the model, including the constant (so that k=2 in our case) and s the number of linear restrictions (so that s=1 since we add only 1 informational regressor - either P or R - in the unrestricted version of the model - that is, Tables 11.16 to 11.19). Now, if the F value obtained from (19) is significantly larger than the value F(5%,1,37) = 4.08 reported in all standard statistic tables (where 5% denotes the test's chosen level of significance), then the null hypothesis of no role for the informational regressor can be rejected. Thus, we could conclude that the availability of complete information about the (other) players has a significant role in stimulating 'fair' offers during the one-shot games of our experiment (that is, our EX prediction is substantially true). This is indeed the case since the application of formula (19) gives values F=6.69 when Table 11.10 is tested against Table 11.16, F=6.71 for Tables 11.11 and 11.17, and F=14.37 for Tables 11.14 and 11.18 (all values being obviously greater than 4.08). Only for Tables 11.15 and 11.19 (relating to Responders' decisions when 'fear' is also considered in the model - recall Figure 9.2) the value found is F=0.01, which is much lower than 4.08: thus, in this case, we must say that the informational variable does not influence much the 'fear' considerations of Responders, while it does indeed for Proposers (see the test of Table 11.14 against Table 11.18). On the other hand, the informational variable is relevant in the taste for fairness of both Proposers and Responders, as the test of Tables 11.10 and 11.11 against respectively Tables 11.16 and 11.17 has consistently shown. At a fairly general level, we can then conclude this commentary (and this section) by saying that also our prediction EX is consistent with the experimental data in the sense that learning does not necessarily lead individuals to strategic behaviour.

Very briefly, we can conclude that, on the lines of our experimental results as well as of previous studies, it is worth stressing what has been already suggested one century ago '...between the frozen pole of egoism and the tropical expanse of utilitarianism, there has been granted to imperfectly-evolved mortals an intermediate temperate region; the position of one for whom in a calm moment his neighbour's happiness as compared with his own neither counts for nothing, nor yet 'counts for one', but counts for a fraction... agreeing with the view suggested that the concrete nineteenth century man is for the most part an impure egoist, a mixed utilitarian' (Edgeworth, 1881, pp. 102-4). This is to say that individuals are not perfect games(wo)men nor perfect fair(wo)men; rather, their behaviour ranges across a wide area in between. In this area many people are observed to be willing to pay (at least to some extent) for fair treatment just as in the same fashion they are willing to avoid free-rider behaviour on quite a few occasions in which such a costless solution would be available.

Conclusions

Moral rules, rules of thumb, self-control rules, procedures, commitment devices: these and others are the repertoire of (voluntarily-imposed) constraints according to which economic agents operate.

Two main questions then arise: why do people constrain their behaviour within a set of rules? And why do people wish other people's behaviour were constrained by a set of rules? When the constitutional choice reflects the second class of preferences, the agent's endogenous constraints (at least a subset of them) become the exogenous constraints for the whole society, a familiar issue usually referred as the 'Hobbesian problem of social order'. From this point of view, the selection of constitutional rules is regarded as a process of rational self-binding, that is enforced through the State's power to prevent deviations which would be detrimental for society.

Thus, (a subset of) endogenous constraints are translated into (although not crowded-out by) exogenous constraints. Through a somewhat parallel process, an 'evolutionary learning-by-doing' technique is translated into a 'social learning-by-enforcing' technique. An interacting relation can be thought between social constitutional rules and private constitutional rules: by reflecting individual preferences, the latter influence the former; on the other hand, with a circulatory feedback, after a certain span of time, the rule is 'forgotten' as a formal or exogenous constraint and, through an evolutionary learning process, it is internalised as a 'private' guide of the agent's behaviour.

As suggested, under uncertainty conditions the technique of rules turns out to be a useful tool in people's decision-making process. Translating this technology of behavioural rules from the individual opportunity set to the social setting, institutional rules dealing with uncertainty provide the economic agents with new opportunities of acting in uncertain contexts. Similarly, in a context of social interactions, translating the technique of behavioural rules of a moral nature from the individual action set to the institutional setting raises the possibility of overcoming recurrent social dilemmas situations of PD type, and thus, to enjoy otherwise non-viable opportunities. More in general, extending the commitment power from a private dimension to a social dimension gives the chance to exploit opportunities precluded to the resource-constrained agent. Hence, 'forced' rules become merit goods: the higher the degree of general acceptance of such rules, the more the government will supply them (Priddat 1992): '...normally the people like to be supplied with merit goods: it is a comfortable way of having no other choice but to follow their ordinary public routine' (p. 67).

Yet, the private dimension of the commitment power still remains important and the shortage of private resources – limited knowledge, calculating, coordination, and information-gathering capacities – must be traded-off against the likely occurrence of government failure.

The present work has addressed the private dimension of (self-enforced) constraints. It has tried to explore the nature, the *raison d'ȇntre* of endogenous constraints as well as their rationality (Part I); their plausibility as a working hypothesis both in a theoretical framework of international cooperation (Part II) and in a laboratory experiment on individuals' fairness (Part III).

It has been argued that both environmental and internal imperfections as well as the evolutionary learning shape the subjective constraints. Innate behaviour patterns and the capacity to form habits through self-constraining rules and routines are adaptive in a broad sense. Rules (of thumb) help agents to deal with environment uncertainty, complexity and evolution. Moreover, within a set of strategic interactions, behavioural rules help agents to form a reputation, which conveys valuable signals and information to the other partners. In all such contexts, rules and commitments associated with cognitive as well as motivational constraints play a crucial role together with preferences, tastes, and even mimicry.

Moral rules can by no means be confined to the sphere of environmental as well as human imperfections; yet, in an evolutionary perspective, their genetic character is the result of agents' attempts to increase their adaptive fit relative to the environmental conditions.

Modelled by the same long-run (survival) objectives, and endowed with the same (more-or-less strictly) bounded capacities, individuals share the same behavioural strategy of following rules. In the same way, these established patterns of behaviour 'preserve knowledge, particularly tacit knowledge in relation to skills, acting through time as a transmission belt of information and knowledge' (Hodgson 1989, p. 31). Hence, social interactions become a network of rule interactions (Vanberg 1989), where institutions provide individuals with information, by establishing predictable patterns of behaviour, thus creating 'for the individual a 'simple' world within which his programmed decision-making can take place' (Simon 1982, p. 3). Ultimately traditions are 'adaptions to the unknown...the key in all evolution' (Hayek 1988, p. 76).

References

Admati, A. and Perry, M. (1987), 'Strategic Delay in Bargaining', *Review of Economic Studies*.

Ainslie, G. (1992), *Picoeconomics*, Cambridge University Press, Cambridge.

Akerlof, G. (1979), 'The Case Against Conservative Macroeconomics: An Inaugural Lecture', *Economica*.

Akerlof, G. (1982), 'Labor Contracts as Partial Gift Exchange', *Quarterly Journal of Economics*.

Alchian, A.A. (1950), 'Uncertainty, Evolution and Economic Theory', *Journal of Political Economy*.

Allais, M. (1953), 'Le Comportement de l'Homme Rationnel devant le Risque: Critique de Postulates et Axiomes de l'École Américaine', *Econometrica*.

Anand, P. (1993), 'The Philosophy of Intransitive Preference', *Economic Journal*.

Anderson, E. (1993), *Value in Ethics and Economics*, Harvard University Press, Cambridge.

Andreoni, J. and Miller, J.H. (1993), 'Rational Cooperation in the Finitely Repeated Prisoner's Dilemma: Experimental Evidence', *Economic Journal*.

Arrow, K. (1971), 'Political and Economic Evaluation of Social Effects and Externalities', in Intriligator, M. (ed.), *Frontiers of Quantitative Economics*, North-Holland, Amsterdam.

Arrow, K. (1973), 'Social Responsibility and Economic Efficiency', *Public Policy*.

Arrow, K. (1975), 'Gifts and Exchanges', in Phelps, S. (ed.), *Altruism, Morality and Economic Theory*, Russel Sage Foundation, New York.

Arrow, K. (1982), 'Risk Perception in Psychology and Economics', *Economic Inquiry*.

Arrow, K. (1986), 'Rationality of Self and Others in an Economic System',

Journal of Business.
Axelrod, R. (1984), *The Evolution of Cooperation*, Basic Books, New York.
Azariadis, C. (1975), 'Implicit Contracts and Unemployment Equilibria', *Journal of Political Economy*.
Banerjee, A.V. (1993), 'The Economics of Rumours', *Review of Economic Studies*.
Banfield, E.C. (1958), *The Moral Basis of a Backward Society*, University of Chicago Research Center in Economic Development and Cultural Change, Glencoe, Illinois.
Barrett, C.R. and Pattanaik, P.K. (1993), 'Decision Making under Complete Uncertainty: The Ordinal Framework', in Sen, S. (ed.), *Uncertainty and Risk in Economic Life*, Edward Elgar, Aldershot.
Battalio, R.C., Kagel, J.H. and McDonald, D.N. (1985), 'Animals' Choices over Uncertain Outcomes', *American Economic Review*.
Bauer, P.T. (1976), *Dissent on Development*, Harvard University Press, Cambridge, Mass.
Becker, G.S. (1992), 'Habits, Addictions and Traditions', *Kyklos*.
Becker, G.S. (1993), 'Nobel Lecture: The Economic Way of Looking at Behavior', *Journal of Political Economy*.
Bergstrom, T.C. and Stark, O. (1993), 'How Altruism Can Prevail in an Evolutionary Environment', *American Economic Review*.
Bernheim, B.D. and Stark, O. (1988), 'Altruism within the Family Reconsidered: Do Nice Guys Finish Last?', *American Economic Review*.
Binmore, K., Shaked, A. and Sutton J. (1985), 'Testing Noncooperative Bargaining Theory: A Preliminary Study', *American Economic Review*.
Bolton, G.E. (1991), 'A Comparative Model of Bargaining: Theory and Evidence', *American Economic Review*.
Bordley, R. and Hazen, G. (1991), 'SSB and Weighted Linear Utility as Expected Utility with Suspicion', *Management Science*.
Borjas, G.J. (1992), 'Ethnic Capital and Intergenerational Mobility', *Quarterly Journal of Economics*.
Bowles, S. and Gintis, H. (1993), 'The Revenge of Homo Economicus: Contested Exchange and the Revival of Political Economy', *Journal of Economic Perspectives*.
Brandenburger, A. (1992), 'Knowledge and Equilibrium in Games', *Journal of Economic Perspectives*.
Breton, A. and Wintrobe, R. (1982), *The Logic of Bureaucratic Conduct*, Cambridge University Press, Cambridge.
Buchanan, J.M. (1975), 'The Samaritan's Dilemma', in Phelps (ed.), *Altruism, Morality and Economic Theory*, Russel Sage Foundation, New York.
Buchanan, J.M. (1975), *The Limits of Liberty*, University of Chicago Press, Chicago.
Buchanan, J.M. (1978), 'Markets, States and the Extent of Morals', *American Economic Review*.

Buchanan, J.M. (1991), *The Economics and the Ethics of Constitutional Order*, The University of Michigan Press, Ann Arbor.

Cadet, B. (1992), 'Contextual Effects and the Influence of the Frame on Decision Making', mimeo, Sixth International Conference on the Foundations and Applications of Utility and Decision Making, Paris, June 15-18.

Camerer, C. and Weber, M. (1992), 'Recent Developments in Modeling Preferences: Uncertainty and Ambiguity', *Journal of Risk and Uncertainty*.

Cudd, A.E. (1993), 'Game Theory and the History of Ideas about Rationality: An Introductory Survey', *Economics and Philosophy*.

Cullis, J.G., Lewis, A. and Winnett, A. (1992), 'Paying to Be Good? U.K. Ethical Investments', *Kyklos*.

Dixit, A. and Nalebuff, B. (1991), 'Making Strategies Credible', in Zeckhauser, R. (ed.), *Strategy and Choice*, MIT Press, Cambridge, Mass.

Dosi, G. and Egidi, M. (1991), 'Substantive and Procedural Uncertainty', *Journal of Evolutionary Economics*.

Edgeworth, F.Y. (1881), *Mathematical Psychics*, Kegan Paul & Co., London.

Egidi, M. and Marris, R. (eds.) (1992), *Economics, Bounded Rationality and the Cognitive Revolution*, Edward Elgar, Aldershot.

Elster, J. (1979), *Ulysses and the Sirens*, Cambridge University Press, Cambridge.

Elster, J. (1989), *The Cement of Society*, Cambridge University Press, Cambridge.

Elster, J. (1993), *Political Psychology*, Cambridge University Press, Cambridge.

Fehr, E., Kirchsteiger, G. and Riedl, A. (1993), 'Does Fairness Prevent Market Clearing? An Experimental Investigation', *Quarterly Journal of Economics*.

Fiocca, M. (1988), 'From the Homo Oeconomicus to the Philanthropic Man', *Economia delle Scelte Pubbliche*.

Fiocca, M. (1990a), 'L'uomo economico, il filantropo, il razionale & co.', *Economia, Società e Istituzioni*.

Fiocca, M. (1990b), 'Il Samaritano, l'individuo avverso al rimpianto e la politica dei dividendi', *Economia, Società e Istituzioni*.

Fiocca, M. (1991), 'Altruism and Efficiency', *Economia, Società e Istituzioni*.

Fiocca, M. (1992a), 'Money vs. Ideals: Are People Games(wo)men or Fair(wo)men?', *Economia, Società e Istituzioni*.

Fiocca, M. (1992b), 'Dai vincoli endogeni alla persona ai risultati economici: il passaggio attraverso la morale, l'incertezza e le strategie', *Economia, Società e Istituzioni*.

Fiocca, M. (1994), 'How Much Does 'Position' Matter in Economics?', forthcoming.

Frank, R.H. (1985), 'The Demand for Unobservable and Other Non-Positional Goods', *American Economic Review*.

Frank, R.H. (1987), 'If *Homo Economicus* Could Choose His Own Utility Function, Would He Want One with a Conscience?', *American Economic Review*.

Frank, R.H. (1988), 'Passions within Reason: The Strategic Role of the Emotions', in Maital, S. (ed.), *Applied Behavioural Economics*, Wheatsheaf Books, Brighton.

Frank, R.H. (1989), 'Beyond Self-Interest', *Challenge*.

Frank, R.H. (1991), 'Positional Externalities', in Zeckhauser, R.J. (ed.), *Strategy and Choice*, MIT Press, Cambridge, Mass.

Frank, R.H., Gilovich, T. and Regan, D.T. (1993), 'Does Studying Economics Inhibit Cooperation?', *Journal of Economic Perspectives*.

Frey, B.S. (1992), 'Tertium Datur: Pricing, Regulating and Intrinsic Motivation', *Kyklos*.

Friedman, M. (1953), *Essays in Positive Economics*, Chicago University Press, Chicago.

Friedman, M. (1962), *Capitalism and Freedom*, University of Chicago Press, Chicago.

Furnham, A. and Lewis, A. (1986), *The Economic Mind*, Harvester Press, New York.

Gauthier, D. (1986), *Morals by Agreement*, Oxford University Press, Oxford.

Gauthier, D. (1991), 'Economic Man and the Rational Reasoner', mimeo, International School of Economic Research, workshop on 'Ethics and Economics', Certosa di Pontignano, July 3-13.

Geanakoplos, J. (1992), 'Common Knowledge', *Journal of Economic Perspectives*.

Gilbert, M. (1989), 'Rationality and Salience', *Philosophical Studies*.

Gradstein, M., Nitzan, S. and Slutsky, S. (1992), 'The Effect of Uncertainty on Interactive Behaviour', *Economic Journal*.

Guth, W., Schmittberger, R. and Schwarze, B. (1982), 'An Experimental Analysis of Ultimatum Bargaining', *Journal of Economic Behavior and Organization*.

Guth, W., Ockenfels, P. and Wendel, M. (1991), 'Multiperiod Ultimatum Bargaining Experiments with an Increasing Cake', mimeo, Goethe University, Frankfurt.

Guth, W. and Tietz, R. (1990), 'Ultimatum Bargaining Behaviour: A Survey and Comparison of Experimental Results', *Journal of Economic Psychology*.

Hammond, P.J. (1976), 'Changing Tastes and Coherent Dynamic Choice', *Review of Economic Studies*.

Hardin, R. (1991), 'Trusting Persons, Trusting Institutions', in Zeckhauser, R.J. (ed.), *Strategy and Choice*, MIT Press, Cambridge, Mass.

Hardin, R. (1993), 'Norms of Exclusion and Difference', mimeo, International School of Economic Research, workshop on 'Economics and Politics', Certosa di Pontignano, July 4-10.

Hargreaves Heap, S. (1989), *Rationality in Economics*, Basil Blackwell, London.

Hargreaves Heap, S. (1993), 'Post-Modernity and New Conceptions of Rationality in Economics', in Gerrard, B. (ed.), *The Economics of Rationality*, Routledge, London.

Hargreaves Heap, S., Hollis, M., Lyons, B., Sugden, R. and Weale, A. (1992), *A Theory of Choice. A Critical Guide*, Blackwell, Oxford.

Hausman, D.M. and McPherson, M.S. (1993), 'Taking Ethics Seriously: Economics and Contemporary Moral Philosophy', *Journal of Economic Literature*.

Hayek, F.A. (1964), 'Kinds of Order in Society', *New Individualist Review*.

Hayek, F.A. (1988), *The Fatal Conceit: The Errors of Socialism*, in *Collected Works of F.A. Hayek*, Routledge, London.

Heath, C. and Tversky, A. (1991), 'Preference and Belief: Ambiguity and Competence in Choice under Uncertainty', *Journal of Risk and Uncertainty*.

Hechter, M., Friedman, D. and Kanazawa, S. (1992), 'The Attainment of Global Order in Heterogeneous Societies', mimeo, Annual Meeting of the Public Choice Society, Torino, April 22-25.

Heiner, R.A. (1983), 'The Origin of Predictable Behavior', *American Economic Review*.

Heiner, R.A. (1990), 'Rule-Governed Behavior in Evolution and Human Society', *Constitutional Political Economy*.

Hey, J.D. (1981), 'Are Optimal Search Rules Reasonable?', *Journal of Economic Behaviour and Organization*.

Hey, J.D. (1982), 'Search for Rules for Search', *Journal of Economic Behaviour and Organisation*.

Hey, J.D. (1993), 'Rationality is as Rationality Does', in Gerrard, B. (ed.), *The Economics of Rationality*, Routledge, London.

Hirsch, F. (1976), *Social Limits to Growth*, Harvard University Press, Cambridge.

Hochman, H. and Rodgers, J. (1969), 'Pareto-Optimal Redistribution', *American Economic Review*.

Hodgson, G.M. (1989), 'Evolution and Institutional Change', mimeo, Swedish Collegium for Advanced Study in the Social Sciences, conference on 'Methodological Problems of Neo-Institutional Economics', Uppsala, August 17-19.

Hodgson, G.M. (1992), 'The Mecca of Alfred Marshall', *Economic Journal*.

Holmes, S. (1990), 'The Secret History of Self-Interest', in Mansbridge, J. (ed.), *Beyond Self-Interest*, University of Chicago Press, Chicago.

Ireland, T. and Johnson, D. (1970), *The Economics of Charity*, Center for the Study of Public Choice, Blacksbugh.

Irwin, J.R., Slovic, P., Lichtenstein, S. and McClelland, G.H. (1993), 'Preference Reversals and the Measurement of Environmental Values',

Journal of Risk and Uncertainty.
Isaac, M., Schmidtz, D. and Walker, J. (1989), 'The Assurance Problem in a Laboratory Market', *Public Choice.*
Kahneman, D. and Tversky, A. (1979), 'Prospect Theory: An Analysis of Choice Under Risk', *Econometrica.*
Kahneman, D. and Tversky, A. (1982), 'The Psychology of Preferences', *Science American.*
Kahneman, D., Knetsch, J. and Thaler, R. (1986a), 'Fairness and the Assumptions of Economics', *Journal of Business.*
Kahneman, D., Knetsch, J. and Thaler, R. (1986b), 'Fairness as a Constraint on Profit Seeking: Entitlements in the Market', *American Economic Review.*
Kahneman, D. and Varey, C. (1991), 'Notes on the Psychology of Utility', in Elster, J. and Roemer, J.E. (eds.), *Interpersonal Comparisons of Well-Being*, Cambridge University Press, Cambridge.
Kavka, G.S. (1983), 'The Toxin Puzzle', *Analysis.*
Kelsey, D. (1993), 'Choice under Partial Uncertainty', *International Economic Review.*
Kelsey, D. and Quiggin, J. (1992), 'Theories of Choice Under Ignorance and Uncertainty', *Journal of Economic Surveys.*
Kennan, J. and Wilson, R.B. (1993), 'Bargaining with Private Information', *Journal of Economic Literature.*
Kimball, M.S. (1993), 'Standard Risk Aversion', *Econometrica.*
Kirman, A. (1992), 'Whom or What Does the Representative Individual Represent?', *Journal of Economic Perspectives.*
Klein, B. and Leffler, K.B. (1981), 'The Role of Market Forces in Assuring Contractual Performance', *Journal of Political Economy.*
Kliemt, H. (1990), *Papers on Buchanan and Related Subjects*, Accedo Verlagsgesellschaft, Munich.
Kreps, D.M., Milgrom, P., Roberts, J. and Wilson, R. (1982), 'Rational Cooperation in the Finitely Repeated Prisoners' Dilemma', *Journal of Economic Theory.*
Laffont, J. (1975), 'Macroeconomic Constraints, Economic Efficiency and Ethics: An Introduction to Kantian Economics', *Economica.*
Lea, S., Tarpy, R. and Webley, P. (1987), *The Individual in the Economy*, Cambridge University Press, Cambridge.
Lewis, D.K. (1969), *Convention: A Philosophical Study*, Harvard University Press, Cambridge, Mass.
Linchtenstein, S. and Slovic, P. (1971), 'Reversal of Preferences Between Bids and Choices in Gambling Decisions', *Journal of Experimental Psychology.*
Lindbeck, A. and Weibull, J.W. (1988), 'Altruism and Time Consistency: The Economics of Fait Accompli', *Journal of Political Economy.*
Long, S. (1976), 'Social Pressure and Contributions to Health Charities', *Public*

Choice.

Loomes, G. and Sugden, R. (1982), 'Regret Theory: An Alternative Theory of Rational Choice Under Uncertainty', *Economic Journal*.

Loomes, G. and Sugden, R. (1983), 'A Rationale for Preference Reversal', *American Economic Review*.

Loomes, G. and Sugden, R. (1986), 'Disappointment and Dynamic Consistency in Choice Under Uncertainty', *Review of Economic Studies*.

Loomes, G. and Sugden, R. (1987), 'Some Implication of a More General Form of Regret Theory', *Journal of Economic Theory*.

Loomes, G. and Taylor, C. (1992), 'Non-Transitive Preferences Over Gains and Losses', *Economic Journal*.

Machina, M. (1981), ' 'Rational' Decision Ranking vs. 'Rational' Decision Modelling?', *Journal of Mathematical Psychology*.

McClennen, E.F. (1983), 'Sure-Thing Doubts', in Stigum, B.P., Wenstop, F. (eds.), *Foundations of Utility and Risk Theory with Applications*, Dordrecht, Reidel.

Neelin, J., Sonnenschein, H. and Spiegel, M. (1988), 'A Further Test of Bargaining Theory', *American Economic Review*.

Ochs, J. and Roth, A.E. (1989), 'An Experimental Study of Sequential Bargaining', *American Economic Review*.

Okun, A. (1981), *Prices and Quantities: A Macroeconomic Analysis*, Brooking Institution, Washington D.C.

Pagano, U. (1992), 'Can Economics Explain Nationalism?', mimeo, Villa Colombella Seminar on Nationalism, Perugia, September.

Pasour, E. (1990), 'External Effects and the Work Ethic: Does Society Gain When an Individual Works Harder?', *Economia delle Scelte Pubbliche*.

Pieters, R. (1988), 'Attitude-Behavior Relationships', in van Raaij, W.F., van Veldhoven, G. and Wärneryd, K. (eds.) *Handbook of Economic Psychology*, Kluwer Academic Publishers, Dordrecht.

Pieters, R. and van Raaij, W.F. (1988), 'The Role of Affect in Economic Behavior', in van Raaij, W.F., van Veldhoven, G. and Wärneryd, K. (eds.), *Handbook of Economic Psychology*, Kluwer Academic Publishers, Dordrecht.

Pollak, R.A. (1968), 'Consistent Planning', *Review of Economic Studies*.

Popper, K.R. (1972), *Objective Knowledge: An Evolutionary Approach*, Clarendon Press, Oxford.

Posnett, J. and Sandler, T. (1986), 'Joint Supply and the Finance of Charitable Activity', *Public Finance Quarterly*.

Prelec, D. and Herrnstein R.J. (1991), 'Preferences or Principles: Alternative Guidelines for Choice', in Zeckhauser, R.J. (ed.), *Strategy and Choice*, MIT Press, Cambridge, Mass.

Priddat, B.P. (1992), 'Behind the Veil of Time Rules, Institutions, and Temporal Stability', in Koslowski, P. (ed.), *Ethics in Economics, Business, and Economic Policy*, Springer Verlag, Berlin.

Pritchett, J.B. and Chamberlain, R.M. (1993), 'Selection in the Market for Slaves: New Orleans, 1830-1860', *Quarterly Journal of Economics*.

Raiffa, H. (1991), 'Coping with Common Errors in Rational Decision Making', in Zeckhauser, R.J. (ed.), *Strategy and Choice*, MIT Press, Cambridge, Mass.

Reny, P.J. (1992), 'Rationality in Extensive-Form Games', *Journal of Economic Perspectives*.

Ritov, I. and Baron, J. (1992), 'Status-Quo and Omission Biases', *Journal of Risk and Uncertainty*.

Ritov, I., Baron, J. and Hershey, J.C. (1993), 'Framing Effects in the Evaluation of Multiple Risk Reduction', *Journal of Risk and Uncertainty*.

Rosenthal, R.W. (1981), 'Games of Perfect Information, Predatory Pricing and the Chain-Store Paradox', *Journal of Economic Theory*.

Ross, S. (1977), 'The Determination of Financial Structure: The Incentive-Signalling Approach', *Bell Journal of Economics*.

Roth, A.E. (1988), 'Laboratory Experimentation in Economics: A Methodological Overview', *Economic Journal*.

Rothschild, K. (1993), *Ethics and Economic Theory*, Edward Elgar, Aldershot.

Rothschild, M. and Stiglitz, J. (1976), 'Equilibrium in Competitive Insurance Markets: An Essay on the Economics of Imperfect Information', *Quarterly Journal of Economics*.

Rowe, N. (1989), *Rules and Institutions*, The University of Michigan Press, Ann Arbor.

Rubinstein, A. (1982), 'Perfect Equilibrium in a Bargaining Model', *Econometrica*.

Rubinstein, A. (1986), 'Finite Automata Play the Repeated Prisoner's Dilemma', *Journal of Economic Theory*.

Rutherford, M. (1988), 'Learning and Decision-Making in Economics and Psychology: A Methodological Perspective', in Earl, P. (ed.), *Psychological Economics. Development, Tensions, Prospects*, Kluwer Academic Publishers, Dordrecht.

Samuelson, P.A. (1993), 'Altruism as a Problem Involving Group versus Individual Selection in Economics and Biology', *American Economic Review*.

Samuelson, W. and Zeckhauser, R. (1988), 'Status Quo Bias in Decision Making', *Journal of Risk and Uncertainty*.

Schelling, T.C. (1960), *The Strategy of Conflict*, Harvard University Press, Cambridge, Mass.

Schelling, T.C. (1973), 'Hockey Helmets, Concealed Weapons, and Daylight Saving: A Study of Binary Choices with Externalities', *Journal of Conflict Resolution*.

Schelling, T.C. (1984a), 'Self-Command in Practice, in Policy, and in a Theory of Rational Choice', *American Economic Review*.

Schelling, T.C. (1984b), *Choice and Consequence*, Harvard University Press,

Cambridge, Mass.

Schoemaker, P.J.H. (1993), 'Determinants of Risk-Taking: Behavioral and Economic Views', *Journal of Risk and Uncertainty*.

Segal, U. (1987), 'The Ellsberg Paradox and Risk Aversion: An Anticipated Utility Approach', *International Economic Review*.

Sen, A. (1977), 'Rational Fools: A Critique of the Behavioural Foundation of Economic Theory', *Philosophy and Public Affairs*.

Sen, A. (1987), *On Ethics and Economics*, Basil Blackwell, Oxford.

Shapiro, C. (1983), 'Premiums for High Quality Products as Returns to Reputations', *Quarterly Journal of Economics*.

Shogren, J. (1989), 'Fairness in Bargaining Requires a Context: An Experimental Examination of Loyalty', *Economics Letters*.

Simon, H.A. (1982), 'The Role of Expectations in an Adaptive or Behavioristic Model', in Simon, H.A., *Models of Bounded Rationality, Behavioral Economics and Business Organization*, The MIT Press, Cambridge, Mass.

Simon, H.A. (1993), 'Altruism and Economics', *American Economic Review*.

Slovic, P. and Tversky, A. (1974), 'Who Accepts Savage's Axiom?', *Behavioral Science*.

Solow, R.M. (1980), 'On Theories of Unemployment', *American Economic Review*.

Spence, A.M. (1974), *Market Signaling*, Harvard University Press, Cambridge, Mass.

Stark, O. (1993), 'Nonmarket Transfers and Altruism', *European Economic Review*.

Strotz, R.H. (1955-56), 'Myopia and Inconsistency in Dynamic Utility Maximization', *Review of Economic Studies*.

Sugden, R. (1984), 'Reciprocity: The Supply of Public Goods through Voluntary Contributions', *Economic Journal*.

Sugden, R. (1985), 'Consistent Conjectures and Voluntary Contributions to Public Goods: Why the Conventional Theory Does Not Work', *Journal of Public Economics*.

Sugden, R. (1986), 'Coordination', in Sugden, R. (ed.) *The Economics of Rights, Co-Operation and Welfare*, Basil Blackwell, Oxford.

Sugden, R. (1989), 'Spontaneus Order', *Journal of Economic Perspectives*.

Sugden, R. (1991), 'Rational Choice: A Survey of Contributions from Economics and Philosophy', *Economic Journal*.

Thaler, R.H. (1988), 'Anomalies: The Ultimatum Game', *Journal of Economic Perspectives*.

Thaler, R.H. and Shefrin H.M. (1981), 'An Economic Theory of Self-Control', *Journal of Political Economy*.

Tiebout, C. (1956), 'A Pure Theory of Local Expenditures', *Journal of Political Economy*.

Titmuss, R. (1971), *The Gift Relationship: From Human Blood to Social Policy*,

Allen and Unwin, London.

Tversky, A. (1975), 'A Critique of Expected Utility Theory: Descriptive and Normative Considerations', *Erkenntnis*.

Tversky, A. and Kahneman, D. (1981), 'The Framing of Decision and the Psychology of Choice', *Science*.

Tversky, A. and Kahneman, D. (1986), 'Rational Choice and the Framing of Decisions', *Journal of Business*.

Tversky, A., Slovic, P. and Kahneman, D. (1990), 'The Causes of Preference Reversal', *American Economic Review*.

Vanberg, V. (1988), 'Morality: Preference or Constraint?', in *Morality and Economics. De Moribus Est Disputandum*, Original Papers n. 7, Transaction Books.

Vanberg, V. (1989), 'Rational Choice, Rule-Following and Institutions: An Evolutionary Perspective', mimeo, conference on 'Methodological Problems of New Institutional Economics', Uppsala, August 17-19.

Vanberg, V. and Buchanan, J.M. (1990), 'Rational Choice and Moral Order', in Nichols, J.H. and Wright, C. (eds.), *From Political Economy to Economics. And Back?*, Institute for Contemporary Studies, San Francisco.

Vanberg, V. and Congleton, R.D. (1992), 'Rationality, Morality, and Exit', *American Political Science Review*.

Vickrey, W. (1962), 'One Economist's View of Philanthropy', in Dickinson, F. (ed.), *Philanthropy and Public Policy*, Columbia University Press, New York.

Wagner, R.E. (1989), *To Promote the General Welfare: Market Processes vs. Political Transfers*, Pacific Research Institute for Public Policy, San Francisco.

Weber, M. (1930), *The Protestant Ethic and the Spirit of Capitalism*, Allen & Unwin, London.

Williamson, O.E. (1975), *Markets and Hierarchies: Analysis and Anti-Trust Implications: A Study in the Economics of Internal Organization*, Free Press, New York.

Williamson, O.E. (1983), 'Credible Commitments: Using Hostages to Support Exchange', *American Economic Review*.

Williamson, O.E. (1985), *The Economic Institutions of Capitalism: Firms, Markets, Relational Contracting*, Macmillan, London.

Wintrobe, R. (1992), 'Some Economics of Ethnic Capital and Conflict', mimeo, Villa Colombella Seminar on Nationalism, Perugia, September.

Witt, U. (1985), 'Economic Behavior and Biological Evolution: Some Remarks on the Sociobiology Debate', *Journal of Institutional and Theoretical Economics*.

Yaari, M.E. (1977), 'Consistence Utilization of an Exhaustible Resource - or - How to Eat an Appetite Arousing Cake', Research Memorandum No. 23, Hebrew University.

Yaari, M.E. (1991), 'Rationality and Morality: A Humean View', mimeo, International School of Economic Research, workshop on 'Ethics and Economics', Certosa di Pontignano, July 3-13.

Young, P.H. (1993), 'The Evolution of Conventions', *Econometrica*.

Zajac, E.E. (1978), *Fairness or Efficiency: An Introduction to Public Utility Pricing*, Ballinger, Cambridge, Mass.

Zemel, E. (1989), 'Small Talk and Cooperation: A Note on Bounded Rationality', *Journal of Economic Theory*.

Appendix

APPENDIX A: EXPERIMENT MATERIAL

Appendix 1: INVITATION

Before the end of the term, we plan to run a new experiment. This is different from any we have done before and you can, if you wish, take part.

Brief details are given below. Those who want to take part will be able to get further details in advance. Since this experiment offers you the chance to earn a substantial amount of money, we strongly advise you to pick up an instruction sheet from the folder, should you sign up for the experiment.

The sheet to be signed and the instructions for the experiment will be located outside the door of the EXEC room D202 in Derwent College.

Ten participants are required for each of the ten sessions. The experiment will require an even number of players, and if for any reason an odd number of people arrive, the last person will not take part in the experiment but will be paid 2 pounds for turning up. *Please note*: you may only take part in *one* of the ten sessions.

Brief details of the experiment:

The experiment consists of a straightforward pie-splitting game with 4 alternative amounts of money (£60, £25, £10, £5) to be divided between pairs of people. The process will be repeated in 8 successive rounds, with different pairs each round.

At the end of the 8 rounds, the actual amount to be divided between the two players will be selected at random, with each amount and each round being equally likely to be selected.

To find out more details, and to sign up for one of the limited number of places, please consult the noticeboard outside the EXEC room. PLEASE DO *NOT* SIGN UP UNLESS YOU ARE COMMITTED TO TAKING PART.

Dates and starting times of the experiment: ...

Appendix 2: INFORMATION ABOUT THE EXPERIMENT

The experiment consists of a straightforward pie-splitting game with 4 alternative amounts of money (£60, £25, £10, £5) to be divided between pairs of people. The process will be repeated in 8 successive rounds (after 2 practice rounds at the beginning) with different pairs each round.

At the beginning of each round, every participant is asked to divide the 4 alternative amounts of money *as if* he/she was the person who makes the offer (called the PROPOSER) and then as if he/she was the person who receives the offer (called the RESPONDER).

Thus, for each of the four amounts, *as* PROPOSER each player has to decide the amount accruing to him/herself and that for the responder; *as* RESPONDER each player has to decide the least amount he/she would accept from any proposer.

Hence, everyone makes all his/her decisions in advance, i.e. before knowing (i) whether he/she will be the actual proposer or responder during the game (the chance to be P or R being equally likely), and (ii) which amount will be selected (each amount being equally likely to be selected).

After this stage, for *each round*:

(i) the random pairing is made and it is randomly selected which member of the pairing turns out to be the Proposer or the Responder. At no stage does anyone know the identity of the person with whom

he/she is paired;
(ii) one of the participants is then asked to pick at random a card which will determine the amount of money to be divided for that round;
(iii) then, the computer screen will show whether the person has been selected to be the Proposer or the Responder; it also shows the amount of money selected and whether the proposal is *accepted* or rejected.

There are *two variants* of the game:
(1) in one variant at the end of each round participants will be told only what happened to themselves: they will be given *no information* about the choices made by the other participants and their results. Hence, what the other players do in each round is not recorded on the screen of a player's terminal;
(2) in the second variant information about what happened to *all* the other pairs (but not their identity) will be shown on the screen of each person's terminal.
Players will not know until they start the experiment which variant they will be playing.

At the end of the 8 rounds, the single round to be chosen for payment will be selected *randomly* (by rolling a die) from the eight rounds previously played. The computer screen will show again the results of that particular round, i.e. the amount to be divided in that round, how it was divided between Proposer and Responder, and whether the offer was accepted or rejected.
(i) If it was *ACCEPTED*, each person in the pair will receive the share decided and payment will be made.
(ii) If it was *REJECTED*, both members of the pair receive zero.

Appendix 3: MOTIVATIONS INDUCING PLAYERS TO DECIDE FOR AN EQUAL DIVISION (10 subjects, session 5, variant 2)

a) (i) Most reasonable figure;
(ii) Other party most likely to offer around this;
(iii) Stayed at 50 per cent constantly to force others to this level.
b) It seemed to be the best option, rather than offering small amounts and accepting large ones. If it worked it would give the best overall profits (that's if everybody thinks like me!)
c) For a start, 'Fair's fair'. But later on, once it developed into a trend, if everyone offered only 1/2, then it was no good asking for

more, and no help to ask for less.
Also, if everyone expects 1/2, then offering less would mean rejection, offering more would be a waste of money.
d) It was obvious that all players were playing for maximum group advantage.
The first two rounds were erratic because some players were a bit greedy!
e) This maximises my probable winning because everyone conforming to 50:50 proposals removes the uncertainty of having a mis-match.
Also, I don't like people being too greedy.
f) It's fair and I thought the probability of getting something was the biggest this way.
g) Less risk I suppose! I think there will be more chance of getting at least some money.
h) Because it's totally fair:
— responder/proposer have equal powers to decide if deal is successful;
— neither has power over other and if the other people thought this way we would have successful deals.
i) Just halved the amount.
l) After round 1, I found that there was a tendency towards an equal split. The responder would not accept less than half, so I had to split equally to obtain my expected amount.
Forced to equilibrium by considerations of fairness.

APPENDIX B: EXPERIMENT DATA

TABLE A: RESERVATION PROPOSALS (RP) AND RESPONSES (RR) PER PERSON (pe), ROUND (r) AND CAKE SIZE; MEAN AND MODE VALUES OF RP AND RR ACROSS PERSONS (ALL FOR VARIANT 1)

SESSION: 1

Cake Size	5		10		25		60	
r pe	RP	RR	RP	RR	RP	RR	RP	RR
1 01	2.50	2.00	5.00	4.00	12.50	10.00	30.00	25.00
1 02	2.50	1.00	5.00	2.00	13.00	5.00	31.00	10.00
1 03	3.00	1.50	5.50	3.50	14.00	10.00	35.00	19.00
1 04	2.50	2.50	5.00	5.00	12.50	12.50	30.00	30.00
1 05	2.50	1.00	6.00	1.00	14.00	1.00	35.00	1.00
1 06	3.00	1.50	5.50	3.00	13.00	10.00	32.00	20.00
1 07	0.00	0.00	0.00	0.00	0.00	0.00	0.00	0.00
1 08	0.00	0.00	0.00	0.00	0.00	0.00	0.00	0.00
1 09	0.00	0.00	0.00	0.00	0.00	0.00	0.00	0.00
1 10	0.00	0.00	0.00	0.00	0.00	0.00	0.00	0.00
mean	2.67	1.58	5.33	3.08	13.17	8.08	32.17	17.50
mode	2.50	1.00	5.00	-	-	10.00	-	-
2 01	2.50	2.00	5.00	4.00	12.00	10.00	30.00	25.00
2 02	2.50	1.00	5.00	2.00	13.00	5.00	35.00	10.00
2 03	3.00	1.50	5.50	3.50	14.00	9.50	32.50	19.00
2 04	2.50	2.00	5.00	4.00	12.50	22.50	30.00	25.00
2 05	3.00	1.00	6.00	1.00	14.00	1.00	35.00	1.00
2 06	3.00	1.80	6.00	3.50	13.00	10.00	32.00	20.00
2 07	0.00	0.00	0.00	0.00	0.00	0.00	0.00	0.00
2 08	0.00	0.00	0.00	0.00	0.00	0.00	0.00	0.00
2 09	0.00	0.00	0.00	0.00	0.00	0.00	0.00	0.00
2 10	0.00	0.00	0.00	0.00	0.00	0.00	0.00	0.00
mean	2.75	1.55	5.42	3.00	13.08	9.67	32.42	16.67
mode	-	-	5.00	-	-	10.00	-	25.00
3 01	2.50	2.00	5.00	4.00	12.50	10.00	30.00	25.00
3 02	2.50	0.10	5.00	1.00	14.00	1.00	35.00	1.00
3 03	3.00	1.50	5.50	3.50	13.50	10.00	33.00	19.00
3 04	2.50	2.00	5.00	4.00	12.50	10.00	30.00	25.00
3 05	2.50	0.50	5.00	1.00	12.50	1.00	30.00	1.00
3 06	3.00	1.50	6.50	3.00	13.00	10.00	32.00	20.00
3 07	0.00	0.00	0.00	0.00	0.00	0.00	0.00	0.00
3 08	0.00	0.00	0.00	0.00	0.00	0.00	0.00	0.00
3 09	0.00	0.00	0.00	0.00	0.00	0.00	0.00	0.00
3 10	0.00	0.00	0.00	0.00	0.00	0.00	0.00	0.00
mean	2.67	1.27	5.33	2.75	13.00	7.00	31.67	15.17
mode	2.50	2.00	5.00	-	12.50	10.00	30.00	-
4 01	1.00	1.00	2.00	2.00	5.00	5.00	10.00	10.00
4 02	2.50	1.00	5.00	2.00	12.50	5.00	31.00	10.00
4 03	3.00	1.50	5.50	3.50	13.00	10.00	31.00	19.00
4 04	2.50	2.00	5.00	4.00	12.50	10.00	30.00	25.00
4 05	2.50	0.10	6.00	1.00	14.00	1.00	35.00	1.00
4 06	3.00	1.50	6.00	3.00	13.50	10.00	32.00	20.00
4 07	0.00	0.00	0.00	0.00	0.00	0.00	0.00	0.00
4 08	0.00	0.00	0.00	0.00	0.00	0.00	0.00	0.00
4 09	0.00	0.00	0.00	0.00	0.00	0.00	0.00	0.00
4 10	0.00	0.00	0.00	0.00	0.00	0.00	0.00	0.00
mean	2.42	1.18	4.92	2.58	11.75	6.83	28.17	14.17
mode	2.50	1.00	-	2.00	12.50	10.00	31.00	10.00

TABLE A (follows)

SESSION: 1

5 01	1.00	1.00	2.00	2.00	5.00	5.00	10.00	10.00
5 02	2.50	0.10	5.00	1.00	13.00	1.00	31.00	1.00
5 03	3.00	0.50	5.50	3.50	13.00	9.00	31.00	19.00
5 04	2.50	2.00	5.00	2.00	12.50	2.00	30.00	2.00
5 05	2.50	0.10	6.00	1.00	14.00	1.00	35.00	1.00
5 06	3.00	1.70	6.50	3.50	13.00	10.00	32.00	20.00
5 07	0.00	0.00	0.00	0.00	0.00	0.00	0.00	0.00
5 08	0.00	0.00	0.00	0.00	0.00	0.00	0.00	0.00
5 09	0.00	0.00	0.00	0.00	0.00	0.00	0.00	0.00
5 10	0.00	0.00	0.00	0.00	0.00	0.00	0.00	0.00
mean	2.42	0.90	5.00	2.17	11.75	4.67	28.17	8.83
mode	2.50	-	5.00	-	13.00	1.00	31.00	1.00
6 01	2.50	2.00	5.00	4.00	12.00	10.00	30.00	25.00
6 02	2.60	0.10	5.10	1.00	13.00	1.00	32.00	1.00
6 03	3.00	0.50	5.50	3.50	13.50	9.00	31.00	19.00
6 04	2.50	2.00	5.00	2.00	12.50	2.00	30.00	2.00
6 05	3.00	1.00	6.00	1.00	14.00	1.00	40.00	1.00
6 06	3.50	1.00	6.00	3.00	13.50	10.00	32.00	21.00
6 07	0.00	0.00	0.00	0.00	0.00	0.00	0.00	0.00
6 08	0.00	0.00	0.00	0.00	0.00	0.00	0.00	0.00
6 09	0.00	0.00	0.00	0.00	0.00	0.00	0.00	0.00
6 10	0.00	0.00	0.00	0.00	0.00	0.00	0.00	0.00
mean	2.85	1.10	5.43	2.42	13.08	5.50	32.50	11.50
mode	2.50	-	-	1.00	13.50	-	30.00	1.00
7 01	2.50	1.00	5.00	2.00	12.00	5.00	25.00	10.00
7 02	2.50	1.00	6.00	2.00	15.00	5.00	40.00	10.00
7 03	3.00	0.50	5.50	3.50	13.00	9.00	31.00	18.00
7 04	2.50	2.00	5.00	2.00	12.50	2.00	30.00	2.00
7 05	3.00	0.50	6.00	0.50	18.00	0.50	40.00	0.50
7 06	3.20	1.00	6.20	3.00	13.00	10.00	32.00	20.00
7 07	0.00	0.00	0.00	0.00	0.00	0.00	0.00	0.00
7 08	0.00	0.00	0.00	0.00	0.00	0.00	0.00	0.00
7 09	0.00	0.00	0.00	0.00	0.00	0.00	0.00	0.00
7 10	0.00	0.00	0.00	0.00	0.00	0.00	0.00	0.00
mean	2.78	1.00	5.62	2.17	13.92	5.25	33.00	10.08
mode	2.50	1.00	-	2.00	-	5.00	40.00	10.00
8 01	2.50	1.00	5.00	2.00	12.00	5.00	30.00	10.00
8 02	2.50	1.00	7.00	2.00	15.00	5.00	40.00	10.00
8 03	3.00	0.50	5.50	3.50	13.00	9.00	31.00	18.00
8 04	2.50	2.00	5.00	2.00	12.50	2.00	30.00	2.00
8 05	3.00	0.10	7.00	0.10	20.00	0.10	45.00	0.10
8 06	3.00	1.00	6.00	3.00	13.00	10.00	32.00	20.00
8 07	0.00	0.00	0.00	0.00	0.00	0.00	0.00	0.00
8 08	0.00	0.00	0.00	0.00	0.00	0.00	0.00	0.00
8 09	0.00	0.00	0.00	0.00	0.00	0.00	0.00	0.00
8 10	0.00	0.00	0.00	0.00	0.00	0.00	0.00	0.00
mean	2.75	0.93	5.92	2.10	14.25	5.18	34.67	10.02
mode	-	1.00	-	2.00	13.00	5.00	30.00	10.00

TABLE A (follows)

SESSION: 2

1 01	3.00	2.00	5.00	3.00	15.00	5.00	30.00	20.00
1 02	3.00	1.00	6.00	4.00	18.00	9.50	43.00	23.60
1 03	2.50	2.00	5.00	3.00	12.50	10.00	30.00	20.00
1 04	3.00	1.00	6.00	2.00	15.00	5.00	36.00	10.00
1 05	2.50	2.50	6.00	5.00	12.50	12.00	35.00	20.00
1 06	3.00	0.00	5.00	0.00	17.00	0.00	35.00	0.00
1 07	2.50	2.00	5.00	4.00	12.50	12.00	30.00	27.00
1 08	3.00	2.00	6.50	3.50	15.00	10.00	40.00	20.00
1 09	3.00	2.00	6.00	4.00	15.00	10.00	25.00	25.00
1 10	2.50	2.50	6.00	4.00	14.00	11.00	35.00	25.00
mean	2.80	1.70	5.65	3.25	14.65	8.45	33.90	19.06
mode	3.00	2.00	6.00	4.00	15.00	10.00	-	20.00
2 01	3.00	2.00	5.00	3.00	15.00	10.00	35.00	25.00
2 02	2.50	1.00	6.50	2.50	12.50	15.50	47.50	23.50
2 03	2.50	1.00	5.00	1.00	12.50	1.00	30.00	1.00
2 04	3.00	0.00	6.00	0.00	15.00	0.00	36.00	0.00
2 05	3.00	2.00	5.00	4.50	15.00	10.00	30.00	30.00
2 06	3.00	0.00	6.00	0.00	20.00	0.00	40.00	0.00
2 07	2.50	2.00	5.00	4.00	12.50	12.00	30.00	27.00
2 08	3.00	1.00	6.00	3.00	15.00	10.00	40.00	15.00
2 09	2.50	2.00	5.00	4.00	15.00	12.00	30.00	25.00
2 10	2.50	2.50	5.00	5.00	13.00	12.00	37.00	23.00
mean	2.75	1.35	5.45	2.70	14.55	8.25	35.55	16.95
mode	3.00	2.00	5.00	-	15.00	-	30.00	25.00
3 01	3.00	2.00	5.00	4.00	15.00	10.00	30.00	25.00
3 02	4.00	1.50	7.50	2.50	17.80	7.90	37.80	32.50
3 03	2.50	1.00	5.00	1.00	12.50	1.00	30.00	1.00
3 04	3.00	0.00	6.00	0.00	15.00	0.00	36.00	0.00
3 05	4.00	1.00	5.00	5.00	10.00	10.00	30.00	30.00
3 06	3.00	0.00	6.00	0.00	12.50	0.00	50.00	20.00
3 07	2.50	2.00	5.00	4.00	12.50	12.00	30.00	26.00
3 08	3.00	1.00	6.00	3.00	15.00	8.00	40.00	15.00
3 09	2.50	2.00	5.00	4.00	15.00	10.00	30.00	25.00
3 10	2.50	2.50	6.00	4.00	13.00	13.00	33.00	20.00
mean	3.00	1.30	5.65	2.75	13.83	7.19	34.68	19.45
mode	-	1.00	5.00	4.00	15.00	10.00	30.00	-
4 01	3.00	2.00	5.00	4.00	15.00	10.00	30.00	25.00
4 02	3.50	1.00	7.60	3.00	15.80	11.50	39.80	24.50
4 03	2.50	1.00	5.00	1.00	12.50	1.00	30.00	1.00
4 04	3.00	1.00	6.00	2.50	15.00	8.00	36.00	10.00
4 05	3.00	2.00	5.00	5.00	12.50	12.00	30.00	28.00
4 06	4.00	0.00	7.00	0.00	20.00	0.00	40.00	20.00
4 07	2.50	2.00	5.00	4.00	12.50	12.00	30.00	26.00
4 08	3.00	1.00	6.00	3.00	15.00	8.00	40.00	15.00
4 09	2.50	3.00	6.00	5.00	14.00	10.00	30.00	25.00
4 10	2.50	2.50	6.00	4.00	13.00	12.00	38.00	20.00
mean	2.95	1.55	5.86	3.15	14.53	8.45	34.38	19.45
mode	-	1.00	-	4.00	-	12.00	30.00	-

TABLE A (follows)

SESSION: 2

5 01	3.00	2.00	5.00	4.00	15.00	10.00	30.00	20.00
5 02	3.70	1.00	7.50	3.50	12.80	7.50	35.90	25.90
5 03	2.50	1.00	5.00	1.00	12.50	1.00	30.00	1.00
5 04	3.00	1.00	6.00	2.00	15.00	4.00	36.00	8.00
5 05	2.50	2.50	5.00	5.00	12.50	12.50	30.00	30.00
5 06	3.00	0.00	6.00	0.00	15.00	0.00	40.00	20.00
5 07	2.50	2.00	5.00	4.00	12.50	12.00	30.00	26.00
5 08	3.00	1.00	6.00	3.00	15.00	8.00	40.00	15.00
5 09	2.50	2.00	5.00	4.50	12.00	10.00	30.00	25.00
5 10	2.50	2.00	7.00	3.00	18.00	5.00	40.00	10.00
mean	2.82	1.45	5.75	3.00	14.03	7.00	34.19	18.09
mode	2.50	-	5.00	-	15.00	10.00	30.00	20.00
6 01	3.00	2.00	5.00	4.00	15.00	10.00	35.00	20.00
6 02	3.70	1.00	8.50	2.50	16.90	12.70	36.80	20.00
6 03	2.50	1.00	5.00	1.00	12.50	1.00	30.00	1.00
6 04	3.00	1.00	6.00	2.00	15.00	4.00	36.00	8.00
6 05	3.00	2.00	6.00	4.00	12.00	11.00	30.00	30.00
6 06	3.00	0.00	6.00	0.00	15.00	0.00	40.00	20.00
6 07	2.50	2.00	5.00	4.00	12.50	12.00	30.00	22.00
6 08	3.00	1.00	6.00	3.00	15.00	8.00	40.00	15.00
6 09	3.00	2.00	6.00	4.40	14.50	9.80	30.00	20.00
6 10	2.50	2.50	6.00	4.00	16.00	12.00	40.00	20.00
mean	2.92	1.45	5.95	2.89	14.44	8.05	34.78	17.60
mode	3.00	-	6.00	4.00	15.00	12.00	30.00	20.00
7 01	3.00	2.00	5.00	4.00	15.00	10.00	35.00	20.00
7 02	3.70	1.00	6.70	3.50	15.80	10.00	35.60	26.70
7 03	2.50	1.00	5.00	1.00	12.50	1.00	30.00	1.00
7 04	3.00	1.00	6.00	2.00	15.00	4.00	36.00	8.00
7 05	3.00	2.00	6.00	5.00	12.00	12.00	30.00	30.00
7 06	3.00	0.00	6.00	0.00	15.00	0.00	40.00	20.00
7 07	2.50	2.00	5.00	4.00	12.50	10.00	30.00	20.00
7 08	3.00	1.00	6.00	3.00	15.00	8.00	40.00	15.00
7 09	3.00	1.80	6.00	3.50	15.00	8.00	33.00	20.00
7 10	2.50	2.00	6.00	4.00	15.00	10.00	40.00	20.00
mean	2.92	1.38	5.77	3.00	14.28	7.30	34.96	18.07
mode	3.00	-	6.00	4.00	15.00	10.00	40.00	20.00
8 01	2.00	2.00	5.00	4.00	15.00	10.00	35.00	20.00
8 02	3.60	1.00	6.70	3.50	14.80	7.80	34.50	26.80
8 03	2.50	1.00	5.00	1.00	12.50	1.00	30.00	1.00
8 04	3.00	1.00	6.00	2.00	15.00	4.00	36.00	8.00
8 05	3.00	2.00	6.00	5.00	12.00	12.00	30.00	30.00
8 06	3.00	0.00	2.00	0.00	15.00	0.00	40.00	15.00
8 07	2.50	1.00	5.00	3.00	12.50	15.00	30.00	20.00
8 08	3.00	1.00	6.00	3.00	15.00	8.00	40.00	15.00
8 09	3.50	1.50	6.50	3.00	17.00	5.00	40.00	15.00
8 10	2.50	2.50	6.00	4.00	15.00	10.00	40.00	10.00
mean	2.86	1.30	5.42	2.85	14.38	7.28	35.55	16.08
mode	3.00	1.00	6.00	3.00	15.00	10.00	40.00	15.00

TABLE A (follows)

SESSION: 3

1 01	2.60	1.50	5.40	3.00	12.50	8.00	31.00	15.00
1 02	2.20	2.20	4.00	4.00	11.00	11.00	23.00	23.00
1 03	3.00	2.00	5.00	5.00	15.00	7.00	40.00	15.00
1 04	3.00	2.00	6.00	4.00	15.00	10.00	35.00	20.00
1 05	2.50	2.00	6.20	3.50	13.50	12.50	40.00	25.50
1 06	2.50	2.50	5.00	5.00	12.50	12.50	30.00	30.00
1 07	3.00	1.00	6.00	2.00	14.00	5.00	35.00	13.00
1 08	2.50	2.00	5.00	5.00	12.50	10.00	30.00	20.00
1 09	2.50	2.40	4.50	4.50	12.40	12.50	30.00	29.90
1 10	2.50	1.50	5.00	3.00	12.50	8.00	30.00	10.00
mean	2.63	1.91	5.21	3.90	13.09	9.65	32.40	20.14
mode	2.50	2.00	5.00	5.00	12.50	12.50	30.00	15.00
2 01	2.60	1.50	5.20	3.00	12.70	9.00	30.00	15.00
2 02	2.00	2.00	4.00	4.00	11.00	11.00	22.00	22.00
2 03	3.00	2.00	5.00	4.00	15.00	10.00	35.00	15.00
2 04	3.00	2.00	6.00	4.00	15.00	10.00	35.00	20.00
2 05	2.80	2.20	6.50	4.00	13.00	11.50	40.00	19.50
2 06	2.50	2.50	5.00	5.00	12.50	12.50	30.00	30.00
2 07	3.00	1.00	6.00	3.00	13.00	10.00	34.00	20.00
2 08	2.50	2.50	5.00	5.00	12.50	12.50	30.00	30.00
2 09	2.50	2.30	4.50	4.50	12.00	12.00	29.90	29.90
2 10	2.50	1.50	5.00	3.50	12.50	10.00	30.00	15.00
mean	2.64	1.95	5.22	4.00	12.92	10.85	31.59	21.64
mode	-	2.00	5.00	4.00	12.50	10.00	30.00	15.00
3 01	2.70	2.00	5.40	3.50	13.00	9.00	31.00	17.00
3 02	2.00	2.00	4.00	4.00	11.00	11.00	22.00	22.00
3 03	3.00	2.00	5.00	4.00	15.00	7.00	35.00	15.00
3 04	3.00	2.00	6.50	4.00	15.00	10.00	36.00	20.00
3 05	2.70	2.30	6.00	4.50	13.00	10.00	40.00	15.00
3 06	2.50	2.50	5.00	5.00	12.50	12.50	30.00	30.00
3 07	3.00	1.00	6.00	2.00	13.00	6.00	35.00	12.00
3 08	2.50	2.50	5.00	5.00	12.50	12.50	30.00	25.00
3 09	2.20	2.50	4.50	4.50	13.00	10.00	30.00	25.00
3 10	2.50	2.00	5.00	3.00	12.50	8.00	30.00	15.00
mean	2.61	2.08	5.24	3.95	13.05	9.60	31.90	19.60
mode	-	2.00	5.00	4.00	13.00	10.00	30.00	15.00
4 01	2.70	1.60	5.30	3.00	13.00	9.00	31.00	18.00
4 02	2.00	2.00	4.00	4.00	11.00	11.00	22.00	22.00
4 03	3.00	2.00	5.00	4.00	15.00	10.00	35.00	15.00
4 04	3.00	2.00	6.00	4.00	15.00	10.00	35.00	20.00
4 05	2.70	2.00	6.30	4.30	13.20	8.40	35.50	16.50
4 06	2.50	2.50	5.00	5.00	12.50	12.50	30.00	30.00
4 07	3.00	1.00	6.00	2.00	13.00	6.00	34.00	13.00
4 08	2.50	2.50	5.00	5.00	12.50	12.50	30.00	25.00
4 09	2.50	2.30	5.00	5.00	13.00	13.00	30.00	30.00
4 10	2.50	2.00	5.00	3.00	12.50	8.00	30.00	10.00
mean	2.64	1.99	5.26	3.93	13.07	10.04	31.25	19.95
mode	2.50	2.00	5.00	4.00	12.50	-	30.00	30.00

TABLE A (follows)

SESSION: 3

5 01	2.60	1.60	5.20	3.00	13.00	8.00	31.00	17.00
5 02	2.00	2.00	4.00	4.00	11.00	11.00	21.00	22.00
5 03	3.00	2.00	5.00	4.00	15.00	7.00	35.00	15.00
5 04	3.00	2.00	6.00	4.00	14.00	10.00	35.00	20.00
5 05	2.50	2.00	6.30	4.20	14.10	10.00	36.00	17.50
5 06	2.50	2.50	5.00	5.00	12.50	12.50	30.00	30.00
5 07	3.00	1.20	6.00	2.30	13.00	6.70	34.00	13.40
5 08	2.50	2.50	5.00	5.00	12.50	12.00	30.00	25.00
5 09	2.50	2.50	5.00	5.00	13.00	12.00	30.00	30.00
5 10	2.50	2.00	5.00	3.00	12.50	7.00	30.00	10.00
mean	2.61	2.03	5.25	3.95	13.06	9.62	31.20	19.99
mode	2.50	2.00	5.00	4.00	12.50	-	30.00	30.00
6 01	2.60	1.50	5.20	3.00	13.00	8.00	31.00	17.00
6 02	2.00	2.00	4.00	4.00	11.00	11.00	22.00	22.00
6 03	3.00	2.00	5.00	4.00	12.50	9.00	35.00	15.00
6 04	3.00	2.00	6.00	4.00	14.00	10.00	35.00	20.00
6 05	3.00	2.00	6.30	4.50	14.00	11.00	39.00	25.50
6 06	2.50	2.50	5.00	5.00	12.50	12.50	30.00	30.00
6 07	3.00	1.50	5.00	2.50	12.50	6.70	31.00	15.00
6 08	2.50	2.50	5.00	5.00	12.50	12.00	30.00	25.00
6 09	2.50	2.30	5.00	4.50	12.50	9.00	30.00	20.00
6 10	2.50	2.00	5.00	3.00	13.00	5.00	35.00	5.00
mean	2.66	2.03	5.15	3.95	12.75	9.42	31.80	19.45
mode	3.00	2.00	5.00	4.00	12.50	11.00	-	-
7 01	2.60	1.70	5.00	3.50	12.50	8.00	30.00	20.00
7 02	2.00	2.00	4.00	4.00	11.00	11.00	22.00	22.00
7 03	3.00	2.00	5.00	4.00	12.50	9.00	35.00	15.00
7 04	3.00	2.00	6.00	4.00	14.00	10.00	35.00	20.00
7 05	3.00	2.00	6.00	4.50	12.50	10.00	35.50	20.00
7 06	2.50	2.50	5.00	5.00	12.50	12.50	30.00	30.00
7 07	3.00	1.20	6.00	2.40	13.00	6.00	32.00	13.90
7 08	2.50	2.50	5.00	5.00	12.50	12.50	30.00	25.00
7 09	2.50	2.30	5.00	4.50	12.50	9.00	30.00	19.00
7 10	2.50	2.00	5.00	3.00	13.00	4.00	35.00	5.00
mean	2.66	2.02	5.20	3.99	12.60	9.20	31.45	18.99
mode	-	2.00	5.00	4.00	12.50	-	30.00	20.00
8 01	2.50	0.00	5.00	0.00	12.50	0.00	30.00	0.00
8 02	2.00	2.00	4.00	4.00	11.00	11.00	22.00	22.00
8 03	3.00	2.00	5.00	4.00	12.50	9.00	30.00	15.00
8 04	3.00	2.00	6.00	4.00	13.00	10.00	35.00	20.00
8 05	3.00	2.00	5.50	4.00	13.50	10.00	30.00	20.00
8 06	2.50	2.50	5.00	5.00	12.50	12.50	30.00	30.00
8 07	2.50	1.00	5.00	2.00	12.50	3.00	30.00	4.00
8 08	2.50	0.10	5.00	0.10	12.50	0.10	30.00	0.10
8 09	2.50	2.00	5.00	4.00	12.50	6.00	30.00	10.00
8 10	2.50	2.00	5.00	3.00	12.50	4.00	35.00	5.00
mean	2.60	1.56	5.05	3.01	12.50	6.56	30.20	12.61
mode	2.50	2.00	5.00	4.00	12.50	10.00	30.00	20.00

TABLE A (follows)

SESSION: 4

1 01	2.50	2.00	5.00	4.00	12.50	10.00	30.00	20.00
1 02	2.50	0.90	5.00	1.00	13.00	3.00	30.00	5.00
1 03	2.50	2.50	5.00	5.00	12.50	12.50	30.00	30.00
1 04	3.00	1.50	6.00	3.50	13.00	10.00	35.00	20.00
1 05	2.50	2.50	5.00	5.00	12.50	12.50	30.00	30.00
1 06	3.00	2.00	5.00	4.00	12.50	10.00	30.00	20.00
1 07	3.20	1.00	6.00	1.00	14.00	1.00	40.00	1.00
1 08	4.00	1.50	7.00	4.00	18.00	10.00	50.00	20.00
1 09	3.00	1.00	5.50	1.00	13.00	1.00	31.00	1.00
1 10	3.00	1.00	6.00	3.00	15.00	5.00	40.00	15.00
mean	2.92	1.59	5.55	3.15	13.60	7.50	34.60	16.20
mode	-	1.00	5.00	1.00	12.50	10.00	30.00	20.00
2 01	2.50	2.00	5.00	4.00	12.50	10.00	30.00	20.00
2 02	2.50	0.80	5.00	1.00	13.00	3.00	30.00	4.00
2 03	2.50	2.50	5.00	5.00	12.50	12.50	30.00	30.00
2 04	2.50	2.00	5.00	4.00	13.00	12.00	30.00	25.00
2 05	2.50	2.50	5.00	5.00	12.50	12.50	30.00	30.00
2 06	3.00	2.00	5.00	4.00	12.50	10.00	30.00	20.00
2 07	4.00	1.00	6.50	1.00	14.00	1.00	40.00	1.00
2 08	3.50	2.00	7.00	3.00	15.00	10.00	50.00	20.00
2 09	2.50	2.50	5.00	5.00	12.50	12.50	30.00	30.00
2 10	3.00	1.00	7.00	4.00	15.00	7.00	45.00	20.00
mean	2.85	1.83	5.55	3.60	13.25	9.05	34.50	20.00
mode	2.50	2.00	5.00	4.00	12.50	-	30.00	20.00
3 01	2.50	2.50	5.00	5.00	12.50	12.50	30.00	30.00
3 02	3.00	0.90	6.00	1.00	13.00	2.00	32.00	3.00
3 03	2.50	2.50	5.00	5.00	12.50	12.50	30.00	30.00
3 04	3.00	2.00	5.00	4.00	12.50	11.00	35.00	25.00
3 05	2.50	2.50	5.00	5.00	12.50	12.50	30.00	30.00
3 06	3.00	2.00	5.00	4.00	12.50	8.00	30.00	20.00
3 07	3.50	1.00	6.50	1.00	15.00	1.00	43.00	1.00
3 08	3.00	2.00	6.00	3.00	15.00	10.00	45.00	20.00
3 09	2.50	2.00	5.00	4.50	12.50	12.00	30.00	29.00
3 10	3.00	1.00	6.00	4.00	15.00	7.00	40.00	20.00
mean	2.85	1.84	5.45	3.65	13.30	8.85	34.50	20.80
mode	3.00	2.00	5.00	5.00	12.50	12.50	30.00	-
4 01	2.50	2.00	5.00	4.00	12.50	10.00	30.00	20.00
4 02	3.00	0.90	6.00	1.00	13.00	2.00	32.00	3.00
4 03	2.50	2.50	5.00	5.00	12.50	12.50	30.00	30.00
4 04	2.50	2.50	5.00	5.00	13.00	12.00	30.00	30.00
4 05	2.50	2.50	5.00	5.00	12.50	12.50	30.00	30.00
4 06	3.00	2.00	6.00	3.00	13.00	8.00	35.00	20.00
4 07	3.20	1.00	6.00	1.00	14.00	1.00	42.00	1.00
4 08	3.00	2.00	6.50	3.00	16.00	10.00	45.00	20.00
4 09	2.50	2.00	5.00	4.50	12.50	12.00	30.00	29.00
4 10	4.00	1.00	6.00	3.00	17.00	10.00	40.00	20.00
mean	2.87	1.84	5.55	3.45	13.60	9.00	34.40	20.30
mode	2.50	2.00	5.00	5.00	12.50	-	30.00	20.00

TABLE A (follows)

SESSION: 4

5 01	2.50	2.00	5.00	4.00	12.50	10.00	30.00	20.00
5 02	3.00	0.80	6.00	1.00	13.00	2.00	32.00	3.00
5 03	2.50	2.50	5.00	5.00	12.50	12.50	30.00	30.00
5 04	3.00	1.50	6.00	3.50	15.00	10.00	35.00	20.00
5 05	2.50	2.50	5.00	5.00	12.50	12.50	30.00	30.00
5 06	3.00	2.00	5.00	4.00	12.50	8.00	30.00	20.00
5 07	3.20	1.00	6.00	1.00	14.00	1.00	35.00	1.00
5 08	3.00	2.00	6.50	3.50	16.00	10.00	45.00	20.00
5 09	2.50	2.00	5.00	4.50	12.50	12.00	30.00	29.00
5 10	3.00	2.00	7.00	4.00	15.00	10.00	40.00	20.00
mean	2.82	1.83	5.65	3.55	13.55	8.80	33.70	19.30
mode	3.00	2.00	5.00	4.00	12.50	10.00	30.00	20.00
6 01	2.50	2.00	5.00	4.00	12.50	10.00	30.00	20.00
6 02	2.50	0.90	5.00	1.00	12.50	2.00	30.00	3.00
6 03	2.50	2.50	5.00	5.00	12.50	12.50	30.00	30.00
6 04	2.50	2.00	5.00	4.00	13.00	11.00	30.00	25.00
6 05	2.50	2.50	5.00	5.00	12.50	12.50	30.00	30.00
6 06	3.00	2.00	5.00	4.00	12.50	8.00	30.00	20.00
6 07	3.00	1.00	5.50	1.00	13.00	1.00	32.00	1.00
6 08	3.00	2.00	6.00	4.00	15.00	10.00	40.00	20.00
6 09	2.50	2.00	5.00	4.50	12.50	12.00	30.00	29.00
6 10	3.00	1.00	6.00	4.00	15.00	10.00	40.00	20.00
mean	2.70	1.79	5.25	3.65	13.10	8.90	32.20	19.80
mode	2.50	2.00	5.00	4.00	12.50	10.00	30.00	20.00
7 01	2.50	2.00	5.00	4.00	12.50	10.00	30.00	20.00
7 02	2.50	0.80	6.00	1.00	12.50	2.00	31.00	3.00
7 03	2.50	2.50	5.00	5.00	12.50	12.50	30.00	30.00
7 04	2.50	2.00	5.00	4.50	12.50	12.50	35.00	25.00
7 05	2.50	2.50	5.00	5.00	12.50	12.50	30.00	30.00
7 06	3.00	2.00	5.00	4.00	12.50	8.00	30.00	20.00
7 07	3.00	1.00	5.50	1.00	13.00	1.00	32.00	1.00
7 08	3.00	2.00	6.50	3.00	15.00	10.00	45.00	19.00
7 09	2.50	2.00	5.00	4.50	12.50	12.00	30.00	29.00
7 10	3.00	2.00	6.00	4.00	15.00	10.00	40.00	20.00
mean	2.70	1.88	5.40	3.60	13.05	9.05	33.30	19.70
mode	2.50	2.00	5.00	4.00	12.50	-	30.00	20.00
8 01	2.50	2.00	5.00	4.00	12.50	10.00	30.00	20.00
8 02	2.50	0.90	5.00	1.00	12.50	2.00	30.00	3.00
8 03	2.50	2.50	5.00	5.00	12.50	12.50	30.00	30.00
8 04	2.50	2.00	5.00	4.00	12.50	12.00	30.00	30.00
8 05	2.50	2.50	5.00	5.00	12.50	12.50	30.00	30.00
8 06	3.00	2.00	5.00	4.00	12.50	8.00	30.00	20.00
8 07	2.50	1.00	5.00	1.00	13.00	1.00	32.00	1.00
8 08	3.00	2.00	6.50	3.00	15.00	10.00	40.00	20.00
8 09	2.50	2.00	5.00	4.50	12.50	10.00	30.00	20.00
8 10	3.00	2.00	6.00	4.00	15.00	10.00	40.00	20.00
mean	2.65	1.89	5.25	3.55	13.05	8.80	32.20	19.40
mode	2.50	2.00	5.00	4.00	12.50	10.00	30.00	20.00

TABLE A (follows)

SESSION: 5

1 01	2.50	0.50	5.00	1.00	15.00	10.00	30.00	20.00
1 02	2.50	1.00	5.00	2.00	15.00	5.00	30.00	10.00
1 03	2.50	0.00	5.00	0.00	12.50	0.00	30.00	0.00
1 04	2.50	1.00	5.00	1.00	12.50	1.00	30.00	1.00
1 05	4.00	1.00	8.00	1.00	20.00	5.00	50.00	10.00
1 06	2.50	2.00	5.00	4.00	12.50	12.00	30.00	25.00
1 07	2.40	1.00	4.00	1.00	12.00	1.00	27.00	1.00
1 08	2.50	1.00	5.00	1.00	12.50	1.00	30.00	1.00
1 09	4.00	1.80	6.00	4.00	15.00	10.00	28.00	30.00
1 10	2.50	2.50	5.00	5.00	12.50	12.50	30.00	30.00
mean	2.79	1.18	5.30	2.00	13.95	5.75	31.50	12.80
mode	2.50	1.00	5.00	1.00	12.50	1.00	30.00	1.00
2 01	2.50	0.50	5.00	1.00	15.00	10.00	30.00	15.00
2 02	2.50	1.00	5.00	2.00	15.00	5.00	30.00	10.00
2 03	2.50	0.00	5.00	0.00	12.50	0.00	30.00	0.00
2 04	2.50	1.00	5.00	1.00	12.50	1.00	30.00	1.00
2 05	4.00	1.00	8.00	2.00	20.00	5.00	50.00	10.00
2 06	3.50	1.00	6.00	1.00	18.00	1.00	40.00	1.00
2 07	2.40	1.00	4.80	1.00	12.30	1.00	29.60	1.00
2 08	2.50	1.00	5.00	1.00	12.50	1.00	30.00	1.00
2 09	3.50	1.00	5.00	3.00	14.00	8.00	32.00	20.00
2 10	2.50	2.00	8.00	3.00	20.00	10.00	35.00	20.00
mean	2.84	0.95	5.68	1.50	15.18	4.20	33.66	7.90
mode	2.50	1.00	5.00	1.00	12.50	1.00	30.00	1.00
3 01	2.50	0.50	5.00	1.00	12.50	5.00	30.00	10.00
3 02	3.00	1.00	6.00	2.00	15.00	5.00	35.00	10.00
3 03	2.50	0.00	5.00	0.00	12.50	0.00	30.00	0.00
3 04	2.50	1.00	5.00	1.00	12.50	1.00	30.00	1.00
3 05	4.00	1.00	8.00	2.00	20.00	5.00	50.00	10.00
3 06	3.50	1.00	8.00	1.00	20.00	1.00	45.00	1.00
3 07	2.40	2.00	4.90	4.00	12.40	10.00	29.80	20.00
3 08	3.00	1.00	5.00	1.00	15.00	1.00	30.00	1.00
3 09	4.00	1.50	7.00	4.50	18.00	12.50	40.00	29.00
3 10	0.00	0.00	0.00	0.00	0.00	0.00	0.00	0.00
mean	3.04	1.00	5.99	1.83	15.32	4.50	35.53	9.11
mode	2.50	1.00	5.00	1.00	12.50	5.00	30.00	10.00
4 01	2.50	0.50	5.00	1.00	12.50	5.00	30.00	10.00
4 02	3.00	1.00	6.00	2.00	15.00	5.00	35.00	10.00
4 03	2.50	0.00	5.00	0.00	12.50	0.00	30.00	0.00
4 04	2.50	1.00	5.00	1.00	12.50	1.00	30.00	1.00
4 05	4.00	1.00	8.00	2.00	20.00	5.00	50.00	10.00
4 06	4.00	1.00	8.00	1.00	23.00	1.00	50.00	1.00
4 07	2.40	2.00	4.90	2.00	12.40	2.00	29.80	2.00
4 08	3.00	1.00	5.00	1.00	15.00	1.00	30.00	1.00
4 09	3.00	1.00	6.00	4.80	13.00	13.00	32.00	25.00
4 10	2.00	2.50	4.00	5.00	12.00	12.50	25.00	30.00
mean	2.89	1.10	5.69	1.98	14.79	4.55	34.18	9.00
mode	2.50	1.00	5.00	1.00	12.50	-	30.00	-

TABLE A (follows)

SESSION: 5

5 01	2.50	0.50	5.00	1.00	12.50	5.00	30.00	10.00
5 02	3.00	1.00	5.00	2.00	15.00	5.00	30.00	10.00
5 03	2.50	0.00	5.00	0.00	12.50	0.00	30.00	0.00
5 04	2.50	1.00	5.00	1.00	12.50	1.00	30.00	1.00
5 05	4.00	1.00	8.00	2.00	20.00	5.00	50.00	10.00
5 06	4.00	1.00	8.00	1.00	20.00	1.00	50.00	1.00
5 07	2.40	1.00	4.80	1.00	12.40	1.00	29.80	1.00
5 08	3.00	1.00	6.00	1.00	15.00	1.00	35.00	1.00
5 09	2.00	1.50	5.00	3.00	12.30	10.00	30.00	24.00
5 10	2.50	2.50	5.00	5.00	12.50	12.50	30.00	30.00
mean	2.84	1.05	5.68	1.70	14.47	4.15	34.48	8.80
mode	2.50	1.00	5.00	1.00	12.50	1.00	30.00	1.00
6 01	2.50	0.50	5.00	1.00	12.50	5.00	30.00	10.00
6 02	2.50	1.00	5.00	2.00	12.50	5.00	30.00	10.00
6 03	2.50	0.00	5.00	0.00	12.50	0.00	30.00	0.00
6 04	2.50	1.00	5.00	1.00	12.50	1.00	30.00	1.00
6 05	4.00	1.00	8.00	2.00	20.00	5.00	50.00	10.00
6 06	4.00	1.00	8.00	1.00	23.00	1.00	50.00	1.00
6 07	2.40	1.00	4.90	1.00	12.40	1.00	29.60	1.00
6 08	3.00	1.00	6.00	1.00	15.00	1.00	35.00	1.00
6 09	1.70	1.00	4.90	4.00	12.00	13.50	27.00	27.00
6 10	2.50	2.50	5.00	5.00	12.50	12.50	30.00	30.00
mean	2.76	1.00	5.68	1.80	14.49	4.50	34.16	9.10
mode	2.50	1.00	5.00	1.00	12.50	1.00	30.00	1.00
7 01	2.50	0.50	5.00	1.00	12.50	5.00	30.00	10.00
7 02	2.50	1.00	5.00	2.00	12.50	5.00	30.00	10.00
7 03	2.50	0.00	5.00	0.00	12.50	0.00	30.00	0.00
7 04	2.50	1.00	5.00	1.00	12.50	1.00	30.00	1.00
7 05	4.00	1.00	8.00	2.00	20.00	5.00	50.00	10.00
7 06	4.00	1.00	8.00	1.00	23.00	1.00	50.00	1.00
7 07	2.40	1.00	4.90	1.00	12.40	1.00	29.90	1.00
7 08	3.00	1.00	5.00	1.00	15.00	1.00	30.00	1.00
7 09	3.00	2.00	6.00	6.00	14.00	14.00	31.00	32.00
7 10	2.50	2.50	5.00	5.00	12.50	12.50	30.00	30.00
mean	2.89	1.10	5.69	2.00	14.69	4.55	34.09	9.60
mode	2.50	1.00	5.00	1.00	12.50	1.00	30.00	1.00
8 01	2.50	0.50	5.00	1.00	12.50	5.00	30.00	10.00
8 02	2.50	1.00	5.00	2.00	12.50	5.00	30.00	10.00
8 03	2.50	0.00	5.00	0.00	12.50	0.00	30.00	0.00
8 04	2.50	1.00	5.00	1.00	12.50	1.00	30.00	1.00
8 05	4.00	1.00	8.00	2.00	20.00	5.00	50.00	10.00
8 06	4.00	1.00	8.00	1.00	23.00	1.00	50.00	1.00
8 07	2.40	1.00	4.90	1.00	12.40	1.00	29.90	1.00
8 08	3.00	1.00	5.00	1.00	12.50	1.00	30.00	1.00
8 09	2.70	1.00	5.80	3.00	12.80	10.00	31.90	25.00
8 10	2.50	2.50	5.00	5.00	12.50	12.50	30.00	30.00
mean	2.86	1.00	5.67	1.70	14.32	4.15	34.18	8.90
mode	2.50	1.00	5.00	1.00	12.50	1.00	30.00	1.00

TABLE B: RESERVATION PROPOSALS (RP) AND RESPONSES (RR) PER PERSON (pe), ROUND (r) AND CAKE SIZE; MEAN AND MODE VALUES OF RP AND RR ACROSS PERSONS (ALL FOR VARIANT 2)

SESSION: 1

Cake Size	5		10		25		60	
r pe	RP	RR	RP	RR	RP	RR	RP	RR
1 01	3.00	2.00	6.00	3.00	15.00	8.00	40.00	20.00
1 02	2.00	2.00	4.00	3.00	10.00	10.00	25.00	20.00
1 03	2.50	1.00	5.00	1.00	12.50	1.00	30.00	1.00
1 04	2.50	1.00	5.00	3.00	12.50	5.00	35.00	10.00
1 05	2.50	1.50	5.00	4.00	16.00	15.00	25.00	20.00
1 06	2.00	2.00	4.00	4.00	13.00	8.00	20.00	15.00
1 07	2.50	2.00	5.00	4.50	12.50	11.00	30.00	25.00
1 08	3.00	1.50	6.50	3.00	15.00	8.00	40.00	15.00
1 09	2.50	1.00	5.00	4.00	12.50	10.00	30.00	15.00
1 10	2.00	1.50	4.50	3.50	12.00	10.00	20.00	20.00
mean	2.45	1.55	5.00	3.30	13.10	8.60	29.50	16.10
mode	2.50	2.00	5.00	3.00	12.50	-	-	20.00
2 01	3.00	2.00	6.00	3.00	15.00	8.00	40.00	15.00
2 02	2.00	2.00	4.00	4.00	10.00	8.00	25.00	20.00
2 03	2.50	1.00	5.00	1.00	12.50	1.00	30.00	1.00
2 04	2.50	1.00	5.50	3.00	13.00	6.00	35.00	15.00
2 05	2.50	2.00	4.00	3.00	17.00	10.00	30.00	20.00
2 06	2.50	1.90	5.50	3.00	13.00	9.00	33.00	15.00
2 07	2.50	2.00	5.00	4.50	12.50	11.00	30.00	25.00
2 08	3.00	1.50	6.50	3.50	15.00	8.00	40.00	15.00
2 09	2.50	1.00	5.00	2.00	12.50	10.00	30.00	20.00
2 10	2.00	2.00	4.00	4.00	11.00	11.00	20.00	20.00
mean	2.50	1.64	5.05	3.10	13.15	8.20	31.30	16.60
mode	2.50	2.00	4.00	3.00	12.50	8.00	30.00	15.00
3 01	3.00	2.00	6.00	3.00	14.00	8.00	35.00	15.00
3 02	2.00	2.00	4.00	4.00	10.00	10.00	25.00	20.00
3 03	2.50	1.00	5.00	1.00	12.50	1.00	30.00	1.00
3 04	2.50	1.00	5.50	2.50	13.00	7.50	35.00	15.00
3 05	2.50	2.00	5.00	4.00	17.00	16.00	30.00	25.00
3 06	2.50	1.90	5.50	3.50	13.00	9.50	33.00	20.00
3 07	2.50	2.00	5.00	4.50	12.50	10.00	30.00	25.00
3 08	3.00	1.50	6.50	3.00	15.00	8.00	40.00	15.00
3 09	2.50	1.00	5.00	2.00	12.50	10.00	30.00	20.00
3 10	2.00	2.00	4.00	4.00	11.00	11.00	20.00	20.00
mean	2.50	1.64	5.15	3.15	13.05	9.10	30.80	17.60
mode	2.50	2.00	5.00	4.00	12.50	10.00	30.00	20.00
4 01	2.50	2.00	6.00	3.00	14.00	8.00	35.00	15.00
4 02	2.00	2.00	4.00	4.00	10.00	10.00	25.00	20.00
4 03	2.50	1.00	5.00	1.00	12.50	1.00	30.00	1.00
4 04	2.50	1.00	5.50	3.00	13.00	8.00	35.00	15.00
4 05	2.50	2.50	5.00	5.00	17.00	17.00	30.00	30.00
4 06	2.50	2.00	4.50	4.00	13.00	9.50	33.00	20.00
4 07	2.50	2.00	5.00	4.00	12.50	10.50	30.00	20.00
4 08	3.50	1.50	6.50	3.00	14.00	8.00	35.00	15.00
4 09	2.50	1.00	5.00	2.00	12.50	10.00	30.00	20.00
4 10	2.00	1.00	4.00	3.50	11.00	10.00	20.00	20.00
mean	2.50	1.60	5.05	3.25	12.95	9.20	30.30	17.60
mode	2.50	-	5.00	3.00	-	8.00	30.30	20.00

TABLE B (follows)

SESSION: 1

5 01	2.50	2.00	5.00	3.00	13.00	8.00	30.00	15.00
5 02	2.00	2.00	4.00	4.00	10.00	10.00	25.00	20.00
5 03	2.50	1.00	5.00	1.00	12.50	1.00	30.00	1.00
5 04	2.50	1.00	5.50	3.00	13.00	8.00	32.50	15.00
5 05	2.50	2.50	3.00	6.00	12.00	17.00	30.00	30.00
5 06	2.50	2.00	5.00	3.50	13.00	10.00	35.00	20.00
5 07	2.50	2.00	5.00	4.00	12.50	10.00	30.00	22.00
5 08	3.00	1.50	6.50	3.00	15.00	8.00	35.00	15.00
5 09	2.50	1.00	5.00	2.00	12.50	10.00	30.00	20.00
5 10	2.00	1.50	4.00	3.50	11.00	10.00	25.00	20.00
mean	2.45	1.65	4.80	3.30	12.45	9.20	30.25	17.80
mode	2.50	2.00	5.00	3.00	-	10.00	30.00	20.00
6 01	2.50	2.00	5.00	3.00	13.00	7.00	35.00	15.00
6 02	2.00	2.00	4.00	4.00	10.00	10.00	25.00	20.00
6 03	2.50	1.00	5.00	1.00	12.50	1.00	30.00	1.00
6 04	2.50	1.00	5.00	3.00	13.00	8.00	32.00	16.00
6 05	2.50	2.50	5.00	5.00	16.00	16.00	30.00	25.00
6 06	2.50	2.00	4.00	3.50	13.00	8.00	33.00	20.00
6 07	2.50	2.00	5.00	4.50	13.50	10.00	32.50	20.00
6 08	3.00	1.50	6.50	3.00	15.00	8.00	35.00	15.00
6 09	2.50	1.00	5.00	2.00	12.50	10.00	30.00	20.00
6 10	2.00	1.50	4.00	3.50	11.00	10.00	25.00	20.00
mean	2.45	1.65	4.85	3.25	12.95	8.80	30.75	17.20
mode	2.50	2.00	5.00	3.00	13.00	10.00	30.00	20.00
7 01	3.00	2.00	5.00	3.00	13.00	7.00	35.00	15.00
7 02	2.00	2.00	4.00	4.00	10.00	10.00	25.00	20.00
7 03	2.50	1.00	5.00	1.00	12.50	1.00	30.00	1.00
7 04	2.50	1.50	5.00	2.50	13.00	6.50	32.00	17.00
7 05	2.50	2.50	5.00	5.00	17.00	16.00	30.00	30.00
7 06	2.50	2.00	5.00	3.50	13.00	8.00	35.00	20.00
7 07	2.50	2.00	5.00	4.50	12.50	10.00	30.00	20.00
7 08	3.00	1.50	6.50	3.00	15.00	8.00	35.00	15.00
7 09	2.50	1.00	5.00	2.00	12.50	10.00	30.00	20.00
7 10	2.00	1.50	4.50	3.50	11.00	10.00	25.00	20.00
mean	2.50	1.70	5.00	3.20	12.95	8.65	30.70	17.80
mode	2.50	2.00	5.00	-	-	10.00	30.00	20.00
8 01	2.50	2.00	5.00	3.00	13.00	5.00	35.00	10.00
8 02	2.00	2.00	4.00	4.00	10.00	10.00	25.00	20.00
8 03	2.50	1.00	5.00	1.00	12.50	1.00	30.00	1.00
8 04	2.50	1.00	5.00	3.00	13.00	6.00	32.00	15.00
8 05	2.50	2.50	5.00	5.00	17.00	17.00	30.00	30.00
8 06	2.50	2.00	5.00	3.50	15.00	8.00	35.00	20.00
8 07	2.50	2.00	5.00	4.50	14.00	10.00	32.00	20.00
8 08	3.00	1.50	6.50	3.00	15.00	8.00	35.00	15.00
8 09	2.50	1.00	5.00	2.00	12.50	10.00	30.00	20.00
8 10	2.00	1.50	4.50	3.50	11.00	10.00	25.00	20.00
mean	2.45	1.65	5.00	3.25	13.30	8.50	30.90	17.10
mode	2.50	2.00	5.00	3.00	-	10.00	-	20.00

TABLE B (follows)

SESSION: 2

1 01	3.00	1.50	6.00	3.00	15.00	8.00	35.00	20.00
1 02	2.50	1.50	5.00	3.00	12.50	8.00	30.00	10.00
1 03	2.50	0.00	5.00	0.00	12.50	0.00	30.00	0.00
1 04	2.10	1.80	5.60	2.70	17.00	10.00	41.00	23.00
1 05	2.50	0.10	5.00	0.10	12.50	0.10	30.00	0.10
1 06	2.50	1.00	5.00	2.00	12.50	5.00	30.00	10.00
1 07	2.50	2.00	5.00	4.00	12.50	10.00	30.00	25.00
1 08	2.50	2.00	5.00	3.00	12.50	8.00	30.00	15.00
1 09	3.00	0.00	6.00	0.00	15.00	0.00	32.00	0.00
1 10	2.50	2.50	5.00	5.00	12.50	12.50	30.00	30.00
mean	2.56	1.24	5.26	2.28	13.45	6.16	31.80	13.31
mode	2.50	-	5.00	3.00	12.50	-	30.00	-
2 01	3.00	1.00	6.50	2.00	17.00	5.00	40.00	5.00
2 02	2.50	1.00	5.00	2.00	12.50	5.00	30.00	5.00
2 03	3.50	0.00	7.00	0.00	15.00	0.00	40.00	0.00
2 04	2.70	1.00	6.00	4.00	16.00	8.00	46.00	28.00
2 05	2.50	0.10	5.00	0.10	12.50	0.10	30.00	0.10
2 06	2.50	1.00	5.00	2.00	12.50	5.00	30.00	10.00
2 07	2.50	2.50	5.00	5.00	12.50	12.50	30.00	25.00
2 08	2.50	1.50	5.00	3.00	12.50	8.00	30.00	15.00
2 09	3.00	0.00	7.00	0.00	13.00	0.00	33.00	0.00
2 10	2.50	2.50	5.00	5.00	12.50	25.00	30.00	30.00
mean	2.72	1.06	5.65	2.31	13.60	6.86	33.90	11.81
mode	2.50	1.00	5.00	2.00	12.50	5.00	30.00	5.00
3 01	3.00	0.50	6.50	2.00	15.00	5.00	35.00	8.00
3 02	2.50	2.00	6.00	3.00	14.00	8.00	35.00	15.00
3 03	3.50	0.00	7.00	0.00	18.00	0.00	45.00	0.00
3 04	4.50	1.00	8.00	2.50	18.00	6.00	49.00	27.00
3 05	2.50	0.10	5.00	0.10	12.50	0.10	30.00	0.10
3 06	3.00	1.00	5.50	2.00	13.00	5.00	35.00	10.00
3 07	2.50	2.50	5.00	5.00	12.50	12.50	30.00	25.00
3 08	2.50	2.00	5.00	3.00	12.50	8.00	30.00	10.00
3 09	3.50	0.00	7.00	0.00	14.00	0.00	35.00	0.00
3 10	4.00	1.00	6.00	2.00	20.00	5.00	50.00	10.00
mean	3.15	1.01	6.10	1.96	14.95	4.96	37.40	10.51
mode	2.50	1.00	5.00	2.00	12.50	-	35.00	10.00
4 01	3.00	0.50	7.00	1.00	15.00	5.00	40.00	5.00
4 02	3.00	1.50	6.00	3.00	15.00	8.00	35.00	15.00
4 03	3.50	0.00	7.00	0.00	18.00	0.00	45.00	0.00
4 04	4.70	0.30	8.00	2.00	21.00	10.00	46.00	36.00
4 05	2.50	0.10	5.00	0.10	12.50	0.10	30.00	0.10
4 06	3.00	1.00	6.00	2.00	13.00	5.00	35.00	10.00
4 07	2.50	2.50	5.00	5.00	12.50	12.50	30.00	20.00
4 08	2.50	2.00	5.00	3.00	12.50	8.00	30.00	15.00
4 09	3.00	1.00	7.00	2.00	15.00	5.00	35.00	15.00
4 10	4.00	1.00	7.00	3.00	20.00	5.00	50.00	10.00
mean	3.17	0.99	6.30	2.11	15.45	5.86	37.60	12.61
mode	3.00	1.00	7.00	2.00	15.00	5.00	-	15.00

TABLE B (follows)

SESSION: 2

5 01	3.00	0.50	6.00	2.00	15.00	3.00	40.00	5.00
5 02	3.00	1.50	6.00	3.00	15.00	7.00	35.00	15.00
5 03	3.50	0.00	7.00	0.00	18.00	0.00	45.00	0.00
5 04	4.20	0.70	7.20	3.00	15.20	10.00	46.20	30.00
5 05	2.50	0.10	5.00	0.10	12.50	0.10	30.00	0.10
5 06	3.00	1.50	6.00	2.50	13.00	5.00	35.00	10.00
5 07	2.50	2.00	5.00	4.00	12.50	12.00	30.00	25.00
5 08	2.50	2.00	5.00	3.00	12.50	8.00	30.00	15.00
5 09	3.00	1.00	7.00	2.00	15.00	5.00	35.00	15.00
5 10	4.00	1.00	8.00	3.00	20.00	5.00	50.00	15.00
mean	3.12	1.03	6.22	2.26	14.87	5.51	37.62	13.01
mode	3.00	-	-	3.00	-	5.00	-	15.00

6 01	3.00	0.50	6.50	1.00	15.00	2.00	40.00	3.00
6 02	3.00	1.50	6.00	3.00	12.50	7.00	30.00	15.00
6 03	3.50	0.00	7.00	0.00	15.00	0.00	35.00	0.00
6 04	4.30	1.00	7.00	4.00	15.00	7.00	45.00	36.00
6 05	2.50	0.10	5.00	0.10	12.50	0.10	30.00	0.10
6 06	3.00	2.00	7.00	4.00	15.00	10.00	40.00	15.00
6 07	2.50	2.00	5.00	4.00	12.50	10.00	30.00	20.00
6 08	2.50	2.00	5.00	3.00	12.50	5.00	30.00	10.00
6 09	3.00	0.00	6.00	0.00	15.00	0.00	35.00	0.00
6 10	4.00	1.00	6.00	3.00	18.00	5.00	50.00	10.00
mean	3.13	1.01	6.05	2.21	14.30	4.61	36.50	10.91
mode	3.00	2.00	-	4.00	15.00	-	30.00	-

7 01	3.00	0.50	6.50	1.00	15.00	2.00	40.00	2.00
7 02	3.00	1.50	6.00	3.00	12.50	7.00	35.00	15.00
7 03	3.50	0.00	7.00	0.00	15.00	0.00	40.00	0.00
7 04	3.90	0.60	6.20	4.00	20.00	13.00	50.00	27.00
7 05	3.00	0.10	5.00	0.10	13.00	0.10	30.00	0.10
7 06	3.00	2.00	6.00	3.00	15.00	8.00	40.00	20.00
7 07	2.50	2.00	5.00	4.00	12.50	10.00	30.00	20.00
7 08	2.50	2.00	5.00	3.00	12.50	5.00	30.00	9.50
7 09	3.00	1.00	6.00	2.00	15.00	5.00	35.00	15.00
7 10	4.00	1.00	7.00	3.00	17.00	5.00	40.00	10.00
mean	3.14	1.07	5.97	2.31	14.75	5.51	37.00	11.86
mode	3.00	2.00	6.00	3.00	15.00	5.00	40.00	-

8 01	3.00	0.50	6.00	1.00	15.00	2.00	35.00	2.00
8 02	3.00	1.50	6.00	3.00	12.50	7.00	35.00	15.00
8 03	3.00	0.00	6.00	0.00	15.00	0.00	35.00	0.00
8 04	4.40	0.50	6.00	4.00	19.00	8.00	50.00	28.00
8 05	3.00	0.10	5.00	0.10	13.00	0.10	30.00	0.10
8 06	3.00	2.00	6.00	3.00	15.00	10.00	40.00	20.00
8 07	2.50	2.00	5.00	4.00	12.50	10.00	30.00	20.00
8 08	3.00	2.00	6.00	3.00	14.00	7.00	33.00	12.00
8 09	3.00	0.00	7.00	0.00	15.00	0.00	35.00	0.00
8 10	4.00	0.00	8.00	0.00	20.00	0.00	50.00	0.00
mean	3.19	0.86	6.10	1.81	15.10	4.41	37.30	9.71
mode	3.00	-	6.00	-	15.00	-	35.00	-

TABLE B (follows)

SESSION: 3

1 01	2.50	2.00	6.00	4.00	15.00	13.00	35.00	25.00
1 02	3.00	0.10	6.00	0.10	15.00	0.10	40.00	0.10
1 03	2.50	1.00	5.00	1.00	12.50	1.00	30.00	1.00
1 04	3.00	1.80	6.20	4.00	13.80	11.00	34.80	24.20
1 05	2.50	2.00	5.00	5.00	12.50	12.00	30.00	25.00
1 06	3.00	1.90	5.90	3.90	13.90	9.90	34.00	22.90
1 07	2.50	2.00	5.00	4.00	12.50	10.00	30.00	23.00
1 08	3.00	1.00	6.80	2.30	13.70	7.00	34.60	12.50
1 09	2.50	1.50	5.00	4.00	12.50	11.00	30.00	25.00
1 10	2.50	1.00	5.00	1.00	13.00	5.00	30.00	5.00
mean	2.70	1.43	5.59	2.93	13.44	8.00	32.84	16.37
mode	2.50	1.00	5.00	4.00	12.50	11.00	30.00	25.00
2 01	2.50	2.00	5.00	4.00	15.00	13.00	35.00	25.00
2 02	3.00	0.00	6.00	0.00	15.00	0.00	40.00	0.00
2 03	2.50	1.00	5.00	1.00	12.50	1.00	30.00	1.00
2 04	3.20	1.00	7.00	2.00	15.00	5.00	38.00	12.00
2 05	2.50	2.00	5.00	5.00	12.50	12.00	30.00	25.00
2 06	3.00	1.90	6.00	3.90	13.90	9.90	34.90	20.00
2 07	2.50	2.00	5.00	4.00	12.50	10.00	30.00	23.00
2 08	2.90	1.00	5.60	2.00	13.80	3.90	34.90	9.90
2 09	2.50	1.50	5.00	3.50	12.50	8.00	30.00	20.00
2 10	3.00	2.00	5.00	5.00	13.00	5.00	30.00	10.00
mean	2.76	1.44	5.46	3.04	13.57	6.78	33.28	14.59
mode	2.50	2.00	5.00	-	12.50	5.00	30.00	-
3 01	2.10	2.00	4.50	4.00	13.00	12.00	28.00	25.00
3 02	3.00	0.00	6.00	0.00	15.00	0.00	40.00	0.00
3 03	2.50	1.00	5.00	1.00	12.50	1.00	30.00	1.00
3 04	3.40	1.00	7.00	2.00	15.00	5.00	38.00	12.00
3 05	2.50	2.00	5.00	5.00	12.50	12.00	30.00	25.00
3 06	3.00	0.00	6.00	0.00	13.90	0.00	34.90	0.00
3 07	2.50	2.00	5.00	4.00	12.50	10.00	30.00	23.00
3 08	2.90	1.00	5.90	1.90	13.90	5.90	34.90	6.90
3 09	2.50	1.00	5.00	2.50	12.50	7.00	30.00	17.50
3 10	2.50	1.00	5.00	3.00	12.50	5.00	30.00	10.00
mean	2.69	1.10	5.44	2.34	13.33	5.79	32.58	12.04
mode	2.50	1.00	5.00	-	12.50	-	30.00	25.00
4 01	2.30	2.00	6.00	4.00	13.00	12.00	35.00	28.00
4 02	3.00	0.00	6.00	0.00	15.00	0.00	40.00	0.00
4 03	2.50	1.00	5.00	1.00	12.50	1.00	30.00	1.00
4 04	3.20	1.00	7.00	1.00	14.30	1.00	37.00	1.00
4 05	2.50	2.00	5.00	5.00	12.50	12.00	30.00	25.00
4 06	3.00	0.00	6.00	0.00	13.90	0.00	34.90	0.00
4 07	2.50	2.00	5.00	4.00	12.50	10.00	30.00	23.00
4 08	2.90	1.00	5.60	1.80	12.50	3.90	30.00	5.00
4 09	2.50	1.00	5.00	3.00	12.50	5.00	30.00	10.00
4 10	2.50	1.50	5.00	3.00	12.50	9.00	30.00	15.00
mean	2.69	1.15	5.56	2.28	13.12	5.39	32.69	10.80
mode	2.50	1.00	5.00	-	12.50	-	30.00	-

TABLE B (follows)

SESSION: 3

5 01	2.20	2.00	4.00	4.00	12.20	11.00	25.00	25.00
5 02	3.00	0.00	6.00	0.00	15.00	0.00	40.00	0.00
5 03	2.50	1.00	5.00	1.00	12.50	1.00	30.00	1.00
5 04	3.00	1.00	6.00	1.00	14.00	1.00	37.00	1.00
5 05	2.50	2.00	5.00	5.00	12.50	12.00	30.00	25.00
5 06	3.00	0.00	6.00	0.00	12.90	0.00	34.90	0.00
5 07	2.50	2.00	5.00	4.00	12.50	10.00	30.00	23.00
5 08	2.90	1.00	5.00	2.00	12.50	2.00	33.00	4.00
5 09	2.50	1.00	5.00	2.00	12.50	5.00	30.00	11.00
5 10	2.50	1.50	5.00	3.00	12.50	5.00	30.00	15.00
mean	2.66	1.15	5.20	2.20	12.91	4.70	31.99	10.50
mode	2.50	1.00	5.00	-	12.50	-	30.00	-
6 01	2.20	2.00	4.00	4.00	12.20	12.20	25.00	25.00
6 02	4.00	0.00	7.00	0.00	15.00	0.00	40.00	0.00
6 03	2.50	1.00	5.00	1.00	12.50	1.00	30.00	1.00
6 04	3.00	1.00	7.00	1.00	15.00	1.00	40.00	1.00
6 05	2.50	2.00	5.00	5.00	12.50	12.00	30.00	25.00
6 06	3.00	0.00	6.00	0.00	14.90	0.00	34.90	0.00
6 07	2.50	2.00	5.00	4.00	12.50	10.00	30.00	23.00
6 08	2.90	1.00	5.00	2.00	12.50	2.00	30.00	3.00
6 09	2.50	1.00	5.00	1.00	12.50	1.00	30.00	1.00
6 10	2.50	1.50	5.00	3.00	12.50	5.00	30.00	10.00
mean	2.76	1.15	5.40	2.10	13.21	4.42	31.99	8.90
mode	2.50	1.00	5.00	1.00	12.50	1.00	30.00	1.00
7 01	2.50	2.50	5.00	5.00	12.50	13.00	30.00	30.00
7 02	3.00	0.00	6.00	0.00	15.00	0.00	40.00	0.00
7 03	2.50	1.00	5.00	1.00	12.50	1.00	30.00	1.00
7 04	3.00	1.00	7.00	2.00	15.00	5.00	39.80	10.00
7 05	2.50	2.00	5.00	5.00	12.50	12.00	30.00	25.00
7 06	3.00	0.00	6.00	0.00	14.90	0.00	34.90	0.00
7 07	2.50	2.00	5.00	4.00	12.50	10.00	30.00	23.00
7 08	3.00	1.00	5.00	2.00	12.50	3.00	30.00	5.00
7 09	2.50	1.00	5.00	1.00	12.50	1.00	30.00	1.00
7 10	2.50	2.50	5.00	5.00	12.50	9.00	30.00	14.00
mean	2.70	1.30	5.40	2.50	13.24	5.40	32.47	10.90
mode	2.50	1.00	5.00	-	12.50	-	30.00	-
8 01	2.20	2.20	4.00	4.50	12.00	12.00	25.00	26.00
8 02	3.00	0.00	6.00	0.00	15.00	0.00	40.00	0.00
8 03	4.00	1.00	8.00	1.00	23.00	1.00	58.00	1.00
8 04	3.00	1.00	6.90	2.00	15.00	5.00	40.00	10.00
8 05	2.50	2.00	5.00	5.00	12.50	12.00	30.00	25.00
8 06	3.00	0.00	6.00	0.00	14.90	0.00	34.90	0.00
8 07	2.50	2.00	5.00	4.00	10.00	10.00	30.00	23.00
8 08	2.50	0.00	5.90	0.00	12.50	0.00	30.00	0.00
8 09	3.00	1.00	6.00	1.00	15.00	1.00	40.00	1.00
8 10	2.50	1.00	5.00	2.00	12.50	5.00	30.00	10.00
mean	2.82	1.02	5.78	1.95	14.24	4.60	35.79	9.60
mode	-	1.00	-	0.00	-	0.00	30.00	0.00

TABLE B (follows)

SESSION: 4

1 01	2.50	2.00	6.00	3.00	15.00	7.00	40.00	15.00
1 02	3.00	1.80	5.50	4.00	13.00	9.50	30.00	21.00
1 03	3.00	2.00	6.00	4.00	14.00	10.00	30.00	25.00
1 04	2.50	1.00	5.00	3.00	13.00	5.00	30.00	10.00
1 05	2.50	2.00	5.50	3.50	13.00	10.00	30.00	15.00
1 06	3.00	2.00	5.50	4.50	12.50	10.00	35.00	25.00
1 07	2.50	2.00	5.00	5.00	12.50	10.00	30.00	20.00
1 08	2.50	2.00	5.00	3.00	12.50	10.00	30.00	20.00
1 09	2.50	1.00	5.00	1.00	12.00	1.00	30.00	1.00
1 10	3.00	1.50	5.00	4.00	15.00	10.00	30.00	25.00
mean	2.70	1.73	5.35	3.50	13.25	8.25	31.50	17.70
mode	2.50	2.00	5.00	-	-	10.00	30.00	25.00
2 01	2.50	2.00	7.00	4.50	15.00	9.00	42.50	15.00
2 02	3.00	1.80	5.50	4.00	13.00	10.00	30.00	21.00
2 03	3.00	3.00	5.00	4.00	13.00	10.00	30.00	28.00
2 04	2.50	1.00	5.00	1.00	13.00	1.00	30.00	1.00
2 05	3.00	2.00	5.00	4.00	13.00	10.00	30.00	20.00
2 06	3.00	2.00	6.00	4.00	12.50	10.00	35.00	20.00
2 07	2.50	2.00	5.00	5.00	12.50	10.00	30.00	20.00
2 08	2.50	2.00	5.00	3.00	12.50	12.00	30.00	15.00
2 09	2.50	1.00	5.00	1.00	12.50	1.00	30.00	1.00
2 10	2.50	2.00	5.00	3.00	15.00	11.00	35.00	20.00
mean	2.70	1.88	5.35	3.35	13.20	8.40	32.25	16.10
mode	2.50	2.00	5.00	4.00	-	10.00	30.00	20.00
3 01	2.70	2.00	6.00	3.00	17.00	10.00	45.00	16.00
3 02	3.00	1.50	5.50	3.00	13.00	10.00	30.00	20.00
3 03	3.00	2.00	5.00	4.00	13.00	12.00	31.50	29.00
3 04	2.50	1.00	5.00	1.00	13.00	1.00	30.00	1.00
3 05	2.50	2.00	5.00	4.00	14.00	10.00	35.00	15.00
3 06	3.00	2.00	6.00	4.00	15.00	10.00	40.00	20.00
3 07	2.50	2.00	5.00	5.00	12.50	10.00	30.00	20.00
3 08	2.50	2.00	5.00	3.00	12.50	12.50	30.00	15.00
3 09	2.50	1.00	6.00	1.00	13.00	1.00	30.00	1.00
3 10	3.00	1.50	6.00	3.50	15.00	10.00	30.00	22.50
mean	2.72	1.70	5.45	3.15	13.80	8.65	33.15	15.95
mode	2.50	2.00	5.00	3.00	13.00	10.00	30.00	20.00
4 01	2.00	1.00	6.00	2.50	15.00	7.00	42.50	12.50
4 02	3.00	1.50	5.50	4.00	13.00	10.00	32.00	20.00
4 03	3.00	1.00	5.00	1.00	13.00	1.00	30.00	1.00
4 04	2.50	1.00	5.00	1.00	13.00	1.00	30.00	1.00
4 05	2.50	2.00	5.50	4.00	13.00	10.00	30.00	17.00
4 06	3.00	2.00	6.00	4.00	15.00	10.00	40.00	20.00
4 07	2.50	2.00	5.00	5.00	12.50	10.00	30.00	20.00
4 08	2.50	2.00	5.00	3.00	12.50	10.00	30.00	20.00
4 09	3.00	1.00	6.00	1.00	13.00	1.00	30.00	1.00
4 10	2.50	1.50	5.00	3.00	13.00	8.00	30.00	20.00
mean	2.65	1.50	5.40	2.85	13.30	6.80	32.45	13.25
mode	2.50	-	5.00	1.00	13.00	10.00	30.00	20.00

TABLE B (follows)

SESSION: 4

5 01	2.70	1.00	6.00	2.00	13.00	7.50	33.00	15.00
5 02	3.00	1.50	5.50	4.00	13.00	10.00	30.00	22.00
5 03	3.00	1.00	6.00	1.00	13.00	1.00	30.00	1.00
5 04	2.50	1.00	5.00	1.00	13.00	1.00	30.00	1.00
5 05	3.00	2.00	5.00	4.00	12.50	10.00	35.00	20.00
5 06	3.00	2.00	6.00	4.00	15.00	10.00	40.00	15.00
5 07	2.50	1.00	5.00	1.00	12.50	1.00	30.00	1.00
5 08	2.50	2.00	5.00	3.00	12.50	10.00	30.00	18.90
5 09	3.00	1.00	6.00	1.00	13.00	1.00	30.00	1.00
5 10	3.00	1.50	7.00	3.00	13.00	10.00	30.00	20.00
mean	2.82	1.40	5.65	2.40	13.05	6.15	31.80	11.49
mode	3.00	1.00	5.00	1.00	13.00	10.00	30.00	1.00
6 01	2.50	1.00	6.00	2.00	12.50	5.00	33.80	8.00
6 02	3.00	1.50	5.50	4.00	13.00	10.00	30.00	19.00
6 03	3.00	1.00	5.00	1.00	13.00	1.00	30.00	1.00
6 04	2.50	1.00	5.00	1.00	13.00	1.00	30.00	1.00
6 05	3.50	2.00	5.00	4.00	12.50	10.00	35.00	20.00
6 06	3.00	2.00	6.00	4.00	15.00	10.00	40.00	15.00
6 07	2.50	1.00	5.00	1.00	12.50	1.00	30.00	1.00
6 08	2.50	2.00	5.00	3.00	12.50	10.00	30.00	20.00
6 09	3.00	1.00	6.00	1.00	13.00	1.00	30.00	1.00
6 10	3.00	1.00	5.00	2.50	13.00	8.00	30.00	15.00
mean	2.85	1.35	5.35	2.35	13.00	5.70	31.88	10.10
mode	3.00	1.00	5.00	1.00	13.00	10.00	30.00	1.00
7 01	2.50	1.00	6.00	2.00	13.00	3.00	35.00	5.00
7 02	3.00	1.50	5.50	3.00	13.00	8.00	31.00	15.00
7 03	3.00	1.00	5.00	1.00	13.00	1.00	31.00	1.00
7 04	2.50	1.00	5.00	1.00	13.00	1.00	32.00	1.00
7 05	2.50	2.00	5.00	4.00	12.50	10.00	30.00	22.00
7 06	3.00	2.00	6.00	4.00	15.00	10.00	40.00	15.00
7 07	2.50	1.00	5.00	1.00	12.50	1.00	30.00	1.00
7 08	2.50	2.00	5.00	3.00	12.50	10.00	30.00	20.00
7 09	3.00	1.00	6.00	1.00	13.00	1.00	30.00	1.00
7 10	2.50	1.00	6.00	2.00	14.00	5.00	30.00	15.00
mean	2.70	1.35	5.45	2.20	13.15	5.00	31.90	9.60
mode	2.50	1.00	5.00	1.00	13.00	1.00	30.00	1.00
8 01	2.50	1.00	6.00	1.00	14.00	3.00	40.00	3.00
8 02	3.00	1.50	5.50	3.00	13.00	8.00	31.00	15.00
8 03	3.00	1.00	6.00	1.00	13.00	1.00	32.00	1.00
8 04	2.50	1.00	5.00	1.00	13.00	1.00	32.00	1.00
8 05	2.50	2.00	5.00	3.50	12.50	10.00	30.00	22.00
8 06	3.00	2.00	6.00	4.00	15.00	10.00	40.00	15.00
8 07	2.50	1.00	5.00	1.00	12.50	1.00	30.00	1.00
8 08	2.50	1.00	5.00	1.00	12.50	5.00	30.00	10.00
8 09	3.00	1.00	6.00	1.00	14.00	1.00	31.00	1.00
8 10	3.00	1.00	5.00	2.00	13.00	8.00	30.00	14.00
mean	2.75	1.25	5.45	1.85	13.25	4.80	32.60	8.30
mode	-	1.00	5.00	1.00	13.00	1.00	30.00	1.00

TABLE B (follows)

SESSION: 5

1 01	2.50	2.00	5.00	4.00	12.50	12.00	30.00	20.00
1 02	3.20	0.10	6.60	0.10	16.20	0.10	38.00	0.10
1 03	2.50	2.50	5.00	5.00	12.50	13.00	30.00	30.00
1 04	2.50	2.50	5.00	5.00	12.50	12.50	30.00	30.00
1 05	2.50	2.50	5.00	5.00	12.50	12.50	30.00	30.00
1 06	2.50	2.50	5.00	5.00	12.50	12.50	30.00	30.00
1 07	2.50	2.50	5.00	5.00	12.50	12.50	30.00	30.00
1 08	2.50	2.50	5.00	5.00	12.50	12.50	30.00	30.00
1 09	2.00	2.00	6.00	6.00	14.00	14.00	30.00	30.00
1 10	2.50	2.00	5.00	4.00	12.50	10.00	30.00	20.00
mean	2.52	2.11	5.26	4.41	13.02	11.16	30.80	25.01
mode	2.50	2.50	5.00	5.00	12.50	12.50	30.00	30.00
2 01	2.50	2.00	5.00	4.00	12.50	12.00	30.00	20.00
2 02	2.80	0.10	6.50	0.10	15.00	0.10	35.00	0.10
2 03	2.50	2.50	5.00	5.00	12.50	12.50	30.00	30.00
2 04	2.50	2.50	5.00	5.00	12.50	12.50	30.00	30.00
2 05	2.50	2.50	5.00	5.00	12.50	12.50	30.00	30.00
2 06	2.50	2.50	5.00	5.00	12.50	12.50	30.00	30.00
2 07	2.50	2.50	5.00	5.00	12.50	12.50	30.00	30.00
2 08	2.50	2.50	5.00	5.00	12.50	12.50	30.00	30.00
2 09	2.00	1.00	4.00	1.00	12.00	1.00	30.00	1.00
2 10	2.50	2.00	5.00	4.00	12.50	10.00	30.00	20.00
mean	2.48	2.01	5.05	3.91	12.70	9.81	30.50	22.11
mode	2.50	2.50	5.00	5.00	12.50	12.50	30.00	30.00
3 01	2.50	2.00	5.00	4.00	12.50	12.00	30.00	20.00
3 02	2.50	0.10	5.00	0.10	12.50	0.10	30.00	0.10
3 03	2.50	2.50	5.00	5.00	12.50	12.50	30.00	30.00
3 04	2.50	2.50	5.00	5.00	12.50	12.50	30.00	30.00
3 05	2.50	2.50	5.00	5.00	12.50	12.50	30.00	30.00
3 06	2.50	2.50	5.00	5.00	12.50	12.50	30.00	30.00
3 07	2.50	2.50	5.00	5.00	12.50	12.50	30.00	30.00
3 08	2.50	2.50	5.00	5.00	12.50	12.50	30.00	30.00
3 09	2.50	2.50	5.00	5.00	12.50	12.50	30.00	30.00
3 10	2.50	2.50	5.00	5.00	12.50	12.50	30.00	30.00
mean	2.50	2.21	5.00	4.41	12.50	11.21	30.00	26.01
mode	2.50	2.50	5.00	5.00	12.50	12.50	30.00	30.00
4 01	2.50	2.00	5.00	4.00	12.50	12.00	30.00	20.00
4 02	2.50	0.10	5.00	0.10	12.50	0.10	30.00	0.10
4 03	2.50	2.50	5.00	5.00	12.50	12.50	30.00	30.00
4 04	2.50	2.50	5.00	5.00	12.50	12.50	30.00	30.00
4 05	2.50	2.50	5.00	5.00	12.50	12.50	30.00	30.00
4 06	2.50	2.50	5.00	5.00	12.50	12.50	30.00	30.00
4 07	2.50	2.50	5.00	5.00	12.50	12.50	30.00	30.00
4 08	2.50	2.50	5.00	5.00	12.50	12.50	30.00	30.00
4 09	2.50	2.50	5.00	5.00	12.50	12.50	30.00	30.00
4 10	2.50	2.50	5.00	5.00	12.50	12.50	30.00	30.00
mean	2.50	2.21	5.00	4.41	12.50	11.21	30.00	26.01
mode	2.50	2.50	5.00	5.00	12.50	12.50	30.00	30.00

TABLE B (follows)

SESSION: 5

5 01	2.50	2.50	5.00	5.00	12.50	12.50	30.00	25.00
5 02	2.50	0.10	5.00	0.10	12.50	0.10	30.00	0.10
5 03	2.50	2.60	5.00	5.00	12.50	12.50	30.00	30.00
5 04	2.50	2.50	5.00	5.00	12.50	12.50	30.00	30.00
5 05	2.50	2.50	5.00	5.00	12.50	12.50	30.00	30.00
5 06	2.50	2.50	5.00	5.00	12.50	12.50	30.00	30.00
5 07	2.50	2.50	5.00	5.00	12.50	12.50	30.00	30.00
5 08	2.50	2.50	5.00	5.00	12.50	12.50	30.00	30.00
5 09	2.50	2.50	5.00	5.00	12.50	12.50	30.00	30.00
5 10	2.50	2.50	5.00	5.00	12.50	12.50	30.00	30.00
mean	2.50	2.27	5.00	4.51	12.50	11.26	30.00	26.51
mode	2.50	2.50	5.00	5.00	12.50	12.50	30.00	30.00
6 01	2.50	2.50	5.00	5.00	12.50	12.50	30.00	25.00
6 02	2.50	0.10	5.00	0.10	12.50	0.10	30.00	0.10
6 03	2.50	2.40	5.00	4.90	12.50	12.50	30.00	30.00
6 04	2.50	2.50	5.00	5.00	12.50	12.50	30.00	30.00
6 05	2.50	2.50	5.00	5.00	12.50	12.50	30.00	30.00
6 06	2.50	2.50	5.00	5.00	12.50	12.50	30.00	30.00
6 07	2.50	2.50	5.00	5.00	12.50	12.50	30.00	30.00
6 08	2.50	2.50	5.00	5.00	12.50	12.50	30.00	30.00
6 09	2.50	2.50	5.00	5.00	12.50	12.50	30.00	30.00
6 10	2.50	2.50	5.00	5.00	12.50	12.50	30.00	30.00
mean	2.50	2.25	5.00	4.50	12.50	11.26	30.00	26.51
mode	2.50	2.50	5.00	5.00	12.50	12.50	30.00	30.00
7 01	2.50	2.50	5.00	5.00	12.50	12.50	30.00	25.00
7 02	2.50	0.10	5.00	0.10	12.50	0.10	30.00	0.10
7 03	2.50	2.40	5.00	4.90	12.50	12.60	30.00	30.00
7 04	2.50	2.50	5.00	5.00	12.50	12.50	30.00	30.00
7 05	2.50	2.50	5.00	5.00	12.50	12.50	30.00	30.00
7 06	2.50	2.50	5.00	5.00	12.50	12.50	30.00	30.00
7 07	2.50	2.50	5.00	5.00	12.50	12.50	30.00	30.00
7 08	2.50	2.50	5.00	5.00	12.50	12.50	30.00	30.00
7 09	2.50	2.50	5.00	5.00	12.50	12.50	30.00	30.00
7 10	2.50	2.50	5.00	5.00	12.50	12.50	30.00	30.00
mean	2.50	2.25	5.00	4.50	12.50	11.27	30.00	26.51
mode	2.50	2.50	5.00	5.00	12.50	12.50	30.00	30.00
8 01	2.50	2.50	5.00	5.00	12.50	12.50	30.00	30.00
8 02	2.50	0.10	5.00	0.10	12.50	0.10	30.00	0.10
8 03	2.50	2.50	5.00	5.00	12.50	12.50	30.00	30.00
8 04	2.50	2.00	5.00	4.00	12.50	10.00	30.00	20.00
8 05	2.50	2.50	5.00	5.00	12.50	12.50	30.00	30.00
8 06	2.50	2.50	5.00	5.00	12.50	12.50	30.00	30.00
8 07	2.50	2.50	5.00	5.00	12.50	12.50	30.00	30.00
8 08	2.50	2.00	5.00	4.00	12.50	10.00	30.00	20.00
8 09	2.50	2.50	5.00	5.00	12.50	12.50	30.00	30.00
8 10	2.50	2.50	5.00	5.00	12.50	12.50	30.00	30.00
mean	2.50	2.16	5.00	4.31	12.50	10.76	30.00	25.01
mode	2.50	2.50	5.00	5.00	12.50	12.50	30.00	30.00

Author index

Subject index